D1337869

# Teaching French Grammar
# in Context

OXFORD BROOKES
UNIVERSITY
LIBRARY

00 942333 0X

# Teaching French Grammar in Context

## Theory and Practice

· · · · · · · · · · · · · · · · · · ·

Stacey L. Katz
University of Utah

Carl S. Blyth
University of Texas at Austin

Yale University Press

New Haven & London

Copyright © 2007 by Yale University. All rights
reserved. This book may not be reproduced,
in whole or in part, including illustrations, in any
form (beyond that copying permitted by Sections
107 and 108 of the U.S. Copyright Law and
except by reviewers for the public press),
without written permission
from the publishers.

Publisher: Mary Jane Peluso
Development Editor: Brie Kluytenaar
Manuscript Editor: Karen Hohner
Production Editor: Ann-Marie Imbornoni
Marketing Manager: Timothy Shea
Cartoons by Walter Moore

Printed in the United States of America
by Sheridan Books, Ann Arbor, Michigan.

Library of Congress Cataloging-in-Publication Data
Katz, Stacey L., 1963–
Teaching French grammar in context : theory and
practice / Stacey L. Katz, Carl S. Blyth.
          p.      cm.
Includes bibliographical references and index.
ISBN 978-0-300-10951-1 (pbk. : alk. paper)
1. French language—Study and teaching.
2. French language—Grammar—Study and teaching.
I. Blyth, Carl S. (Carl Stewart), 1958–   II. Title.
PC2066.K38 2007
445'.071—dc22
2007008073

A catalogue record for this book is available
from the British Library.

The paper in this book meets the guidelines
for permanence and durability of the Committee
on Production Guidelines for Book Longevity
of the Council on Library Resources.

10   9   8   7   6   5   4   3   2   1

ACC. NO.
9423330x
FUND
EDUG
LOC.
ET
CATEGORY
STAN
PRICE
20.00

27 APR 2012

CLASS No.
445   KAT
OXFORD BROOKES
UNIVERSITY LIBRARY

To Charlie, Max, and Sarah.
—SLK

To my mother, Dorothy Rhyne Blyth, a dedicated teacher,
Francophile and grammarian.
—CSB

We would also like to dedicate this book to the memory of Laura Jackson,
our dear friend and colleague, and the French teacher
we wish everyone could have had.

# Contents

# Acknowledgments

SLK:

I would like to thank Knud Lambrecht, an extraordinary and generous mentor and friend, who taught me to think about how people say what they mean. This book would never have come to fruition without his insights and help.

Thanks especially to my family: to my parents, Bill and Sandra Katz, for their endless and remarkable patience; to Missy Hudson, for her support and pep talks; to Andy Hudson, for his technological help and insider access to the Yale library; to Jim and Charlotte Katz, for the room by the sea; to Gigi Stein, for the chocolate-chip cookies and travel breaks; to Leila and David Fisher, for the use of their Cape Cod and Miami homes; and to the DiLallas, the Fishers, the Rosenbaums, and the Steins.

Many colleagues and friends contributed greatly to this project, whether through reading chapter drafts and giving feedback, or by offering encouragement. I would particularly like to thank Elizabeth Emery, Randall Gess, and Johanna Watzinger-Tharp.

My thanks also go to the following people for helping to facilitate the writing of this book in various ways: Todd Anderson, for being my personal chauffeur in Austin during the fall of 2003; Ginny and Bill Crabtree, for taking me on a working vacation to Hilton Head Island in 2003; Celia Donatio, for her generous hospitality and friendship; Alon and Betsy Kasha, and Pounce the cat, for the use of their Paris apartment during the summer of 2005 (and Dan Kasha and Leigh Mercer for introducing us); Howard Mayer, for the use of his University of Hartford library office during the summer of 2004; Ed Rubin, for driving me cross-country; Jonathan and Irwin Singer, for the Sox study breaks; and Bill Tortorelli, for creating PDF files of many of my materials. I would also like to thank David Black, Olivier Bourderionnet, Ellen Bromberg, Ann Marie Cotton, Kent Dickson, Kristina de la Ferrière, Eve Dubrow, Sally Hoffer, Christine Jones, Debbie Jones, Mehdi Khorrami, Kent Kirk, Kathy McKinley, Lois Oppenheim, Corky Reeser, and Don Robinson for their help and support in various ways. I am grateful as well to my very first French teachers at the Loomis Chaffee School, Anne Sbarge, the late Edie Treadway, and Danièle Tzeutschler, for sharing their joy of the French language with me.

I appreciate the financial backing that I received from the University of Utah in the form of a University research grant (fall 2003) and a faculty fellowship (fall 2005). I would like to thank the French and Italian Department of the University of Texas at Austin for granting me visiting professor status in the fall of 2003.

And finally, sincere and heartfelt thanks to my big *papi*, David Ortiz, and the 2004 World Series Champion Boston Red Sox, for the inspiration.


CSB:

Writing this book has made me realize what a debt of gratitude I owe to my own French teachers: Dorothy Rhyne Blyth, Alice Battle, and Simone Creech. I also would like to thank the inspiring teacher educators who supervised my development as a graduate teaching assistant: Clare Tufts, Hannelore Jarausch, and Nancy Gabriel. And last, thanks to my colleagues at the University of Texas at Austin, Karen Kelton and Nancy Guilloteau, for their support and collaboration over the years.

Thanks most of all to my wonderful family: To Joe for teaching me how to punch cows and tend my garden, and to my kids—Sarah, Katie, and Claire—for teaching me never to take myself too seriously. You guys are the best.


We would both like to thank the following colleagues for their help: Aidan Coveney, Thérèse De Raedt, Gwénaëlle Dinspel, Françoise Ghillebaert, Alain Giacomi, Sandra Katz, Dale Koike, Cheryl Krueger, Kevin Lemoine, Cory Lyle, Walter Moore, Kaye Murdock, Lindsy Myers, Nicole Rambaud, Rafael Rios, Fernando Rubio, Muriel Schmid, and Jay Siskin. Particularly, we would like to thank Betsy Kerr and Nadine O'Connor Di Vito for sharing their research and pedagogical materials with us.

We would also like to thank the following no-longer-anonymous reviewers, who offered helpful suggestions on our book prospectus and early chapters: Nadine O'Connor Di Vito, University of Chicago; Cheryl Krueger, University of Virginia; Cynthia Fox, SUNY Albany; Elizabeth Emery, Montclair State University; and Jay Siskin, Cabrillo College.

Finally, we would like to express our gratitude to our publisher at Yale University Press, Mary Jane Peluso, for her enthusiasm, her encouragement, and her expertise. We would also like to thank our editors, Karen Hohner, Brie Kluytenaar, and Ann-Marie Imbornoni, for their competence, efficiency, and good humor.

Some of the sections in this book are based on articles we have published previously (see Bibliography). Although we have expanded upon the ideas expressed in our earlier publications, some of our assertions and examples may be similar.

# 1 · Introduction

Have you ever found yourself in the following situation? You are teaching a French language class, and a student asks, "Why it is wrong to say **J'aime des chats et des chiens**?" You respond that one should say **les chats** and **les chiens,** citing the rule that after verbs of liking, disliking or preferring (the well-known **aimer, adorer, détester, préférer** list), one uses the definite article. The student then informs you that he does not like dogs and cats in general; he likes SOME dogs and SOME cats. Now, if you think quickly on your feet, you reply that one should then say **certains chats** and **certains chiens.** The truth is, though, you are not quite sure why **des** does not work in this context. If you are a novice instructor and you panic, you might even reply, "OK, well then, **des** would be acceptable." Yet you know in your heart that it is not. You just don't know why.

Perhaps you are a language program director or a course supervisor, and a teaching assistant asks which sentence is correct: **Je ne sais pas de quoi tu as besoin,** or **Je ne sais pas ce dont tu as besoin.** Both sound pretty good, and since you are not sure which one is actually "correct," you ask a few native French speakers. They too find them both acceptable and have no idea which structure is indeed prescriptively "right." So you pose the same question to your friendly departmental syntactician (if you are lucky enough to have one). He or she gets very excited and goes off into a long discussion about indirect questions and their use in the spoken language. You nod as though you are following, but actually you understand precious little. More discouraged after your conversation, you still do not know which form one should use.

If you can relate to the awkward situations just described, we have written this book for you. As TA trainers and applied linguists with a background in formal linguistics and sociolinguistics, we have come to the conclusion that something should be done about grammar. Instructors need resources that not only facilitate their teaching of French grammar but also help them come to a better understanding of how French grammar functions in discourse. If you are a literature specialist, or perhaps an applied linguist who has never studied French syntax, pragmatics, or sociolinguistics extensively, we want to help fill in the gaps. If you are a new TA and are overwhelmed by your students' questions, our goal is to enhance your understanding of French grammar. You will probably find that our approach is quite different from the methods you have seen before.

A common complaint we hear from colleagues is that while many recent French textbooks have made great strides in teaching reading, writing, vocabulary, and culture, the presentation of grammar remains problematic. As Cheryl Krueger, director of the French language program at the University of Virginia, observes:

> Have you noticed that textbooks (elementary and often intermediate) tend to present vocabulary in a way that would allow a confused, unprepared, or unsure teacher to open the book and "walk" through a fairly interactive presentation? In fact, that teacher might even pick up on some ways of teaching vocabulary (how to group and map related words, how to involve students in the presentation phases, etc.) by following the presentation in the book. In other words, the teacher finds an organization, a context, visual back-up, and prompts—all applicable to use in class, and in fact, all providing a model for preparing presentations of vocabulary. The vocabulary presentations reinforce at least some of the theories and methods TA's have learned in their methods course.
>
> However, the grammar is presented (usually in English) in a sort of ref-

erence grammar format, with model sentences in French. If the same un-prepared/uncertain teacher relies on the book, he or she will end up read-ing or having students read an explanation in English. In other words, there is no model for presenting grammar in class implicit in the textbook pre-sentation—no reinforcement of the methods or techniques studied in the methods course (and here, I am not even concerned about what method is reinforced, as long as it involves thinking, interaction, use of French). (per-sonal correspondence)

Textbook grammar explanations are usually either overly simplified, or they contain grammatical terms that are not adequately defined or ex-plained. In addition, instructors sometimes do not know how to integrate these explanations (or their accompanying activities, for that matter) into their lesson plans and classroom presentations. Instructors simply have not been provided with the tools or the support to make grammar acces-sible to their students.

There are two major reasons why teaching grammar has become such a difficult undertaking, and these issues are reflected in textbook gram-mar explanations. First, with the advent of the communicative approach in the 1980s, grammar took a backseat to communication. It was as-sumed that students would pick up grammatical structures through studying succinct grammar explanations at home and then performing communicative activities, which did not focus on grammar, in class. Re-search has shown that students do indeed acquire some grammar with-out explicit instruction or focused attention, but it has also demonstrated that there are grammar points that may require more than just a good deal of input in order for students to master them.

Second, most textbooks continue to teach grammatical constructions at the sentence level, even though such an approach cannot account for many of the phenomena that make grammar confusing and complicated from the learner's perspective. Although some grammatical items are straightforward and easily learned at the word or sentence level (such as verb or adjective endings, for example), other topics are more complex and are impossible to master without considering the greater discourse environments in which they are found. Put differently, this book is not so much about traditional grammar rules per se, but rather about usage: when to use the **passé composé** or the **imparfait** in recounting past events, when to use the definite or the indefinite article, when to use dif-ferent word order constructions or interrogative constructions in communication. This book also makes no attempt to provide a comprehensive guide to all aspects of French grammatical usage. Only those areas that have been recognized as being the most problematic for learners to acquire and for instructors to explain have been included.

It is important to point out that our goal is not to advocate a return to traditional methods for teaching grammar. On the contrary, we aim to demonstrate how grammar can be taught using methods that are currently showing great promise in the foreign and second language classroom. Intended to help instructors and teacher trainers develop a knowledge of French discourse that is grounded in recent theoretical and sociolinguistic research, this book explains various approaches to teaching discourse grammar that may be easily incorporated into today's French language classrooms. At the same time, we propose an approach that is eclectic; not all French grammar needs to be studied as "discourse grammar." It is important to distinguish between topics that require a discourse approach and those that do not.

In particular, the goals of this book are to help instructors

- acquire a metalanguage for explaining discourse-conditioned grammar;
- distinguish when a grammar item requires a sentential vs. a discourse frame and consequently develop different types of treatments in the classroom for each;
- become aware of the importance of pragmatic and sociolinguistic factors that influence the use of grammatical forms in discourse;
- develop their own discourse activities as needed;
- adapt sentential textbook activities in textbooks to focus on discourse;
- guide students to discover discourse patterns and properties on their own (and allow students to work as "language researchers"—see Riggenbach 1999).

The book is divided into two sections: the initial Background chapters and the Grammar chapters. In the Background chapters, the goal is to define discourse grammar and explain why it is necessary to conceive of grammar as connected discourse. We begin in Chapter 2 with a discussion that shows the influence of the attitudes of linguists, students, and instructors on the ways grammatical topics are taught and learned (or not learned). Chapter 3 presents various methods for teaching French grammar and includes a discussion of which methods seem to work best for different types of grammar points. Most important in Chapter 3 is a discussion of the disparity in the complexity of grammatical constructions. Although some grammatical constructions are highly conditioned by context, others can be profitably studied at the word or sentence level. It is important for instructors to be able to differentiate between various types of grammatical structures and thus choose the most effective techniques for teaching them.

The second part of the book concentrates precisely on the grammatical structures that are best studied and more effectively learned within discourse. Chapter 4 treats the noun phrase and its components. We pay specific attention to determiners, a particularly difficult topic for instructors to explain and students to master. Chapter 5 contains an analysis of narration in the past, focusing on the linguistic topics of *tense* and *aspect*. Chapters 6 and 7 both stress the importance of distinguishing between the features of spoken and written French in order to communicate in a manner that is pragmatically and sociolinguistically appropriate. Chapter 6 treats word-order constructions; much of this material will be new for readers, as non-linguists do not usually study this topic. Chapter 7 treats the topic of interrogation, stressing that not all interrogative forms are appropriate in various settings and situations. Finally, Chapter 8 offers practical advice for instructors about integrating the study of grammar into the communicative classroom. Suggestions are provided for creating lesson plans where grammar is no longer treated as a peripheral, unrelated component of a content- or task-based language program.

The grammar chapters (Chapters 4–7) all follow the same format, which is as follows:

1. *Overview/Key Considerations*
   To begin, we provide a short overview of the major points of the chapter (the road map).
2. *Difficulties for the Learner*
   This section contains a description of the problems that students have with the structure at hand, focusing on the structures and concepts that confuse students, as well as student (and teacher) misconceptions. In addition, some background knowledge is provided for the topics that will be discussed throughout the chapter.
3. *Basic Forms and Meanings*
   Here we provide the reader with a short summary of the grammar point from a traditional perspective. The goal is to lay out for the reader the

various forms and pair them with their basic meanings, before getting into the important pragmatic and/or sociolinguistic considerations that will condition the use of these forms in discourse.

4. *Meanings in Context*

This section is the heart of every chapter, since it focuses on discourse pragmatics. Its goal is to describe how native speakers use the target forms in natural contexts and to point out their associated meanings. Form, meaning, and function come together in this section.

5. *Going Beyond: For the Advanced Learner*

This section contains a more sophisticated, linguistically driven discussion of the topics. Some instructors may choose to skip these sections (they are less relevant for the introductory and intermediate levels), but they are helpful for those who wish to enhance their own knowledge and gain a broader understanding of how the French language functions in discourse.

6. *Classroom Applications*

This section addresses practical matters such as how to

a. present particular grammar points in class;

b. develop activities that allow students to

• discover the properties of grammatical structures in discourse, and

• incorporate these structures into their developing linguistic repertoire;

c. teach various topics at different levels of instruction (beginning to advanced).

7. *Consolidation Exercises*

This section helps readers to verify their mastery of the grammatical and pragmatic topics presented in the chapter. It includes samples of French discourse that are to be analyzed according to pragmatic principles.

8. *Typical Student Errors*

This section provides a list of typical student errors for the instructor to correct, along with the contexts in which they were made. It is followed by an answer key.

9. *Discussion Topics/Projects*

Here we provide a more open-ended section containing topics for discussion and projects that help instructors develop their own knowledge and create pedagogical materials.

10. *Further Reading*

  At the end of every chapter is a list of relevant books and articles.

Readers may find certain content chapters more relevant than others to the classes they teach or their personal interests. Chapter 6, for example, is geared more toward advanced learners, as it focuses on spoken vs. written grammatical constructions and analyzes some "non-standard" forms. It is considerably more challenging than the other chapters, because it presents many new terms and concepts. On the other hand, every chapter contains information that may be applied even to the most elementary levels of language instruction. It is recommended to read the chapters in order, although it is not essential to do so.

# 2 · What Is Grammar?

*Grammar is like sex. It's a basic fact of life for both language teacher and language learner. It casts a huge shadow over both teacher and learner, often dominating the relationship. And it has become taboo.* (Robin 2004)

## OVERVIEW / KEY CONSIDERATIONS

This chapter focuses on attitudes toward grammar: the feelings and opinions of scholars, instructors, and students. Central to the discussion is the ongoing debate in the foreign language teaching profession about the most effective way to teach grammar. We describe different types of "grammars," including an "instructional grammar" for teachers. An introduction to "discourse grammar" is incorporated: what it is, how it can help solve problems, and why it is essential in bridging the gaps between communicative competence and grammatical accuracy.

## THE PROBLEM WITH GRAMMAR

*[The] claim that the teaching of grammar is of limited use (or even counter-productive) in teaching communicative competence is the cause of considerable uneasiness in the field today . . . "Grammar" is clearly a thorny issue. (Garrett 1986, 134)*

What is it about the topic of grammar that ruffles so many feathers? Ask certain French instructors if they "teach grammar" in their language classes, and one may be met with a condescending glare and a response along the lines of "No, of course I don't *teach* grammar. We use the communicative approach in our program, where students learn grammar through task-based activities." For some, admitting to "teaching grammar" is paramount to acknowledging being old-fashioned, traditional, or passé. Others, when responding to the same question, may explain that they do indeed teach grammar in their classes: "I have to explain the grammar to my students, because they don't understand the descriptions in the book." They sometimes add, however, that they wish that they could make their grammar explanations and activities more communicative.

Teaching assistants and new instructors want and need to know how they are supposed to present and teach grammar to their students, yet they seem to get mixed messages from supervisors, colleagues, and researchers. Should they assume that students can master a given grammar point by studying at home and then launching into the book's activities in class, or should instructors provide students with metalinguistic explanations of the target structures? What should instructors do if students come to class claiming that they simply did not understand the book's explanation of, for example, the difference between **qu'est-ce que, qu'est-ce qui,** and **quel?** What if the instructors themselves do not completely understand the book's grammar descriptions? Where should they turn for help?

Beginning instructors are often advised to try to convince their students not to focus too much on grammar. Many language instructors remember being told by their supervisors to discourage students from asking questions about grammar in class: "If they insist on wanting you to explain grammar to them, tell them to come to your office hours for extra help." As Robin (2004) points out, however, many students, especially adults, want to acquire an understanding of the rules of grammar: "Ten-year-olds don't want the big picture, but college students are more likely to demand an analytical treatment of the morphological system of the target language. It behooves instructors to play to the best styles of each learner. A few charts and basic manipulation drills on each point [do] take away from valuable time that might otherwise be spent in communicative activities. But this kind of basic structural handholding appeals to many learners, especially older ones, who find more chaos than solace in a less structured environment." It may be a battle trying to get students to assimilate grammar rules entirely through input/communicative activities, but many instructors are not convinced that students should receive more explicit instruction when it comes to studying certain, more complicated, grammar points.[1]

To make matters even more challenging, colleagues who teach upper-level classes often exert pressure on directors of first- and second-year language programs to prepare students better for more advanced courses. Complaints abound that students arrive in upper-level classes ill-prepared: "They can't write!" "They can't spell!" "Their grammar is atrocious!" The list goes on and on.[2] At many universities one can find a camp of faculty members, often made up of those who began their careers using more traditional, grammar-based methods, which feels that the communicative approach is a sham. They complain that students cannot express themselves with accuracy or precision. "Students don't even know what a preposition or a pronoun is!" they lament. They claim that students come out of the lower-division program ready to reserve a hotel room or order a glass of Beaujolais, but that they are unable to write grammatically correct sentences. "Why don't we teach them grammar anymore?" they ask.

What these colleagues do not realize is that within the communicative approach, grammar instruction is often accomplished using *implicit*, not *explicit*, techniques. One such technique is Lee and VanPatten's (2003) structured input, which will be outlined in detail in Chapter 3. In brief, structured-input activities are designed to help students focus on and subsequently internalize a particular grammatical structure without receiving a long grammatical explanation to accompany the activities. People for whom teaching grammar must include explicit presentations followed by mechanical drills and metalinguistic commentary may not see structured-input activities as a legitimate way to teach grammar. We strongly disagree. It may not be the *only* way to teach grammar (see Chapter 3), but it is indeed a valid technique. There are others as well. The real issue is not *whether* grammar should be taught, but *how* (see Lee and Van-Patten 2003 and Nassaji and Fotos 2004). Instructors must first acquire an understanding of what grammar is and then determine what it means to teach grammar. And most important, instructors need to have an open mind as to what constitutes "grammar instruction."

## TYPES OF GRAMMAR

So what exactly is grammar? It is perplexing that the term "grammar" means different things to different people depending on their perspectives and backgrounds. In other words, students, instructors, teacher trainers, and linguists all use the word "grammar," but they usually are referring to a range of concepts and constructs. Linguists even use the term differently among themselves, depending on whether they consider their research to be theoretical or applied and whether their approaches and analyses are based in cognitive/psychological or syntactic/pragmatic frameworks. As a consequence, people often end up talking about dissimilar issues using comparable terminology, thus dooming discussions about grammar from the onset. In this section we have two goals: to present the various types of "grammars" that exist and to elucidate the debate about the teaching of grammar over the last three decades.

*Prescriptive or normative grammars* describe what one should and should not say in order to speak and write a language "correctly." For French, such grammars have been around almost as long as there has been a discernible French language. The Académie française fulfills the modern-day role of deciding what is correct and acceptable in the French language. There are other respected grammars of the French language, however, that are more descriptive than "normative." Grevisse's *Le Bon Usage*, for example, includes grammar that is conventional, even though it may not be prescriptively "proper."

Linguists have their own *academic grammars*, which tend to be technical in their discussions of particular aspects of the language. These books are usually inaccessible to those who have not mastered linguistic terminology, as they focus on such syntactic notions as argument structure, adjuncts, and copulas, or such phonological notions as codas, metathesis, and elision.

Grammar books written for students are called *pedagogical grammars*. These books concentrate not only on the structure of the language but also on the interaction between the language (in the form of explanations, examples, and exercises) and the learners' "developing system."

These kinds of grammars select and sequence grammar points according to a predetermined pedagogical agenda, the so-called grammatical syllabus. There is no attempt to give exhaustive detail. In other words, the aim of pedagogical grammars is to be practical and to provide rules of thumb that seem to work reasonably well as long as one does not pay too much attention to the exceptions. Unfortunately, determining how much detail is enough for a given lesson is a daunting challenge, since the users of pedagogical grammars, the learners, are typically a heterogeneous group. Pedagogical grammars also differ markedly from other grammars in their emphasis on exercises, activities, or tasks. The ultimate goal of a pedagogical grammar is not so much to help students *understand* the grammar point but to encourage them to practice using a given structure, develop a feel for it, and use it when communicating.

Modern textbooks all contain grammatical explanations of some sort, as well as activities to practice the target grammar point. Grammatical paradigms and brief descriptions appear throughout textbooks, but less apparent is the presence of any consistent method of instruction. There is no consensus among linguists and instructors as to how grammar should be taught or learned in the communicative classroom, and this uncertainty has been passed along to the textbook authors and the instructors. New and experienced instructors alike often struggle with the dilemma of whether to explain grammatical rules to their classes.

Supervisors and language trainers are often surprised and disappointed to come across teaching assistants (who have been trained to teach using the communicative method) who completely disregard what they have learned in their methods courses when teaching their own classes. A teaching assistant might even present a grammatical item using long, complicated descriptions reminiscent of the grammar-translation method. Some offenses are even more disturbing. One supervisor reported, "I observed a TA today who decided it would just be easier to open the book and read the English explanation (very quickly and with no examples) of demonstrative adjectives, rather than present them in any other way" (personal correspondence, anonymous language program director, 2004). Unfortunately, many supervisors tell similar stories. Why does this type of situation occur? Some of the blame can be placed on the grammar descriptions found in textbooks. Despite writers' and publishers' insistence that their books reflect the tenets of the "communicative" approach (and many of the books are indeed communicative when it comes to teaching topics other than grammar), there is a general tendency to teach grammar in an outdated manner. Such a presentation encourages an ineffective type of classroom pedagogy, consisting of dry, traditional, and tedious explanations.

The presentation of grammar in textbooks has evolved very little over the years. The main difference between what one finds today and what was included twenty-five years ago is the amount of detail that authors employ to explain grammatical phenomena. Often under pressure from the publishers, today's textbook writers try to keep explanations "concise." Their rationale is that they should stress communication and not get bogged down in lengthy discussions about grammar. This justification, however, is merely an excuse for superficial and incomplete work. (For criticisms of traditional textbook grammar, see Walz 1986; Herschensohn 1988; Di Vito 1991; Glisan and Drescher 1993; Cirko 2002; and Giessing 2003.) As can be seen in many cases, textbook writers provide explanations of grammatical topics that are oversimplified and at times linguistically unsound. Often students ask their instructors to fill in the gaps, forcing instructors to come up with ad hoc explanations. New instructors sometimes panic and convey incorrect information when they find themselves in this kind of situation (see Fox 1993).

Equally problematic are the exercises following modern textbook grammar explanations, which sometimes are not only uninspiring and monotonous, but also pedagogically flawed. Mechanical exercises, such as drills or fill-in-the-blank type activities, are not uncommon, despite a general consensus among researchers that such tasks are ineffective—not to mention boring and incompatible with the "communicative approach" pedagogy. Despite the numerous studies that have been conducted on teaching grammar, little of this research has been incorporated into the textbooks. Why is there such a disparity between the findings in Second Language Acquisition (SLA) and Applied Linguistics research and their application to the classroom? The answer is not clear.

An anonymous reviewer has pointed out to us that the issue of how textbooks teach grammar goes deeper than the preferences of the individual textbook writers. He or she explains that "there is a sort of complicity between textbook publishers and language teachers; some innovations that textbook publishers would like to introduce would not be supported by the market. So unless a critical mass of potential adopters reveals a desire for materials that incorporate more research from SLA, textbook publish-

ers will not take that risk . . . The point remains that French teachers as a
group are very conservative. Their attachment to prescriptive grammar
comes only in part from the textbook tradition. Rather, they are
influenced by a prescriptivist culture that fetishes [sic] correct language. I
do think this 'pedagogical culture' is another important explanation as to
why more SLA research isn't incorporated into pedagogical materials.
SLA's research methods and findings are not consonant with the ideal-
ized, written language that French teachers call correct French" (personal
correspondence). VanPatten (1996) illustrates this "complicity" between
publishers and language teachers with a personal anecdote: "Once I was
engaged in a conversation with a publisher over the sales of a French version of a very popular Spanish textbook based on the Natural Approach.
During the conversation I found out that the French sales were 'disappointing' and that, in general, the French teaching profession was slower
to adopt innovations than was the Spanish teaching profession" (4).

Some researchers and instructors feel ambivalent about advocating that
more attention be paid to grammar. Few want to run the risk of being labeled "elitist" or too "traditional" if they express the desire to focus on
grammatical forms. Lee and VanPatten (2003) comment: "What then of
all our treasured notions of teaching language, especially our insistence
that people have to 'master the grammar'? One possible conclusion is that
our ideas about language teaching, especially the teaching of grammar as
a necessary part of language acquisition, may be artifacts of the culture of
institutionalized education" (117). Nassaji and Fotos, however, cite research that reaches the opposite conclusion (2004): "A recent meta-
analysis of 49 studies on the effectiveness of L2 instruction (Norris and
Ortega, 2000) concludes that explicit instruction (presenting the structure, describing and exemplifying it, and giving rules for its use) results
in substantial gains in the learning of target structures in comparison to
implicit instruction (usually consisting of communicative exposure to
the target form) alone, and that these gains are durable over time" (129).
The issue of how much "explicit" instruction to provide when teaching
grammar is one of the most controversial topics in the field today. In contrast to Norris and Ortega (above), Lee and VanPatten (2003) insist that
instructors should not teach grammar explicitly: "Aside from the knowledge of abstract rules that we all develop without any explicit instruction,
research on nontraditional approaches to grammar strongly suggests that
explicit information (explanation of forms and rules) is not necessary"

(125). Like Krashen (1982), whose influence on today's communicative language instruction has been tremendous, some believe that if students are given enough input in the target language, and if the input is structured properly, students will acquire the grammatical forms in question along the way. But do they?

The truth is that many students who are products of today's communicative classrooms appear to have great difficulty mastering certain grammatical structures. Studies have suggested that communicative, entirely input-based programs may not provide enough guidance for students to acquire problematic elements of grammar. This research has justified the persistent conviction of many foreign language practitioners, both experienced instructors and neophytes, that it is indeed beneficial to provide students with explicit instruction for certain grammatical structures and concepts. Ellis (1998) explains that: "how best to teach grammar is a question that many teachers feel the need to address. Investigating different options is a better way of tackling the problem of grammar teaching than simply abandoning it in favor of communicative language teaching, as some have suggested (for example, Krashen, 1982). Williams (1995) points out that the current research suggests ways in which a focus on form can be incorporated into communicative activities. However, research findings do not provide a basis for proclaiming solutions to practical problems" (55).

Ellis's call to explore options for teaching grammar is also an appeal to bring people with various perspectives together and find some common ground. In The Language Teaching Matrix, published in 1990, Richards observed that the language teaching profession at that time was divided into two rather distinct camps: the direct camp vs. the indirect camp. At the risk of oversimplifying Richards's discussion, the direct camp (also called the traditional camp) favored the teaching of an explicit grammar rule accompanied by decontextualized example sentences followed by a sequence of mechanical drills. In contrast, the indirect or nontraditional camp largely spurned explicit grammar instruction as irrelevant to acquisition and emphasized the importance of comprehensible input. Richards generally classifies advocates of Communicative Language Teaching (CLT) as belonging to the indirect camp. Celce-Murcia et al. (1997) describe the CLT methodology in the following manner: "The typical teaching practice for CLT in the late 1970s and 1980s involved setting up and managing lifelike communicative situations in the language classroom (for example, role plays, problem-solving tasks, or information-gap activities) and leading learners to acquire communicative skills incidentally by seeking situational meaning" (141). Teachers who favored the direct approach never really adopted CLT's innovations but instead remained faithful to the structural syllabus and its related practices: first, present new grammar explicitly; next, practice grammar via drills; and finally, have students produce the targeted grammar item in a quasi-communicative situation (the so-called 3 Ps: present, practice, and produce).

Even as the role and importance of communication gained widespread acceptance in the profession, research in the 1990s began uncovering a disturbing trend: entirely meaning-based approaches that dispensed with a traditional focus on linguistic forms led to less than perfect grammatical accuracy. Perhaps the best example of this research was Harley (1992), a detailed description of a French immersion program in Canada. Harley noted that the program's more than 6000 hours of meaningful input resulted in impressive communicative gains. And yet, despite communicative ability, students still exhibited surprising difficulty with common elements of French morphosyntax, such as articles, past tenses, and gender agreement.

Such findings might have led to a pendulum swing back to traditional methods emphasizing grammatical accuracy, had it not been for a group of researchers who articulated a sensible middle ground between the two extremes. Following an influential article in 1991 by Michael Long, this middle ground, referred to as *focus on form*, sought to focus learners' attention on grammatical form during communication. Proponents of focus on form were adamant that such an approach was not a return to traditional methods of grammar instruction, despite the approach's emphasis on drawing attention to linguistic structure (Long 1991). Basically, the focus on form approach attempts to create ideal conditions for grammar learning by drawing students' attention to a linguistic form *in a real communicative context*. In other words, students who engage in communication invariably experience moments when they need a particular form or construction in order to express their message. The teachable moment arises whenever students realize the gap between their communicative need and their limited linguistic repertoire. It is this "Aha!" moment when a linguistic form becomes cognitively salient. As such, Doughty and Williams (1998) explain how focus on form activities differ crucially from traditional grammar exercises: "Focus on form entails a prerequisite engagement in meaning before attention to linguistic features can be expected to be effective . . . the learner's attention is drawn precisely to a linguistic feature as necessitated by a communicative demand" (3). In Chapter 3, we describe some of the wide variety of innovative techniques that may be used to guide students.

Although the direct and indirect approaches are opposites in many ways, they actually share an important commonality: they both are based on an either/or conception of the teachability of grammar: either grammar can or cannot be taught. The focus on form approach, the so-called middle ground between these two extremes, is based on a more realistic conception of grammar as heterogeneous, that is, comprised of qualitatively different phenomena. The real problem, in our view, is that grammar instruction in most approaches is limited to a small set of pedagogical practices. In contrast, we advocate a pedagogy that profitably mixes explicit and implicit techniques, depending on the grammar item and the communicative task.

In short, the kind of pedagogy we suggest requires the instructor to think about the nature of each grammatical item and to ask some difficult questions:

- Is this form amenable to instruction?
- Can this form be learned without pedagogical intervention?
- What combination of implicit and explicit techniques gives the best results?

Thus in creating this *instructional grammar* specifically for instructors, our goal is to lay out the problems of teaching French grammar and propose solutions for the instructors who teach these structures. The solutions offered are based on our own practical experience and our best efforts at applying the most recent and the most pertinent research on language learning. We do not claim that our solutions amount to a foolproof recipe for success in every French language classroom. In fact, we have taken care to avoid what one reviewer referred to as "the discourse of pedagogical triumphantalism," that is, the notion that there is a well-known best way to present a given grammar point (for example, "The most effective way to present definite articles is . . . "). Unlike the prescriptive, academic, and pedagogic grammars discussed above, this grammar book focuses both on theory and on practice. Its purpose is to help instructors find out what works best for their own classrooms by challenging them to think through the many options in grammar instruction. In particular, we hope to lead instructors to construct a grammar pedagogy that is more consonant with the idiosyncracies of each grammatical item.

The various types of grammars discussed in this section are summarized below:

### Types of Grammars

---

• *Prescriptive or Normative Grammars*: Grammars that describe what one should and should not say in order to speak and write a language correctly.
• *Academic Grammars*: Grammars written for linguists, containing technical descriptions about various aspects of the language (syntax, phonology, etc.).
• *Pedagogical Grammars*: Grammars written for students that explain grammar rules that are accessible to learners.
• *Instructional Grammars*: Grammars that are written for instructors in order to guide them to teach grammar effectively.

---

## WHAT INSTRUCTORS NEED TO KNOW ABOUT GRAMMAR

*There is no natural end to [the] grammar education process . . . The best language teacher is one who remains a student of language and languages. (Leech 1994, 29)*

With the exception of Celce-Murcia and Larsen-Freeman's *Grammar Book* (1999) for ESL, grammar books designed for teachers have had limited success over the years. Leech (1994) claims that the real problem with most grammar books written for instructors is that they are either too academic or too pedagogical; that is, they are better suited either for practicing linguists or for language students:

Although there are some grammatical books and materials written specifically for teachers, all too often, I suggest, it is assumed that grammar for teachers is a variant either of academic grammar on the one hand or of pedagogical grammar (grammar for learners) on the other . . . I suppose it could be argued that teachers should ideally be well-versed in both [academic grammar] and [pedagogical grammar]; that they should have a sound, detailed academic knowledge of the language; and that they should also be thoroughly skilled in the methodologies of mediating grammar to learners at different stages. But perhaps, in the real world, this is too much to hope for; and in any case, it does not solve the problem of the necessarily indirect relation between academic knowledge and the way it can be put to use in the classroom. (17)

Leech's comments raise the following question: What kind of grammar knowledge does the language instructor need or want? Following Leech, we suggest that, in order to be most effective, a teacher should have a mature communicative knowledge of grammar. In addition to knowledge of the correct grammatical forms of the target language, a teacher who possesses a mature communicative knowledge of grammar should have a keen understanding of the following:

- The basic components of syntax, including the terms used to designate various word-, phrase-, and sentence-level phenomena
- The concepts of register and sociolinguistic variation
- The many differences between the grammars of the spoken and written forms of the target language
- The various types of structures that are used in specific pragmatic situations

This kind of knowledge far surpasses the traditional way of understanding grammar, which usually includes only a general mastery of rules of word and sentence formation (*morphology* and *syntax*).

## PROBLEMATIC STRUCTURES

It is often puzzling to language instructors why students have such difficulty mastering certain grammar points but not others. For example, students tend to learn adjectival endings or verb conjugations (or at least understand the need to make these correspondences, even if they have not memorized the exact forms). On the other hand, the topics focused on in this book—the use of determiners, the selection between the **passé composé** and the **imparfait** in narration, the choice of the most felicitous interrogative structure or word order construction—remain troublesome for instructors to teach and for students to learn. These grammar points are qualitatively different from the other grammar points because they are first and foremost about *usage* rather than *formation*. Formation rules are axiomatic; they are simple to describe and easy to apply. Usage, however, is anything but simple. To explain grammatical usage to students requires an in-depth understanding of language as a communicative system. Such a sophisticated approach to language goes beyond what beginning textbooks typically provide.

Herschensohn (1988) calls for changes in the types of grammar presentations that are found in textbooks: "A linguistically informed revision of language text grammars is desirable both for its clarity and for the communicative benefits it would afford. Linguistic insight is compatible with a functional approach to language teaching, and can enrich it by providing accurate grammatical information and a more efficient pedagogical grammar" (412). Most textbooks, however, ignore discussion of the function of these grammatical constructions in discourse. Our focus in this book is to examine the most problematic parts of grammar and to make them comprehensible to instructors so that they, in turn, may teach grammatical usage to their students in a more coherent way. To help instructors accomplish this goal, we not only provide tools and strategies for presenting these parts of grammar more effectively, we also provide discussion about language as discourse. In our experience, beginning instructors are frequently not well-acquainted with the notions of language as discourse or discourse competence.

## DISCOURSE COMPETENCE

> Using a language entails the ability to both interpret and produce discourse in context in spoken and written communicative interaction, which is why we assign such a central role to discourse in our discussion of frameworks that should inform language teaching. (Celce-Murcia and Olshtain 2000, 4)

Even though most language instructors believe that they teach using the communicative approach, which, as we stated earlier, is an approach that we do not advocate eliminating, there is some disagreement about the definition of "communicative competence" and about the procedures one should use to help one's students become "communicatively competent." In Canale and Swain's (1980) and Canale's (1983) seminal articles, "communicative competence" is divided into the following categories (see Canale, 7–9):

• *Grammatical competence:* The mastery of the language code (vocabulary, word formation, sentence formation, pronunciation, spelling, and semantics).

• *Sociolinguistic competence:* The extent to which utterances are produced and understood appropriately in different sociolinguistic contexts, depending on contextual factors such as the status of the participants, the purposes of the interaction, and the norms or conventions of interaction.

- *Strategic competence:* The mastery of verbal and non-verbal communication strategies that may be called into action for two main reasons: to compensate for breakdowns in communication due to limiting conditions/insufficient competence (for example, if one cannot think of a word and needs to use circumlocution) or to enhance effectiveness of communication (for rhetorical purposes).

- *Discourse competence:* The mastery of combining grammatical forms and meanings to achieve a unified spoken or written text in different genres.

Canale (1983) explains that all four types of competence are vital: "The primary goal of a communicative approach must be to facilitate the integration of these types of competence for the learner, an outcome that is not likely to result from over-emphasis on one area of competence over the others throughout a second language programme" (18). According to Celce-Murcia and Olshtain (2000), discourse competence is the core or central competence in the Canale and Swain (1980) framework, because it is the place where everything else comes together. They explain that "it is in discourse and through discourse that all of the other competencies are realized. And it is in discourse and through discourse that the manifestation of the other competencies can best be observed, researched and assessed" (16). Unfortunately, most pedagogical grammars have not incorporated the concept of discourse competence, with the exception of materials created for the ESL classroom (see McCarthy 1991; McCarthy and Carter 1994; Riggenbach 1999; and Celce-Murcia and Olshtain 2000).

## UNDERSTANDING DISCOURSE AS A DISTINCT LEVEL OF GRAMMATICAL ORGANIZATION

In 1993, applied linguist Cynthia Fox published a cogent article in the *Modern Language Journal* based on a large-scale survey examining the language beliefs of graduate teaching assistants (GTAs) in French. According to her survey, GTAs are adept at explaining sentence-level phenomena (so-called formation rules), but they are at a loss when it comes to explaining language use in discourse (for example, speaker choice of de-

terminers, tenses, moods, etc.) Fox asserts that: "besides pointing to a serious inability to provide articulate explanations for how French works,
these survey responses indicate that 'discourse competence' is not understood as a distinct level of organization" (318). As a language program
director, Fox questioned the wisdom of adopting a so-called "communicative approach" to language teaching when so many of her instructors
were largely unaware of Canale and Swain's theoretical model of communicative competence, which forms the basis of such an approach. Fox
explains that: "the results indicate that the TA conception of language differs from the Canale and Swain model in several important ways. They
also suggest that these differences have the potential to interfere seriously
with a TA's ability to teach in a manner consistent with communicative
goals" (314).

A year after Fox's article appeared, Dörnyei and Thurrell (1994) outlined what they believed to be the major trends occurring in the language
teaching profession as a whole:

1. Adding specific language input to communicative tasks
2. Raising learners' awareness of the organizational principles of language use within and beyond the sentence level
3. Sequencing communicative tasks more systematically in accordance
   with a theory of discourse-level grammar (41)

Taken together, these two articles point to a serious disjuncture between
professional realities and pedagogical trends. How it is possible for instructors to participate in the shifts that Dörnyei and Thurrell describe
without receiving proper instruction to fill the gaps in their training and
knowledge? How are instructors supposed to raise "learners' awareness
of the organizational principles of language use . . . beyond the sentence
level" without textbooks and other materials that support such a goal?
And how can instructors sequence "tasks . . . in accordance with a theory
of discourse-level grammar" if they have never been exposed to such a
theory? As Di Vito (1991) posits, only through understanding the importance of the discourse setting in which linguistic forms are used can
students even begin to approach true mastery of the target language:
"Even if one knows every grammatical structure and rule, native-like
mastery of a second language is impossible unless one knows the discourse and social norms governing their use. To help our students understand not only what is grammatically possible but what is appropriate in

a given discourse context, we must distinguish among those contexts in our explanations, in our examples, and in our spoken and written classroom exercises" (393). Valdman (1997) explains that envisioning language as discourse may serve to lead students to a more sophisticated understanding of the target language, which will be reflected in their use of the language. In addition, he believes that a focus on discourse grammar in the intermediate and advanced courses would be a welcome change from the sentential grammatical syllabus so common in beginning foreign language courses.

We believe that discourse-level grammar should be integrated into language programs from the very beginning, and this book is designed to help you do just that. In order to teach grammar at the discourse level, you should be willing to look at grammar in an entirely new way. For example, you must begin to examine various pragmatic notions that rarely appear in current textbooks. When analyzing grammatical forms, you will be asked to consider issues such as

- whether the speaker assumes that his addressee can identify a particular object or notion;
- what the speaker presupposes his addressee already knows and what should be considered new information;
- whether the speaker is referring to an entire proposition or to a particular noun when using a pronoun or article;
- whether a particular narrative event is considered mainline or collateral material;
- the attitude/epistemic stance of the speaker toward a particular topic.

Throughout this book you will be led to

- discover the underlying pragmatic properties of difficult French grammatical constructions in discourse;
- frame explanations to students in terms of context and information structure;
- create activities that lead students to discover important discourse-based phenomena.

Even if one makes relatively few grammatical errors when speaking French, to understand and be able to explain French grammar in context is another skill entirely. Native speakers, for example, rarely reflect on their native grammar and often have not developed the ability to verbalize their tacit grammatical knowledge. Thus, being a native speaker is no guarantee that one knows all the "right" answers to students' questions about grammar. For the many non-native speakers among us who teach French, as well as for the native speakers, there is always more to discover. And as most of us come to realize at some point in our careers, simply knowing how to use French grammar correctly is not enough to be effective in the classroom.

## DISCUSSION TOPICS / PROJECTS

1. Why do you think that many instructors say that they enjoy "teaching grammar" in a traditional manner? What do they mean by this, and why do you suppose they feel this way? In addition, many instructors report that their students often ask for grammar instruction ("They want grammar!"). Why do students want to study grammar, and what do they mean by "grammar"?

2. Reflect upon the pedagogical grammars you used in your language learning/language teaching career. How did you find the grammar explanations: opaque, lucid, ambiguous, boring, remedial, funny? Was there too much or too little information? Did you find some items explained better than others? Which ones proved problematic? Do you think that you would answer these questions differently depending on your perspective as a student or an instructor?

3. What are the most common grammatical problems that you face as an instructor? Do you believe that all language instructors face these same problems, or are they particular to French?

4. What grammar skills are required to be an effective foreign language instructor; for example, the ability to make up extemporaneous examples, the ability to contextualize grammar items, the ability to explain grammar, etc.? Do you possess these skills? About which of these skills do you feel most confident? About which of these skills do you feel least confident? Do you think that some skills just come with practice, or are there ways you can improve your skill set, outside the classroom, before you begin your teaching career?

5. Is it possible to discuss grammar skills in the abstract? Is a teacher's skill in explaining grammar dependent on the grammar point in question?

6. Do you teach grammar as you were taught? If you have adopted meth-

ods used by your previous teachers, which ones do you find effective or ineffective?

7. How do instructors' opinions and attitudes about language learning and about grammar as an object of study affect their pedagogical choices? Give as many concrete examples as possible.

## FURTHER READING

### On Teaching Grammar

Leech, Geoffrey. "Students' Grammar—Teachers' Grammar—Learners' Grammar." In *Grammar and the Language Teacher*, edited by Martin Bygate, Alan Tonkyn, and Eddie Williams, 17–30. New York: Prentice Hall, 1994.

Nassaji, Hossein, and Sandra Fotos. "Current Developments in Research on the Teaching of Grammar." *Annual Review of Applied Linguistics* 24 (2004): 126–145.

Yule, George. *Explaining English Grammar*. Oxford: Oxford University Press, 1999.

### On Discourse Grammar

Celce-Murcia, Marianne, and Elite Olshtain. *Discourse and Context in Language Teaching*. Cambridge: Cambridge University Press, 2000.

McCarthy, Michael, and Ronald Carter. *Language As Discourse: Perspectives for Language Teaching*. London: Longman, 1994.

### On the Problem with Textbooks

Giessing, Jürgen. "Learning a Foreign Language in Spite of the Textbook: Further Notes on the Role of Textbooks in Foreign Language Learning." *Praxis des neusprachlichen Unterrichts* 50 (2003): 91–93.

Herschensohn, Julia. "Linguistic Accuracy of Textbook Grammar." *Modern Language Journal* 72 (1988): 409–414.

Walz, Joel. "Is Oral Proficiency Possible with Today's French Textbooks?" *Modern Language Journal* 70 (1986): 13–20.

# 3 · Methods for Teaching Grammar

*I sometimes wonder if the methods we use really matter. Do today's students have better communicative skills than the grammar-translation students from the 1970s did? Just give students some exposure to French using any method and then send them to France for a year. Tell them to hang out in a bar and meet the locals. They'll pick up the language. (anonymous, and perhaps jaded, French program director)*

OVERVIEW / KEY CONSIDERATIONS

This chapter examines recent research on the most effective methods for teaching grammar. To begin, we provide a critique of the grammar presentations and activities that are found in modern textbooks. Next we describe and assess the approaches that methodology textbooks (written for those preparing to be language teachers) advocate for teaching grammar, comparing these strategies to the techniques that are found in recent studies in second language acquisition and applied linguistics. Subsequently, we apply some of these findings to the teaching of French grammar, providing suggestions for their integration into textbooks and classrooms. The goal is to show how teachers can draw from different approaches to create a methodology that is eclectic yet firmly grounded in findings from the field of applied linguistics. French grammatical constructions are broken down into categories according to whether they should be studied at the lexical, word, sentence, or discourse levels. We provide sample activities for teaching various types of grammar points, employing techniques from a variety of frameworks.

## THE TROUBLE WITH TEXTBOOKS

Choosing a first- or second-year French textbook can be daunting. There are a great number of books on the market, each promising an approach that will make students both communicatively competent and culturally sensitive. It is only after selecting and actually teaching with a given textbook that instructors often become painfully aware of its weaknesses and flaws. In many cases, the area in which the textbook in question is deficient is in the teaching of grammar.

It has been said that successful instructors can adapt any textbook to suit their needs, but it is counterproductive and frustrating for students to work with a book that does not teach grammar in a pedagogically sound manner. Unfortunately, the lack of agreement in the field as to how to teach grammar finds its way into the textbooks. In contrast to other parts of textbooks, which are based on current findings in the field of applied linguistics (sections on reading, writing, learning vocabulary, etc.), grammar segments often remain out-of-date.

The following list summarizes some of the most serious problems with many textbooks' grammar presentations and activities:[1]

- Explanations are overly simplified, incomplete, and/or pedagogically unsound.
- Explanations are constructed at the word or sentence level and do not take greater discourse factors into consideration.
- Students do not receive enough input before being asked to produce target structures.
- Students are asked to produce language that would never be found in naturally occurring discourse situations.
- Exercises require students to attend to too many issues at once, thus not focusing their attention on the target structure.
- Exercises are not contextualized.

We do not wish to imply that all textbooks fail in presenting every grammar point; some books are successful in teaching certain topics. It is important, however, for teachers to recognize problems in textbooks and learn strategies to fill in the gaps and modify ineffective grammar sections. As Herschensohn (1988) explains: "As for the role of grammar in classroom presentation . . . both the quality of the textbook grammar and the teacher's techniques contribute to the effectiveness of the grammar presentation. A good textbook grammar—one which is clear, concise, and linguistically motivated—constitutes a pedagogically efficient tool in the classroom. The teacher's presentation is also crucial" (411). Instructors should consider the grammar sections in a textbook as introductions to topics, not as the main or only information students will receive.

## WHERE METHODS BOOKS FALL SHORT

The two most popular and widely used methodology books for foreign language teaching on the market today are Lee and VanPatten's *Making Communicative Language Teaching Happen* (2003) and Omaggio Hadley's *Teaching Language in Context* (2001). Both books have contributed greatly to the field of communicative language teaching, providing instructors-in-training with the knowledge and tools they need to teach various aspects of a foreign language (listening, speaking, writing, reading, etc.) within the Communicative Language Teaching (CLT) framework. Some would argue, however, that both books could be improved in the area of teaching grammar. There are three major problems with the way "methods" books in general present grammar:

- *Problem 1*: Only one method or approach for teaching grammar is advocated.
- *Problem 2*: Strategies for actually *teaching* grammar have been ignored, while the overwhelming focus is on developing "communicative" activities to accompany the grammar sections.
- *Problem 3*: Books are not language-specific, but most grammatical problems *are* specific to each particular language.

Lee and VanPatten (2003) have fallen into the trap of Problem 1. They assert that a processing instruction/structured input approach is the be-all and end-all to teaching grammar. They outline the three components of processing instruction:

- Learners are given information about a linguistic structure or form.
- Learners are informed about a particular processing strategy that may negatively affect their picking up of the form or structure during comprehension.
- Learners are pushed to process the form or structure during activities with structured input—input that is manipulated in particular ways to push learners to become dependent on form and structure in the input so that learners have a better chance of attending to it (i.e., learners are pulled away from their natural processing tendencies toward more optimal tendencies). (142)

Based on studies of how learners derive meaning from input, VanPatten (1996) suggests that instruction be based on "structured input activities in which learners are given the opportunity to process form in the input in a controlled situation so that better form-meaning connections might happen compared with what might happen in less controlled situations" (60). In other words, structured-input activities do not require students to produce the targeted forms. Instead, these activities lead learners to attend to the grammar within a meaningful context and to demonstrate comprehension in some nonlinguistic way. Lee and VanPatten (2003) provide the following guidelines for developing structured-input (and eventually -output) activities:

- Present one thing at a time.
- Keep meaning in focus.
- Move from sentences to connected discourse.
- Use both oral and written input.
- Have the learner do something with the input.
- Keep the learner's processing strategies in mind. (154)

According to Lee and VanPatten, input eventually becomes intake, leading learners to integrate the target structure into their developing system. It is at this point that learners may begin producing the structure (creating output), but not before. We provide some examples of structured-input and -output activities later in this chapter.

Lee and VanPatten provide various types of input and output activities that they believe are effective in teaching grammar. Despite the efficacy of their sample exercises, they do not address an issue that may arise when one attempts to create structured-input activities for various types of grammatical constructions: certain grammar points may not be amenable to this type of instruction. Although some studies have shown that input-based programs may be highly effective in leading students to master certain types of grammatical points (see Lee and VanPatten 2003, Chapter 7), one of the tasks of current research in Second Language Acquisition (SLA) is to differentiate between the structures in various languages that are difficult to acquire through input alone, as opposed to the forms and rules that are relatively easy to learn via input-based instruction. Some aspects of grammar, particularly those that are intricate or where there is not necessarily a clear form-meaning correspondence, are resistant to entirely input-based communicative language teaching techniques. As scholars have noted, the failure of students in French immersion programs in Canada to master various grammatical structures strongly indicates that input may not always be sufficient in and of itself to facilitate acquisition in classrooms. As Nassaji and Fotos (2004) comment: "This research suggested that some type of focus on grammatical forms was necessary if learners were to develop high levels of accuracy in the target language. Thus, communicative language teaching by itself was found to be inadequate" (128). Nassaji and Fotos, along with others (Hulstijn 1995; Ellis 1997 and 1998; Hinkel and Fotos 2002) argue that there are times when grammar instruction must go beyond simply supplying meaningful input, especially when the grammar point in question is complex.

Lee and VanPatten (2003) do not provide guidelines for teaching more complicated constructions, such as those that require attention to discourse phenomena. They dismiss the assertion that "explicit instruction," the explaining of grammatical phenomena, is useful: "The evidence is indicating that explicit information—although we may like it and it makes us feel good about what we are doing—is not necessary for successful acquisition" (124). In a later section, however, when they discuss strategies for teaching verb endings, they posit that "after learners receive *a brief explanation* [emphasis ours] of how past-tense endings work, they might first practice attaching the concept of past time to verb forms in an activity" (143). It is unclear what exactly they mean by a "brief explanation" and what such an explanation should include. Should it be given in English or in the target language? Should it come from the teacher or the students? Why is an explanation not inherently "explicit"? Finally, Lee and VanPatten do not address the issue of monotony (Fernando Rubio, personal correspondence). If all grammar is taught and practiced the same way (through structured input and output), it is likely that students will eventually tire of such activities. In order to maintain students' motivation and interest, it is better to vary techniques for teaching grammar. In addition, some types of strategies usually work better for particular grammatical structures. It is important to point out, however, that very little empirical research has been done to investigate which types of techniques are most effective for teaching particular types of grammar. Currently, much of what is proposed is hypothetical and subject to future research. By the same token, not all grammar items have the same level of complexity (see Hulstijn 1995); therefore, it would be misguided to believe that they should all be taught in exactly the same way. While we strongly advocate a structured-input approach for some types of grammatical constructions (which we discuss below), one should recognize the limitations along with the strengths of this approach. Structured-input activities have their place, but they are not always the only or the best way to teach grammar.

In her book, *Input Enhancement: From Theory and Research to the Classroom*, Wong (2005) has a section entitled "What Are the Advantages and Disadvantages of Structured Input Activities in the L2 Classroom?" Here she provides only one caveat to structured-input activities: "A disadvantage of this technique is that structured input activities do require a lot of planning and thought. Any old input activity will not do. In order for the activity to be effective, the instructor must determine what inefficient strategy learners are using to process a particular form and then manipulate the input so that learners will be forced to use more optimal strategies" (74). This "disadvantage" is indeed an issue. At present there are no textbooks on the market that contain a structured-input approach for French; thus, teachers would have to create all their own structured-input activities for every grammar point they were to teach. Most instructors do not have the time or expertise to devote to such an enterprise. Therefore, it is frustrating, especially for new French teachers, to be exposed to only one way of teaching grammar, particularly when currently no textbook exists that integrates this framework.

As mentioned above, a more important issue is that not all grammar points are amenable to a structured-input approach. The key is figuring out which ones are and which ones are not. As Nassaji and Fotos (2004) explain: "DeKeyser and Sokalski (1996) suggest that the effectiveness of processing instruction depends on the morphosyntactic complexity of the target structure as well as the length of the testing time, suggesting that input processing is more effective for promoting comprehension skills, whereas production-based instruction is more effective for promoting production skills. Thus, the effectiveness of this type of instruction may depend on the nature of grammatical form as well as the type of skill involved. More research is required to explore the exact effect of input processing and the ways in which it may influence different language skills" (132). Even though Wong (2005) is a strong proponent of structured input–based instruction, she concedes that consciousness-raising tasks, which lead students to focus on grammatical rules (see below), are often necessary to help students understand the properties of grammatical structures.

Omaggio Hadley (2001) is less specific than Lee and VanPatten (2003) about how to teach grammar; in fact, she advocates no particular approach. In an earlier edition of her book, Teaching Language in Context (Omaggio 1986), there is a section entitled "The Place of 'Grammar' in a Proficiency-Oriented Lesson Plan." In this section she explains that: "traditionally, two approaches to the teaching of grammar have been advocated by various methodologists and learning theorists: (1) the inductive approach, which encourages learners to draw conclusions about the underlying rules of the language from the many examples they see and practice, and (2) the deductive approach, which moves from the explicit statement of a rule to its application in many examples. Although practitioners and methodologists have, across the years, argued in favor of one approach or the other, it seems that a blend of the two might make the most sense" (419). Omaggio is absolutely correct in advocating a multifaceted approach for teaching grammar, and her comments are in line with research findings almost two decades later. Hinkel and Fotos (2002) echo Omaggio Hadley's perspective: "There may be no single best approach to grammar teaching that would apply in all situations to the diverse types of learners a teacher can encounter. However, teachers' familiarity with different approaches to grammar instruction and language learning can allow them to apply to their particular situation the most effective blend of features that each has to offer. In addition, familiarity with a variety of views and approaches can lead to recognition that many approaches share common features and appreciation of an eclectic view [emphasis ours] of teaching grammar" (1).

Although Omaggio Hadley is on track by advocating a varied approach to the teaching of grammar, it is disappointing that she never actually shows instructors how to employ different approaches in the classroom. Her discussion, especially in the 2001 volume, is really an overview of the literature, and it is more theoretical than applied. In other words, there are no descriptions or examples of the ways in which various types of grammar instruction can be implemented into the second language classroom. Even more striking, the section entitled "The Place of 'Grammar' in a Proficiency-Oriented Lesson Plan" has been removed from the latest edition of the book, and any discussion of grammar presentation/teaching has been relocated to a chapter entitled "On Teaching a Language: Principles and Priorities in Methodology." Again, new teachers are expected to figure out on their own how to interpret theoretical findings and integrate them into their lesson plans.

Teaching Language in Context thus falls into the trap of Problem 2. Omaggio Hadley provides a plethora of useful suggested activity types for teaching grammar communicatively, but, like Lee and VanPatten, she supplies the activities without any explanation of what kind of grammar presentation should take place before they are conducted (or any discussion of whether or not a grammar presentation should take place). Unlike Lee and Van-Patten, most of the activities she suggests are of the output variety. The goal is to have students communicate, and it is not clear whether grammatical accuracy should be stressed. In addition, students must concentrate on so many different elements of the communicative act that there is no focus on one particular form (the target grammar point). Take, for example, the following sample activity (238), which Omaggio Hadley calls a "Sentence Builder":

---

**Sample 1 (Novice)**

Context: Discussing clothing choices

Function: Expressing preferences

Grammatical Features: -**er** verbs in French, **faire** expressions, **aller, jouer à**

Student Task: Students discuss in pairs what they and people they know like to wear when doing certain activities, using the sentence-builder frame below.

*Follow-up:* Students can be asked to write out some of their sentences to share orally with the class in a report-back activity.

*Student Task:* **Qu'est-ce que vous portez?** Using elements from each of the columns below, make up five sentences that express what you and your friends and family like to wear when doing various activities. The question mark (?) invites you to add other people, clothing items, or activities if you would prefer to do so.

*Modèle: Je porte un jean et un tee-shirt quand je fais de la bicyclette.*

| Sujets | Verbe | Vêtements | Activités |
| --- | --- | --- | --- |
| Je | | une robe | faire du jardinage |
| Ma mère | | un tee-shirt | aller au cinéma |
| Mon père . . . | porter . . . | un costume . . . quand . . . | faire de la bicyclette |
| Mes amis | | un jean | dîner dans un restaurant élégant |
| Ma sœur | | un chapeau | aller à la plage |
| Mes amis et moi | | un short | jouer au basket-ball |
| Mon frère | | un maillot de bain | aller au bureau |
| ? | | ? | ? |

Source: *Teaching Language in Context,* 3rd edition, by Omaggio Hadley. © 2001. Reprinted with permission of Heinle, a division of Thomson Learning: www.thomson.com. Fax 800-730-2215.

Students must attend to so many different aspects of the sentences they are forming that there is no clear focus on either the grammar or the vocabulary. Furthermore, this activity is ostensibly for "novice" learners. Perhaps it would work well as a culminating task, but it is not clear where in the sequence of activities this one should take place.

To summarize, although the Lee and VanPatten and Omaggio Hadley methods books offer some useful strategies and models for creating certain types of communicative grammar activities, neither book provides instructors with guidelines as to how to prepare students *before* they begin a series of activities. Furthermore, since grammar points vary in their complexity, it follows that they should receive different pedagogical treatments. In the following section, we explore various techniques that researchers have advocated for teaching grammar. In this chapter's final section, we address Problem 3; strategies are provided to help teachers decide which methods are the most effective for certain types of French grammatical structures.

## TECHNIQUES FOR TEACHING GRAMMAR

Recent studies in Second Language Acquisition have increasingly shown that some degree of learner awareness or attention is a necessary, but not a sufficient, condition for adult language learning (Rutherford 1987; Schmidt 1990, 1993, 2001; Tomlin and Villa 1994; Leow 1997, 1998). Doughty (2003) coins the term "attention-oriented instruction" to refer to two lines of research—processing instruction (structured input) and focus-on-form studies—that both address the central question of SLA: what is the best way to focus learner attention on surface forms in the input that may go unnoticed? These studies are largely motivated by the so-called Noticing Hypothesis: "SLA is largely driven by what learners pay attention to and notice in target language input and what they understand the significance of noticed input to be" (Schmidt 2001, 3–4). The growing interest in the attentional processes of learners has in turn given rise to empirical studies that attempt to operationalize the notion of learner awareness. Nassaji and Fotos (2004) note how this trend is affecting grammar instruction. They explain that: "traditional structure-based grammar teaching approaches have been replaced by treatments which may or may not include an explicit discussion of target forms and the rules for their use, but present the forms in numerous communicative contexts designed to promote learner awareness of meaning-form relationships and to permit processing of the form to occur over time" (137).

While Nassaji and Fotos avoid advocating specific pedagogical techniques, they contend that current research findings suggest three conditions essential for effective pedagogical interventions: "(1) Learner noticing and continued awareness of target forms, (2) Repeated meaning-focused exposure to input containing them, and (3) Opportunities for output and practice" (137). In a similar vein, Ellis (2002a, 2002b) contends that the emphasis of grammar instruction should be placed largely on awareness rather than performance. In particular, Ellis favors "discovery-type grammar tasks for raising learners' consciousness about grammar, data in the form of structured input to induce noticing of target structures and input-processing tasks" (2002b, 176).

One aspect of grammar teaching that has been particularly controversial is the role of explicit instruction. Ellis (1998) breaks down the category of explicit instruction into two types: direct and indirect. He differentiates between them in the following way: "Direct explicit instruction takes the form of oral or written explanations of grammatical phenomena. They can stand by themselves or can be accompanied by exercises in which learners attempt to apply the rule they have learned. In indirect explicit instruction, learners complete consciousness-raising tasks in which they analyze data illustrating the workings of a specific grammatical rule" (48). Most foreign language textbooks provide a great deal of direct explicit instruction, although explanations are often simplified to the point where they may be incomplete or confusing. Many instructors, especially those teaching at the post-secondary level, expect students to study the grammar explanations in the book at home and then come to class prepared to participate in communicative output activities using the given structure. Numerous researchers now believe that some class time should be spent going over grammar rules explicitly to make sure that students have understood the concepts. The students themselves may be made responsible for coming up with hypotheses about grammatical rules; the instructor's role may be that of a guide/facilitator. Ellis explains why he favors indirect explicit instruction: "An invitation to discover rules for themselves may be more motivating to learners than simply giving them the rules. Also, if consciousness-raising tasks are performed in groups and the target language is used as the medium for solving the problems they pose, the tasks double as communicative tasks. Learners can as well talk about grammar as talk about other topics" (48–49). Thus, students take responsibility for their learning, instead of having materials spoon-fed to them.

Researchers generally agree that grammar should be an interactive process through which learners create and confirm hypotheses about how forms correspond to communicative functions and needs. Studies have shown that explanations accompanied only by drill type activities do not lead to the mastery of grammatical structures. Insights into grammar must become part of the student's developing system. As McCarthy and Carter (1995) explain: "The 'three Ps' of Presentation-Practice-Production may need to be supplemented or extended to include procedures which involve students in greater language awareness of the nature of spoken and written distinctions, and thus a range of grammatical choices across and between these modes. A 'three Is' methodology may be appropriate here, standing for Illustration-Interaction-Induction. Students need to be involved in the process of learning grammar, and strategies for leading students along this path need to be as carefully constructed as those processes for teaching reading or writing" (217). McCarthy and Carter define the three Is as follows:

- Illustration: looking at data
- Interaction: discussing hypotheses
- Induction: positing a rule for a particular pattern or regularity in the data (217)

Research has shown that leading students to *notice* and then become *conscious* of various grammatical rules may greatly bolster their developing systems and improve their output. This type of grammar instruction is called "consciousness raising." Wong (2005) explains that "the goal of grammar consciousness-raising tasks is to make learners aware (or conscious) of the rules that govern the use of particular language forms while providing them with opportunities to engage in meaningful interaction . . . It is important to point out that in GCR tasks, students are not given explicit information about the L2. Instead, they are encouraged to discover the rules on their own by performing an interactive task with input" (79).

Ellis (1997) stresses that "the goal of consciousness-raising (CR) tasks is explicit knowledge of grammatical structures, including some metalingual knowledge . . . One major advantage of this discovery approach is that it provides opportunities for learners to interact in the target language while learning about it. Grammar becomes both the object of learning and a topic for communicating about" (160). He provides the following definition of a consciousness-raising task: "A CR task is a pedagogic activity where the learners are provided with L2 data in some form and required to perform some operation on or with it, the purpose of which is to arrive at an explicit understanding of some linguistic property or properties of the target language" (160). Thus, the purpose is to focus on grammar itself and to come up with hypotheses based on the data that one receives.

Some proponents of CR tasks have suggested giving students examples of incorrect as well as correct data (clearly labeled as such) in order to lead students to induce rules and regularities. Until more research has been done on the efficacy of this technique, we would suggest having students focus entirely on "good input," that is, "correct" grammatical exemplars. In other words, students should be provided with enough good data for them to generate the corresponding grammatical rule. Sometimes the data may be minimal, as in Activity 3.1 below, where the goal is to make students realize that, while all indefinite and partitive articles become **de** following a negative expression, the definite article remains as it is. This activity could be done after students have already been exposed to the forms of the definite, indefinite, and partitive articles in affirmative sentences.

• • • • •

### Activity 3.1: Moi et les autres.

Read the following sentences, and then answer the questions below.

1. Indiana Jones aime **les** serpents. Moi, je n'aime pas **les** serpents.
2. Les Espagnols font **la** sieste tous les jours. Moi, je ne fais pas **la** sieste. Je travaille.
3. Ma mère boit **du** thé chaque soirée. Moi, je ne bois jamais **de** thé.
4. Mon professeur a lu **un** roman ce week-end. Moi, je n'ai pas lu **de** livre.
5. Les Français mettent **des** lardons dans leurs omelettes. Moi, je ne mets pas **de** lardons dans mes omelettes.

Questions:
1. What is the major difference between the first and second sentences of each group?
2. How do the negative sentences in 1 and 2 differ from those in 3, 4, and 5?
3. What general rule can you hypothesize from the data given above?

Answers:
1. The second sentences are all negative.
2. In sentences 1 and 2, **les** and **la** remain **les** and **la,** whereas in 3, 4, and 5, **du, un,** and **des** become **de** following negation.
3. Definite articles remain the same following negation whereas the indefinite article and the partitive become **de** following negation.

Note that the articles are highlighted to draw students' attention to them. Students should be asked to work in groups to formulate the given rule, based on the examples given above.

There are many techniques that provide instructors with options for teaching various types of grammar. We have divided these techniques, which are presented below, into two groups. The first group of activity types (structured input, input flood, textual enhancement, and discourse analysis) consists primarily of input activities. Their goal is to give students exposure to the target forms, without forcing the students to produce these forms. Textual enhancement and discourse analysis activities are often considered consciousness-raising exercises as well; they require students to make hypotheses about grammatical phenomena, based on the data that they receive. The second group of activity types is concerned with output. Some types require students to produce output that is structured very carefully (garden pathing and structured output), whereas other types are more open-ended and thus less structured (task-essential language and dictogloss). Both input and output activities are important at all levels of instruction, and we strongly advocate supplying students with as much input as possible before asking them to produce output.

### Group 1: Input

#### Structured Input

As mentioned above, Lee and VanPatten's structured input is an excellent tool for focusing students' attention on grammatical form. The goal is for students to make a connection between form and meaning; in other words, they focus on one particular element of a word or sentence in order to construct its message. The following is an example of a structured-input activity, which we have adapted into French from the Spanish activity provided by Lee and VanPatten (2003, 144). This activity should be done after students have already studied the difference in pronunciation between the masculine and feminine forms of adjectives.

• • • • •

#### Activity 3.2: Qui est-ce?

Listen to each sentence in which either a French woman or a French man is described. Decide whether the speaker is referring to a man or woman or whether one cannot tell from the given information. Then decide whether the sentiments expressed in each statement are stereotypical of French men or women, or of French people in general.

[Students hear the following statements:]

1. Claude est très beau.
2. Danièle est grosse.
3. Frédéric est grand.
4. Dominique est riche.

[Students receive a sheet with the following choices for each statement:]

a. homme     femme       pas évident
b. typique     pas typique

An activity such as this one allows students to focus on one form-meaning feature: the adjectival ending which denotes the gender of the noun in question. Note that in this activity students need not produce any forms of the target structure; the goal is for them to receive carefully structured input to enhance their assimilation of the target grammar point. Having to decide whether each statement is stereotypical personalizes the activity and forces students to process the meaning of the adjective, in addition to noting its gender.

Lee and VanPatten (2003) present various types of structured-input activities: binary options, matching, supplying information, selecting alternatives, surveys, and ordering/ranking (160–165). Activity 3.2 above is an example of binary options (although one could argue that the **pas évident** category would actually make it more of a threefold option). Some of the other structured-input activity types are found in the activities accompanying the French-specific strategies below.

Input Flood

Wong (2005) defines the input-flood technique as follows: "In input flood, the input learners receive is saturated with the form that we hope learners will notice and possibly acquire. We don't usually highlight the form in any way to draw attention to it nor do we tell learners to pay attention to the form. We merely saturate the input with the form. The basic idea here is that by flooding the input with many exemplars of the form, learners will have an increased chance to notice it" (37). Students become familiar with a given grammatical item, but the input is not structured in such a way that they must make a form-meaning connection in order to complete a given task. Note that an input-flood activity is much easier to create than a structured-input exercise. In the following activity, students are "flooded" with many examples of the article **de** preceded by negation:

• • • • •

## Activity 3.3: Les aliments interdits.

Read the dialogue, and answer the questions that follow it.

ALICE: Hé, Marie, j'ai entendu que tu suis le régime Atkins. Alors, ça marche?

MARIE: Oui, ça marche bien mais, c'est dur comme régime. C'est-à-dire, je perds beaucoup de poids mais je souffre!

ALICE: Ah bon? Pourquoi ça?

MARIE: Eh bien, je (ne) peux pas manger beaucoup de choses que j'adore. Par exemple, absolument pas de féculents. Pas de pommes de terre, pas de riz, pas de pain. Alors ça veut dire que je ne mange plus de croissants le matin. Et surtout pas de pâtisseries.

ALICE: Pas de pâtisseries?! À quoi bon vivre si on ne peut pas se régaler de temps en temps?

Questions:

1. Selon Marie, quels sont les avantages et les inconvénients du régime Atkins?
2. Est-ce que le régime Atkins marche? Qu'est-ce qu'il faut faire?
3. Avez-vous jamais suivi un régime comme celui de Marie? Quels étaient les aliments interdits?
4. Avez-vous de bonnes habitudes alimentaires? Mangez-vous un peu de tout? Y a-t-il des aliments que vous ne mangez jamais ou presque jamais? Pourquoi?
5. Est-ce qu'il est plus important pour Alice d'être mince ou d'apprécier la bonne cuisine? Et pour vous? Et dans la culture américaine?

### Textual Enhancement

Textual enhancement is accomplished by using italics, boldface, under-lining, or any other device that can make certain elements of a particular written text stand out (Wong 2005, 49). Wong explains: "Textual en-hancement directs learners' attention to form while also encouraging them to process meaning-bearing input for meaning" (56). For example, students could be asked to read a passage in which agreements either with subject pronouns (in the case of **être** verbs) or with the preceding direct object are highlighted. Students would then perform a consciousness-raising activity in which they choose the appropriate reason for the agreement in each case. Note that it would be better to use an authentic text, but sometimes it is easier simply to construct the text and integrate as many exemplars as possible:

• • • • •

### Activity 3.4: Pourquoi l'accord?

Decide whether the agreement boldfaced in each sentence is (a) un accord avec le sujet; or (b) un accord avec l'objet direct.

Contexte: Un étudiant de l'Université de l'Utah parle d'une conférence récente à sa fac.

> Catherine Cusset, écrivaine très connue en France, est (1) venue nous parler des romans qu'elle a (2) écrits. Les étudiants qui les ont (3) lus ont été surpris de l'aspect très personnel de ses romans. Un étudiant explique: «Elle est (4) sortie avec quelqu'un, et puis elle a raconté toute l'aventure qu'elle a (5) eue avec lui—tous les détails intimes! Elle ne s'est pas (6) retenue . . .» Est-ce que la meilleure littérature est le résultat d'une vie intéressante ou plutôt d'une imagination puissante? Madame Cusset nous a (7) encouragés à nous poser cette question.

### Discourse Analysis

Discourse analysis is a broad category and may consist of various types of activities. Blyth (1999) points out: "in a nutshell, the goal is to change the role of the student into that of a language researcher who works to discover patterns and induce rules from authentic data" (205). Using authentic materials from both written and spoken sources, students are asked to look for particular trends and occurrences within the data and to come to conclusions about specific grammatical topics based on what they have found. For example, as we discuss in Chapter 6, differences between spoken and written French may become more apparent to students when they are asked to look for, highlight, and analyze specific features of the spoken language in a transcription of dialogue from a film.

### Group 2: Output

#### Structured Output

Lee and VanPatten (2003) explain that the two major characteristics of structured output are that "1. They involve the exchange of previously unknown information [and] 2. They require learners to access a particular form or structure in order to express meaning" (173). Structured-output activities are not mechanical drills in which students exchange meaningless (and often fabricated) information. On the contrary, their goal is to get students to communicate in an informative manner while focusing on one particular form-meaning component. Lee and VanPatten contrast a traditional output drill with a structured-output activity (173):

---

**Example of a Communicative Drill**

Use the following verbs to describe what you have or have not done this weekend.
Model: study →*I have not studied chemistry this week.*
1. open
2. write
3. leave
4. break
5. speak

---

Source: Lee/VanPatten, *Making Communicative Language Teaching Happen.* © 2003 McGraw-Hill. Used with permission of The McGraw-Hill Companies.

---

**Structured-Output Activity for French**

*Activity A: What You Used to Do*

*Step 1:* You are attempting to find out if a fellow classmate was a model student in high school. Think of questions that you can ask about what he or she used to do or about events that used to happen involving your partner that would help you gather the information. You should come up with about eight good questions.
Modèle: Est-ce que tu faisais [sic—should be **posais**] des questions
    quand tu ne comprenais pas quelque chose?
    (*Did you usually ask questions when you didn't understand something?*)

*Step 2:* Now, interview the person of your choice. Be sure to jot down your partner's responses because you will need them later.

---

Source: Lee/VanPatten, *Making Communicative Language Teaching Happen.* © 2003 McGraw-Hill. Used with permission of The McGraw-Hill Companies.

Note that in the structured-output activity above, the students are directed to perform a very specific task, and they will be responsible for the information they gather. In addition, students focus on only one form: the imperfect second-person singular verb ending. Finally, Lee and Van-Patten stress that it is important to "move from sentences to connected discourse" (174). They explain that "learners should not be forced to string utterances together at the outset" (174), but that eventually they will be asked to produce discourse beyond the sentence level.

### Garden Pathing

Blyth (1999) describes the garden-path technique as follows: "In this technique, the instructor purposefully leads students down the grammatical garden path with the goal of getting them to commit errors (Tomasello and Herron 1988). More precisely, this technique requires the instructor to present a grammatical pattern or rule in such a way that students overgeneralize the rule . . . The basic goal of garden pathing is to render the exceptions to a rule more salient, thereby making them easier to learn" (193). An example of this technique would be having students come up with a list of questions to ask their peers using the expression **penser à.** The teacher would then ask students to write some of these questions on the board. The other students would attempt to answer them, using the pronoun **y.** Students will probably come up with questions such as: **Penses-tu souvent à la politique/à tes devoirs/à tes projets pour le week-end,** etc. It is almost certain that someone will propose a question that contains a person as the object of the preposition **à,** such as **Penses-tu à ton professeur de français pendant le week-end?** When the incorrect answer **! J'y pense**[2] is provided, the instructor has the opportunity to explain to students that the stressed pronoun is used instead of **y** when the object of the preposition is animate, thus making the answer to the question given above either **Je pense à elle** or **Je pense à lui.** Because students have made the overgeneralization, the correction becomes particularly salient; it is hoped that even if they make this mistake again, when prompted, they will remember why it is incorrect and be able to make the necessary adjustments.

### Task-Essential Language

Task-essential language refers to linguistic items or grammatical forms that are inevitably or obligatorily produced by a speaker while accomplishing a given task. For example, according to speech act theory, performative speech acts require the utterance of a specific sentence in accordance with cultural conventions in order for the actual act to be performed ("I now pronounce you husband and wife," "I nominate you to be president," "I sentence you to a jail stay of four months"). Of course, performative speech acts are an exception to the norm. For the most part, specific linguistic forms are rarely required for the execution of a task or action. As such, applied linguists Loschky and Bley-Vroman (1993) identify three degrees of linguistic involvement in a given task: naturalness, utility, and essentialness. They explain that "in task-naturalness, a grammatical construction may arise naturally during the performance of a particular task, but the task can often be performed perfectly well, even quite easily, without it. In the case of task-utility, it is possible to complete a task without the structure, but with the structure, the task becomes easier. The most extreme demand a task can place on a structure is essentialness: The task cannot be successfully performed unless the structure is used" (132).

Recounting a story may seem like a rather natural way for getting students to produce narrative tenses. However, research on natural storytelling in French demonstrates that native French speakers typically recount personal narratives in a complex mixture of the present and past tenses (Fleischman 1990). It is not unusual for narrators to switch to the present tense immediately upon setting the past time frame at the opening of their story (**"Quelque chose de bizarre m'est arrivé hier. Alors, figure-toi . . . Je suis en classe devant le tableau noir quand j'entends un bruit horrible dehors . . . "**). Teachers must design tasks carefully in order to constrain natural linguistic variation of this sort that may defeat a task's pedagogical agenda.

### Dictogloss

A dictogloss, a consciousness-raising activity with a metalinguistic goal, calls for students to listen to a short text read aloud several times and then work together in small groups to reconstruct the text as faithfully as possible. Students are encouraged to discuss and justify their linguistic choices with each other. When all the groups have finished, the teacher compares the various reconstructed versions with the original in order to determine whose text is most faithful. The point of the activity is to prompt collaborative metatalk that focuses on various targeted items within the text (grammatical, pragmatic, rhetorical, etc.). Swain (1998) defines metatalk as any discussion about the linguistic properties of the text. Swain cautions that texts must be chosen carefully since studies have shown that some texts elicit more metatalk than others. In addition, teachers should monitor the metatalk for any erroneous hypotheses about the targeted grammatical items. This technique is demonstrated in Chapter 5, which deals with understanding the differences between the use of the **passé composé** and the **imparfait** in discourse.

## FRENCH-SPECIFIC STRATEGIES

As mentioned above, very few foreign language methods textbooks are language specific.[3] Because authors do not focus on the grammatical intricacies of a particular language, they have no choice but to make generalizations about the best way to teach "grammar." It is not our goal to dictate to teachers exactly which types of activities should be used to teach each and every type of French grammatical construction, but in certain cases, we suggest that particular treatments may be more effective than others. Ultimately, the instructor should decide which techniques to use. As Ellis (1998) points out, teachers need better tools to enable them to make decisions about integrating pedagogical research into their classroom activities: "The social worlds of the teacher and the researcher are often very different (Crookes 1997) . . . Teachers require and seek to develop *practical knowledge*, researchers endeavor to advance *technical knowledge*. This distinction, then, encapsulates the divide that often exists between the two" (39). In this section, we wish to lead teachers to make informed decisions about the types of grammar "presentations" they should use in class and the best kinds of activities to help students learn various grammatical structures. More research needs to be conducted to determine what truly works best; perhaps there is no way to come to a definitive answer on the matter, because there is so much individual variation among instructors' personalities and teaching styles (not to mention the variable characteristics of groups of students). Nonetheless, we provide below some guidance for teachers in order to help them to

• distinguish among different types of grammatical constructions (those that should be considered lexical items, those that are best taught at the word or sentence level, and those that require a discourse-based treatment);

- acquire strategies for keeping grammar explanations brief when they are simple, and interactive and inductive when they are more complicated;
- choose activity types that are most efficient for the grammar points in question;
- vary activity types in order to decrease student boredom.

In addition, it is of course important to note that teaching strategies should vary somewhat according to the level of the course and the age, background, and ability of the students.

We have categorized various types of French grammatical constructions below as being either lexical, morphological, syntactic, or discursive. However, as Celce-Murcia and Olshtain (2000) point out, even the most basic mechanical formation rule is not truly independent of the discourse environments in which it is found. For example, every pronoun that occurs in every sentence is linked to its discourse setting. Thus, although one might be able to make the necessary adjectival agreement at the sentence level in an utterance such as **Elle est belle,** the word **elle** is linked to a referent in the surrounding discourse; the fact that one is speaking about a woman is discourse-conditioned. Therefore, it is important to note that the categories we suggest for teaching grammar are not always clearly delineated. What teachers need to determine is whether the grammar point in question needs to be situated in a larger discourse environment in order for students to master it.

It is important to emphasize here that we do not believe that every grammar point requires a discourse-based treatment, especially in beginning courses. Rather, our intent in categorizing grammar into four separate levels—lexical, morphological, syntactic, and discursive—is to raise instructors' awareness of the heterogeneity of grammatical phenomena typically discussed in textbooks. For the most part, instructors are well acquainted with the first three levels of grammatical organization. Our book simply endeavors to add the fourth level of grammatical organization— discourse.

### Grammatical Structures As Lexical Items

Some researchers advocate teaching various grammatical rules as lexical items. In other words, the goal is for students to commit these structures to memory as they would vocabulary items. Hulstijn (1995) asserts that: "for lexical rules, regardless of their scope, there is, in principle, an alternative to teaching them explicitly. This alternative is simply that learners are told to learn the lexical, morphological forms separately" (372). He asserts that certain grammatical constructions should be learned as "lexical blocks" early in students' training. For example, he explains that "in a French course for beginners, the teacher might postpone a grammatical analysis of the expression 'asseyez-vous' (sit down) by presenting this expression as if it were one, unanalyzable word" (372). Even entire sentences may be best presented and learned initially as blocks, such as **Comment ça va?** or **Quelle heure est-il?** There is no advantage in outlining the intricacies of interrogative expressions in the earliest semesters of language study (when students clearly do not have the metalinguistic capability to understand such constructions); at the same time, students often have the communicative need to ask such questions.

Hulstijn stresses that instructors should not withhold rules from students who indicate a desire to know them; he claims that sometimes, however, especially with high-frequency forms, it is better simply for students to memorize them. He explains that "the more frequently individual flectional forms (of verbs, nouns and other lexical categories) occur in normal language use, the better candidates they are for the alternative route of vocabulary learning without rules. There is growing evidence from the psycholinguistic literature that native speakers produce frequently occurring flectional forms automatically, as they appear to be readily available and accessible in their mental lexicon" (370). Thus, the question is how students can gain this type of automaticity and build up a mental lexicon like that of a native speaker. Lee and VanPatten (2003) believe that the answer is comprehensible input: students must receive a great deal of input of the targeted forms and be forced to attend to the input in a meaningful way.

French nouns are usually presented along with their accompanying definite or indefinite articles to help students remember the nouns' gender. Another grammatical category that would benefit from this kind of treatment is prepositions, particularly those that are required after certain verbs (before either a noun or another verb). Usually the preposition **à** translates as in, at, or to in English, and **de** translates as from or of. Of course there are exceptions to the rule, as well as idiomatic expressions. It is important that students begin very early on to associate certain common and frequently used verbs with their required corresponding prepositions (for example, **téléphoner à, réussir à, regretter de, choisir de,** etc.). As Celce-Murcia and Larsen-Freeman (1999) assert for English, "at the beginning and intermediate levels, it probably suffices to make sure that when new verbs or adjectives are introduced, any prepositions that occur with them are also taught. At the advanced level, it would be helpful to systematically review the particular patterns of verb + preposition and adjective + preposition clusters that are common" (417). In French as well, verbs should be taught along with their accompanying prepositions relatively early in the curriculum. If students learn that **téléphoner** is always followed by the preposition **à,** for example, they will make fewer mistakes at the sentence level when it comes to using object pronouns, interrogative pronouns, and relative pronouns. Common student errors include:

- *Je l'ai téléphoné instead of Je lui ai téléphoné.
- *Qui téléphones-tu? instead of À qui téléphones-tu?
- *L'homme que j'ai téléphoné instead of L'homme à qui/auquel j'ai téléphoné.[4]

It is important to note that English-speaking students are generally able, without too much difficulty, to learn to use prepositions in French that are similar to those in English constructions, such as using **à** after **aller** before a location (for example, **Je vais à la plage**). They have more trouble when there is not a one-to-one correspondence with English, for example, when there is a preposition in French, but not in English (as in **téléphoner à, obéir à, regretter de,** etc.) or in the opposite case, when there is a preposition in English but no preposition in French (as in **chercher, regarder, voir, écouter,** etc.). It may be helpful to teach these lexical items using mnemonic devices or semantic groupings. For example, **chercher, regarder,** and **voir** all involve some sort of "looking." Therefore, students could be asked to hypothesize a semantic rule to remember these lexical items. In addition, it is sometimes useful for students to learn lexical grammar items through pairs of oppositions. Thus one finds **réussir à** but **rater** (with no preposition), or **téléphoner à** but **appeler,** etc. By focusing their attention on pairs, students may process and remember various items better.

Similar techniques, such as formulating pairs and semantic groupings, can be helpful for teaching students to remember the gender of nouns, one of the most difficult lexical-grammatical topics for English-speaking

students to memorize. For example, advanced students sometimes benefit from seeing pairs of words that they often confuse contrasted. Thus,
they may learn **une espèce** and **un espace** as a pair, or **un souvenir** and
**une mémoire.** The word **mémoire** is sometimes difficult for students, because it may have two different meanings: either a memory (female gender) or a thesis (masculine). Similarly **un mémoire** (masculine—*thesis*)
may be contrasted with **une thèse** (feminine—*dissertation*). Semantic
groupings may also be helpful in learning gender. Advanced learners
benefit from recognizing that many expressions denoting the body are
masculine: **un corps, un cadavre, un squelette,** etc. Similarly, many expressions involving the mouth are feminine: **une bouche, une dent, une
lèvre, une langue, une gorge, une gencive.** These categorizations, combined with structured-input activities, can help students internalize these
grammatical "rules."

Another strategy to teach grammatical lexical items involves asking
students to imagine vivid scenes in order to remember groups of exceptions. For example, the following nouns and adjectives do not follow the
usual pattern of the ending **-al** becoming -**aux** in the plural form: instead, **un récital** becomes **des récitals; un carnaval, un festival, un bal,
naval, banal, final, fatal** also use the **s** plural (see Barson 1996, 221). In
groups, students should be asked to imagine three different stories/sce-
narios, each of which combines one noun and one adjective. Therefore
one might perhaps have **un récital final,** after which all the musicians
will burn their instruments; **un carnaval banal,** where everyone is walking around looking bored and wearing exactly the same costume; **un bal
fatal,** where everyone is poisoned by arsenic in the punch or stabbed in
the gut on the way out; and **un festival naval,** where handsome young
sailors are given out to depraved women as parting gifts. The outra-
geousness of the stories and scenes will make them and the grammatical
rule easier to remember.

These types of strategies for learning grammar as lexical items or patterns can be highly successful and enduring, especially if items recur frequently in follow-up input and output activities. In addition, it is useful
for students to receive input that will make it easier for them to integrate
rules into their developing systems later on. If students get used to hearing and using certain expressions, the rules may come to them more easily later on because of the intuitions they have developed. For example, if
students have received a great deal of input that contains the prepositions

en before **France** and **à** before **Paris,** when they eventually learn that **en** is used before feminine countries and **à** before cities, the rule will seem logical, and they will assimilate it more easily. Learning a song such as the Canadian national anthem **O Canada** may also be helpful, since the **O** sounds like **Au.**

## Word-Level Constructions (Morphology)

Morphological rules (for example, verb endings, adjectival agreements, pronoun agreements) are usually not particularly difficult for students to understand. As many experienced teachers know, however, getting students to apply these rules to the language that they produce is another story. This issue is related to the decades-old question of *competence* vs. *performance*: if students understand a grammatical rule, why don't they apply this rule when speaking or writing? Is it carelessness, laziness, or forgetfulness? Most students would argue that there are just too many details to consider. The only way that teachers can get students to make agreements and use correct verb endings is to make these forms particularly salient to them. One way to do so is to use a garden-path approach to lead students to remark the form-meaning correspondence contained in morphological units. For example, to teach students adjectival agreements, one could begin with the adjectives that do not vary in form due to gender (adjectives that already end in **e,** such as **jeune, sociable, bête, sévère,** etc.). Students could be asked to describe various celebrities (both male and female) using these endings. Next, regular adjectives ending in a consonant are added to the list: **intelligent, américain, intéressant,** etc. When a student comes up with an utterance such as \***Jodie Foster est intelligent,** the teachable moment for focusing on feminine endings has occurred. The Lee and VanPatten structured-input activity given above (Activity 3.2, where students must decide whether Claude is male or female based on the adjectival ending) is an excellent follow-up activity at this point. It is important to give students enough input of these forms, and to focus students' attention on the form-meaning connection, before asking them to produce output.

Some researchers have suggested teaching irregular adjectival forms (for example **blanc** vs. **blanche**) as lexical items instead of presenting them as irregular patterns. Other researchers have argued for breaking with the tradition of teaching the masculine form as the base. Instead, they claim that it is cognitively easier for learners to memorize the feminine form as the base form from which the masculine is derived by a simple process of deletion of the final consonantal phoneme (**blanche→blanc, heureuse→heureux**). A consensus has not yet been reached on this matter, so teachers will have to make their own decision.

Likewise, using minimal pairs as a springboard for students to discover the rules works well with a variety of types of grammatical structures. For example, this technique may be useful to make students cognizant of agreement rules, as in the following table:

---

### Past Participle Agreement

---

Group 1: (Rule: Add an **-e** to the past participle when the subject of an **être** verb is feminine.)

> Franck est venu à la fête.
> Nancy est venu**e** à la fête.

Group 2: (Rule: Add an **-s** to the past participle when the subject of an **être** verb is masculine plural or composed of a mix of masculine and feminine elements; add an **-es** only if the entire subject is feminine plural.)

> Franck et Nancy sont venu**s** à la fête.
> Nancy et Karine sont venu**es** à la fête.

---

Notice that these sentences are simple and need not be contextualized beyond the sentence level. The goal is to focus students' attention on a particular morpheme and then have them generalize the rule.

To help students internalize these patterns, structured-input activities, such as Activity 3.2 above, work effectively because they force students to make the form-meaning connections that the various morphemes reflect (gender, number, person, etc.). It is not difficult to construct structured-input activities to help students focus on morphemes, but one needs to be careful that it is indeed the morpheme, and not another element in the sentence, that contains the meaning in focus. For example, consider Activity 3.5 below. The instructor wishes to lead students to recognize the difference between the **passé composé** and the **futur.** In this listening activity, the students must distinguish between the auxiliaries **avoir** and **aller** to determine the appropriate tense:

• • • • •

### Activity 3.5: Hier ou demain?

Does the action take place in the past (hier) or in the future (demain)?

1. Joseph va acheter une voiture.
2. David a mangé des pistaches.
3. Franck va préparer un bon dîner.
4. On a regardé un film à la maison.
5. Tu as dansé avec mon ami.

Note that only **-er** verbs are used (since the endings **é** and **er** sound the same), and students are thus required to focus on the auxiliary verb to determine the correct tense. Note also that no other indication of time frame is given; never does one actually hear **demain** or **hier.** As Lee and VanPatten (2003, Chapter 7) point out, lexical items such as these would provide enough information for students to process when the action is taking place, thus thwarting the point of the activity, which is to gain meaningful input from the auxiliary.

## Sentence-Level Constructions (Syntax)

This category is troubling because it contains simple constructions as well as structures that may be considered more difficult.[5] The main concern in sentence-level constructions is their *syntax,* that is, the way the words are organized within the sentence. Some sentence-level constructions are mechanical and relatively easy for students to master. Consider, for example, the topic of basic negation (in written French). Students seem to have little difficulty inserting **ne** and **pas** around a given verb or auxiliary; it is a rather straightforward exercise. In fact, one could argue that there is no point in spending a lot of time doing input activities containing negative structures, since students acquire this structure rather quickly. A structured-input activity to ensure that students have understood the meaning contained in the negative particles, such as Activity 3.6, is a good way to begin:

• • • • •

### Activity 3.6: Comment est-il/elle?

Which of the following statements describe your French professor?

1. Elle n'aime pas les devoirs.

2. Elle ne chante pas en classe.

3. Elle ne travaille pas le week-end.

4. Elle ne veut pas parler français.

5. Elle n'est pas très belle.

6. Elle n'accepte pas les devoirs en retard.

[One could also intersperse affirmative assertions among the negative ones to be sure that students are focusing on the negative particles:]

7. Elle déteste parler anglais.

8. Elle peut parler espagnol aussi.

(etc.)

It would be reasonable to move from an activity such as this one to another structured-output activity where students must respond either affirmatively or negatively, as in Activity 3.7:

• • • • •

**Activity 3.7: Comparaisons.**

Compare yourself to the following people, using either affirmative or negative responses.

Modèle: Notre professeur dit: «Je suis francophile, moi.» Et vous?

*Moi aussi, je suis très francophile.*

*Moi, non. Je ne suis pas très francophile.*

1. Notre chien Bayou dit: «Je suis bête, moi.» Et vous?

2. Jodie Foster dit: «Je parle bien le français, moi.» Et vous?

3. Le chef dit: «J'aime les frites, moi.» Et vous?

4. Un étudiant de votre classe dit: «Je veux étudier tout le week-end, moi.» Et vous?

5. Votre professeur de français dit: «J'adore conjuguer les verbes français!» Et vous?

[Note that all the adjectives are invariable, and the verb conjugation does not change; therefore students focus only on the issue of negation.]

There is one flaw, however, with these exercises concerning negation. As we discuss in Chapters 6 and 7, the negative particle **ne** is a written convention, and it is found only in formal registers of spoken French. Students should learn about this phenomenon as early as the first semester of language study, knowing that they will be held responsible for writing **ne** but that they need not *say* it when the communicative setting is not formal.

Other sentence-level grammar points are not quite as simple and mechanical as basic negation. Consider, for example, the divergent functions of the relative pronouns **qui** and **que.** It might be effective to present this grammar point using a consciousness-raising activity, as in Activity 3.8 below. First, provide students with a list of example sentences that contain **qui** and **que.** Then tell students that their task is to hypothesize the relevant rules, or have them choose the correct rules from a list given at the bottom of the page. Note that it is not vital that the sentences used here be contextualized. The input is structured to serve the need of focusing students' attention on differences between the use of the two relative pronouns.

• • • • •
### Activity 3.8: Qui ou que?

Read the following sentences, and then answer the questions below.

- Elle cherche l'homme **qui** est sous ton lit.
- Elle cherche l'homme **que** tu as câché sous ton lit.
- Elle cherche le livre **qui** est sous ton lit.
- Elle cherche le livre **que** tu as câché sous ton lit.
- Elle cherche le chien **qui** fume.
- Elle cherche le chien **qui** t'aime.
- Elle cherche le chien **qui** lui appartient.

Questions:
1. Where are the relative pronouns **qui** and **que** located within the sentence (beginning, middle, or end)? Are they found elsewhere in any of the examples given above?
2. What do you notice about the grammatical categories (nouns, verbs, prepositions, etc.) that follow **qui** and **que?**
3. What do you notice about what precedes **qui** and **que** (the antecedent)?
4. Do you notice a difference between the use of **qui** and **que** when the antecedent is human, animate (living, but not necessarily human), or inanimate (that is, an object)?
5. Construct a hypothesis that summarizes the use of the relative pronouns **qui** and **que.**

Answers:

1. **Qui** and **que** are always found in the middle of a sentence, never at the beginning or the end.
2. **Que** is always followed by a subject and a verb, and **qui** is always followed by a verb (or a verb preceded by a direct or indirect object pronoun).
3. **Qui** and **que** are always preceded by a noun.
4. The antecedent's being human, animate, or inanimate is irrelevant.
5. Hypothesis: **Qui** and **que** are found following a noun. **Qui** is followed by a verb (or a verb preceded by an object pronoun), and **que** by a subject and a verb. (Some stronger students may hypothesize that **qui** is the subject of what follows it and **que** the direct object, but this type of analysis is not required for students to understand the use of **qui** and **que** in relative clauses.)

Structured-input activities are useful to give students exposure to this construction, followed by structured-output activities to ensure the students' ability to use them properly in discourse. Activity 3.9 is an example of a structured-input activity, and Activity 3.10 of a structured-output activity. Note that in Activity 3.9 the students are required to finish the sentences, but they are not required to choose between **qui** and **que.** They do need to understand the functions of **qui** and **que,** however, in order to complete the sentences. Note also that although this activity is not based on authentic discourse; there is a context; and the input is structured to fit appropriately into the context.

• • • • •

### Activity 3.9: Les préférences des étudiants et des jeunes d'aujourd'hui.

Complete the following sentences logically.

Modèle: En général, on n'aime pas les devoirs que nos professeurs

_____.

       *donnent* (réponse possible)

En général,

On apprécie les amis qui sont _____.

On préfère les camarades de chambre qui font _____.

On déteste les chiens qui aboient _____.

On aime les fêtes que nos amis _____.

On apprécie les dîners que notre mère _____.

On achète les CDs qu'on _____.

• • • • •

**Activity 3.10: La vie est dure.**

*Step* 1: Make a list of things people do that annoy you.
Modèle: *Je n'aime pas les gens qui parlent au téléphone au cinéma.*
    *J'ai horreur des enfants qui crient dans les restaurants.*
You may find some of the following verbs useful: **siffler, manger, conduire, dormir, courir, chanter, téléphoner**

*Step* 2: Compare your list with that of a partner. Are you similar or different? Who is more tolerant? Who is more easily annoyed?

Only after students have mastered **qui** and **que** are they ready to be introduced to **dont** and other preposition + **qui/quoi** constructions. Lee and VanPatten (2003) stress throughout their methods book that it is best not to introduce an entire paradigm at once.

### Discourse-Level Grammar

Discourse-level grammatical constructions have received the least amount of attention in the literature on teaching grammar, yet it is precisely these structures that students need to master in order to attain more proficiency in speaking and writing French. In Chapters 4–7, we identify and focus on the grammatical aspects of French grammar that must be taught using a discourse-based approach: determiners, narrative past tenses, word-order constructions, and interrogative expressions. We believe that these elements are, without question, the most difficult areas of French grammar and that the only way students will master them is through becoming aware of their use and purpose in discourse.

This raises the interesting question of whether students should be exposed only to authentic discourse in order to learn about discourse phenomena. We believe that it is sometimes more efficient to use pedagogically doctored or invented texts to teach certain discourse phenomena, particularly at lower levels of instruction. The point of structuring input is to make it more accessible to learners and to allow them to focus on particular phenomena. A successful pedagogical plan can seamlessly lead students to work with structured to more open-ended discourse materials. Since all grammar is related to the discourse in which it is found, it is always important to provide a meaningful context for activities that focus on grammar. It should be kept in mind, however, that if discourse information is not structured appropriately, students may end up being overwhelmed.

In the chapters that follow, we not only explain the discourse properties of various constructions, but we also provide suggestions for activities for teaching them, based on the discussion above of input and output exercise types. Celce-Murcia and Olshtain (2000) explain that: "the biggest problem . . . is that there are very few materials currently available that show the teacher how to teach grammar using discourse-based and context-based activities and formats" (61). We hope that the types of activities proposed throughout the chapters to come will help fill some of this void, as well as give teachers some guidelines and options, for creating their own activities. In the following table we summarize the four levels of grammatical organization discussed in this chapter: lexical, morphological, syntactic, and discursive.

### Levels of Grammatical Organization in Foreign Language Curricula

| | |
|---|---|
| Lexical: | Unanalyzed parts of language that require memorization rather than rule-based learning, such as verbs followed by a preposition (**téléphoner à**) |
| Morphological: | Formation rules of inflectional and derivational morphology such as gender inflection (**chanteur→chanteuse**) or adverbial derivation (**heureuse→heureusement**) |
| Syntactic: | Rules governing word order such as negation of affirmative sentences (**Elle travaille le week-end.→Elle ne travaille pas le week-end.**) |
| Discursive: | Grammatical choices that depend on textual and contextual variables such as the selection of **passé composé** or **imparfait** |

### DISCUSSION TOPICS / PROJECTS

1. Hulstijn (1995) differentiates between language courses that are designed either for those seeking "survival knowledge" (of the Berlitz variety) or for learners with a "low educational background" (not more

than a few years of secondary school) and courses for students at the late secondary or college level (381). He believes that a focus on grammar may not be useful for the survival/low educational background groups. Do you agree? What should be the goal of language courses offered at the college/university level? Is the goal to teach students to speak a language? To become literate in a language?

2. There is not much room for the teaching of grammar (even of English grammar) in modern American primary or secondary classroom curricula. Consequently, it is not unusual to find students in college classrooms who do not know the grammatical parts of speech, such as prepositions, direct objects, articles, etc. Do you believe that we are doing students a disservice by not providing them with this knowledge, or do you think that this type of training is unnecessary? Do you feel that the foreign language classroom should be the place where students learn grammatical terminology and functions?

3. What should a new high school teacher do when asked to teach using a textbook that is twenty years old and steeped in audiolingual or grammar-translation pedagogy? How can such a textbook be integrated into today's communicative classroom? More important, how can grammar activities be updated from the traditional fill-in-the-blank variety into more pedagogically valid options? For example, try to modernize the following activity:

**Exercice de genre.** Changez la forme de l'adjectif pour que cela corresponde au genre du nom qu'il modifie:

1. une _____ femme (beau)

2. une classe _____ (intéressant)

3. des amis _____ (américain)

4. les _____ tantes (vieux)

5. les _____ hommes (beau)

6. les tables _____ (ancien)

7. la chaise _____ (léger)

4. What criteria would you suggest for evaluating the presentation of grammar and the accompanying activities in a prospective textbook? Are there particular grammar points that you would want to assess in order to make a final decision about whether to adopt the book?

5. Do you agree with Lee and VanPatten (and others) that students should

not be required to produce output until they have received a significant amount of input and have incorporated the given structure into their "developing system"? What might be the disadvantage of producing output too early? Can you think of any advantage of having students produce output immediately?

6. Think back to when you first started studying French. What was the most difficult grammatical point for you to master? Do you remember how it was introduced in your textbook and how your teacher presented it in class? Was this a word-, sentence-, or discourse-level issue? How would you teach this structure to your students today? What type of activities would you prepare?

## FURTHER READING

### General Methods Textbooks

Lee, James, and Bill VanPatten. *Making Communicative Language Teaching Happen.* New York: Mc-Graw-Hill, 2003.

Omaggio Hadley, Alice. *Teaching Language in Context.* Third Edition. Boston: Heinle, 2001.

### On Focus on Form

Doughty, Catherine, and Jessica Williams. *Focus on Form in Classroom Second Language Acquisition.* Cambridge: Cambridge University Press, 1998.

Long, Michael. "Focus on Form: A Design Feature in Language Teaching Methodology." In *Foreign Language Research in Cross-Cultural Perspective,* edited by Kees de Bot, Ralph B. Ginsberg, and Claire Kramsch, 39–52. Amsterdam: John Benjamins, 1991.

### On Input and Structured Input

VanPatten, Bill. *Input Processing and Grammar Instruction in Second Language Acquisition.* Norwood, NJ: Ablex, 1996.

———. *From Input to Output: A Teacher's Guide to Second Language Acquisition.* New York: McGraw-Hill, 2003.

Wong, Wynne. *Input Enhancement: From Theory and Research to the Classroom.* New York: McGraw-Hill, 2005.

### On Consciousness-Raising and Noticing

Fotos, Sandra. "Integrating Grammar Instruction and Communicative Language Use through Grammar Consciousness-Raising Tasks." *TESOL Quarterly* 28 (1994): 323–351.

Schmidt, Richard W. "Attention." In *Cognition and Second Language Instruction,* edited by Peter Robinson, 3–32. Cambridge: Cambridge University Press, 2001.

Sharwood Smith, Michael. "Consciousness-Raising and the Second-Language Learner." *Applied Linguistics* 2 (1981): 159–169.

# 4 · Articles

## OVERVIEW / KEY CONSIDERATIONS

The following grammatical topics are covered in this chapter:

- Definite articles (**le/la/les**)
- Indefinite articles (**un/une/des**)
- Partitive articles (**du/de la/de l'**)
- Zero article
- Topics for the advanced learner

## DIFFICULTIES FOR THE LEARNER

It is striking that even anglophone students who have spent a long period of time in a French-speaking country and obtained a high level of proficiency in French often make mistakes when choosing articles. It is therefore unreasonable to expect classroom learners to master the French article system through input alone. While the forms of French articles are not especially difficult, the function of articles in discourse is particularly opaque. Thus students typically make mistakes such as the following:

(1) *Context:* A discussion about favorite things.
Speaker A: Quel animal préfères-tu?
Speaker B: ! Je préfère des chiens.
[*Correct answer:* Je préfère les chiens.]

(2) *Context:* A student joins friends who are already seated in a restaurant.
Speaker A: Qu'est-ce qu'on boit, alors?
Speaker B: ! Jacques a commandé une bouteille du vin.
[*Correct answer:* Jacques a commandé une bouteille de vin.]

(3) *Context:* A student returns to her dorm room carrying a backpack that contains groceries.
Speaker A: Qu'est-ce que tu as acheté au marché?
Speaker B: ! J'ai pris les tomates et les oignons.
[*Correct answer:* J'ai pris des tomates et des oignons.]

(4) *Context:* A hostess is pouring coffee into her guest's cup.
Speaker A: Qu'est-ce que tu prends dans ton café?
Speaker B: ! J'aimerais le sucre.
[*Correct answer:* J'aimerais du sucre.]

(5) *Context:* A student has just ordered a pizza over the phone, and her roommate walks into the room.
Speaker A: Je viens de commander une pizza végétarienne.
Speaker B: ! Super! Mais je ne mange pas des olives.
[*Correct answer:* Super! Mais je ne mange pas d'olives.]

(6) *Context:* A discussion about animals.
Speaker A: Qu'est-ce que tu sais à propos des éléphants?
Speaker B: ! Je sais que les éléphants sont les animaux.
[*Correct answer:* Je sais que les éléphants sont des animaux.]

Errors such as these signal the need for techniques that lead learners to understand the use of determiners in discourse; many of the structures students produce are not necessarily *grammatically* ill-formed, but rather *pragmatically* inappropriate. An utterance is said to be pragmatically ill-formed when it sounds inappropriate in a particular discourse environment. The responses given above are not grammatically incorrect in and of themselves; they are just inappropriate in these particular discourse settings. For example, **Je préfère des chiens** would be pragmatically acceptable in the following context:

(1a) *Context:* Also talking about preferences.
 Speaker A: Qu'est-ce que tu préfères avoir dans la maison? Des chiens ou des chats?
 Speaker B: Je préfère des chiens.

Likewise, **une bouteille du vin** would be perfectly acceptable in the following discourse setting:

(2a) *Context:* Also in a restaurant.
 Speaker A: J'adore le vin qu'on sert dans ce restaurant.
 Speaker B: Moi aussi. Tu as jamais goûté une bouteille du vin qu'ils gardent dans leur cave privée? C'est superbe.

Therefore, it is important to make the distinction between pragmatically odd and grammatically incorrect utterances.

Articles are difficult to master in many languages. Some researchers, for example, believe that there is no point in trying to teach English articles using explicit instruction; the topic is simply too complicated. Doughty and Williams (1998) remark that: "[the English article system] seem[s] strangely impermeable to instruction and so, for that reason alone, perhaps should not take up valuable class time" (201). Other studies, however, strongly advocate teaching the properties of articles. Master (1994) posits that: "it is perhaps the systematic presentation of the article system that makes the difference [in its being learned]" (245). We agree with Master, adding that the presentation must include a methodical discussion of discourse-based criteria for article selection. In addition, activities to accompany the study of articles should focus on raising students' consciousness of the pragmatic properties of articles. Finally, the articles being learned should be placed within a clear context, if possible, using snippets of authentic discourse (especially at more advanced levels of instruction).

## BASIC FORMS AND MEANINGS

It is important to note that many students (and teachers, and even linguists) are unsure of the difference between the terms *articles* and *determiners*. This confusion arises because grammarians are not always clear in their explanations of what is meant by each term; unfortunately, text-books often use one or both expressions without defining them. Some-times certain determiners are incorrectly called *adjectives*, which contrib-utes further to the misunderstanding. Grevisse and Goosse (1995) define the article as "le déterminant minimal, le mot qui permet à un nom de se réaliser dans une phrase, si le sens ne rend pas nécessaire un autre déterminant. On distingue trois classes: l'article *défini*, l'article *indéfini* et l'article *partitif*; mais les deux dernières peuvent être jointes" (177). Celce-Murcia and Larsen-Freeman (1999) propose a similar categoriza-tion for English: "We will use the term *determiner* to refer to that special class of words that limits the nouns that follow them. Various types of words fit into this category: articles (*the, a[n]*), demonstratives (*this, that, these, those*), and possessive determiners (*my, your, his, her, its, our, their*) to cite the major ones" (19). We will adopt the same terminology as Celce-Murcia and Larsen-Freeman, including the partitive in the articles group, and including the *Quantifiers* category in our list of determiners. The following chart contains an overview of the basic forms of French determiners:

### Determiners

1. Articles
   a. Definite article
        **le, la, l', les**                                          (*the, ø*)
   b. Indefinite article
        **un, une, des**                                            (*a, some, ø*)
   c. Partitive article
        **du, de la, de l'**                                    (*some, any, ø*)
2. Demonstratives
        **ce, cette, cet, ces**                                (*this, these*)
3. Possessives
        **mon, ma, mes, ton, ta, tes,** etc.               (*my, your,* etc.)
4. Quantifiers
   a. Numbers
        **un** (meaning *one*), **deux, trois,** etc.        (*one, two, three,* etc.)
   b. Others
        **quelques, certain(e)s, plusieurs,** etc.     (*some, certain, several*)

Demonstratives, possessives, and quantifiers may be better taught and learned as vocabulary items, rather than as grammatical categories. Therefore, we do not focus on them in this chapter except occasionally in contrast with definite, indefinite, and partitive articles.

## MEANINGS IN CONTEXT

It is crucial to differentiate between articles based on their functions in discourse, using specific pragmatic criteria. At the same time, instructors must steer students away from the confusing and often incorrect terminology presented in many textbooks. The following terms appear frequently in textbook chapters on articles: *general, specific, specified, unspecified,* etc., but usually they are undefined (see Herschensohn 1988 for a discussion of the flaws of such terminology). If these terms are to be used (we advocate some, but not others), they must be clearly explained and supplemented with examples of contextualized language. From the beginning, it is important to clear up any misconceptions that students may have due to overgeneralizations they may have made or faulty explanations given in textbooks.

In addition, knowing how to use English articles correctly does not necessarily facilitate the acquisition of the French system. As Katz (2001) explains, the French article system is markedly different from its English counterpart. At first glance, the distinction between the definite article **le/la/les** and the indefinite article **un/une/des** appears to be parallel to what one finds in English. Many elementary textbooks explain that the definite article corresponds to the English word *the*, and the indefinite article to *a, any,* or *some*. However, this is not always the case. Consider example (7), where this rule does not necessarily work:

(7) J'aime les serpents.

When taken out of context, example (7) is ambiguous. It may be translated either as *I like the snakes* or *I like snakes*, depending on the discourse environment in which it is found. Students may thus hypothesize that **le, la,** and **les** are used either when one wishes to say *the* or when no article is used in English. The second part of this hypothesis is only partly correct, however, since **des** can also be found when there is no article in English, as in example (8):

(8) Les serpents sont des reptiles.

This sentence is best translated without any articles: *Snakes are reptiles.*[1]

Thus, what is the rule for the use of either **les** or **des** when there is no article in the corresponding English sentence? We discuss this issue below.

Katz (2001) also explains that some textbook grammar descriptions of the partitive can be even more confusing: "In many textbooks the partitive is defined as the equivalent of *some* or *any*, a part of a larger whole, or an unspecified amount of an item. Because of these vague explanations, students often do not understand why one would say, for example, **du riz,** but **des haricots verts.** Both expressions contain articles meaning *some*, refer to entities that are part of a larger whole, and are of unspecified quantities, but one noun is preceded by **du** and the other by **des.** Furthermore, students tend to be puzzled when **des** is presented as both an indefinite and a partitive article, often with no explanation as to why it fits into both categories" (291–292).

In the following sections we provide guidelines for explaining the use of definite, indefinite, and partitive articles in discourse. Our explanations are based on various pragmatic concepts concerning assumptions that speakers have about what their addressees already know, what entities their addressees are able to identify, and whether the speaker and the addressee possess presuppositions or expectations related to a particular situation.

## The Definite Article: Identifiability and Genericness

### Identifiability

Lambrecht (1994) explains that "an identifiable referent is one for which a shared representation already exists in the speaker's and the hearer's minds at the time of utterance, while an unidentifiable referent is one for which a representation exists only in the speaker's mind" (77–78). A referent is a word or expression that *refers* to an entity that exists in the world or to an idea. A French speaker will use a definite article if he believes that his addressee is able to identify a particular entity. Therefore if a speaker makes a statement such as (9), he can assume that his addressee already knows of the train in question:

(9) Je vois le train.     (*I see the train.*)

The train may be identifiable because it has been mentioned in previous discourse, or it may be a specific, identifiable train to which the speaker can point. The third way that an entity may be considered identifiable is through an association that the speaker and his addressee can easily make with what one usually finds in a certain situation. Lambrecht calls this last case "common ground" (personal correspondence). For example, if two people usually take the train together to go to work, one could say to the other upon arriving at the station that he sees **le train,** even if the conversation at that given moment is not about the train. Here the speaker assumes that his addressee shares the same mental frame about a specific train in a particular station.

To summarize: there are three types of assumptions that a speaker can make about his addressee's ability to identify a given referent. His addressee can identify a referent due to

1. its being mentioned in prior discourse;
2. its being present and thus identifiable physically in the speaker and addressee's world;

or

3. its being part of a *common ground* that the speaker and addressee share.

If the noun in question fulfills one of these criteria, the definite article is used.

### Genericness

The identifiability distinction makes the choice of the definite article clear in the majority of cases. There is one common situation, however, in which the definite article is used, but not because the noun in question is identifiable. As Lambrecht (1994) explains: "the DEFINITE article, which is normally used to designate specific identifiable individuals out of a particular class, can sometimes also be used with noun phrases that refer *generically* [emphasis ours] to the whole class" (83). Therefore, one can find utterances such as (10):

(10) Les enfants aiment les bonbons.     (*Children like candy.*)

Lambrecht's explanation is straightforward: students should be told that when the noun refers to all the members of a particular group in a *generic* sense, the definite article should be used. Genericness means that all the members of a group are included as the referent of the given noun. This means that if the group in question is but a subset of a larger group, the definite article cannot be used. This concept is illustrated in example (8), repeated below:

(8) Les serpents sont des reptiles.     (*Snakes are reptiles.*)

The definite article **les** precedes **serpents,** but the indefinite article **des** precedes **reptiles.** The reason for the distinction is that all snakes are but a subset of the reptile group. All reptiles are not snakes!

Finally, it is important to point out that genericness is often used for stereotyping. Therefore, one may say that all the members of a particular group act or think in a certain way, even if such a statement is clichéd and not necessarily true. Thus one finds statements such as (11)–(13):

(11) Les Américains aiment la malbouffe.
(12) Les Français sont très chics.
(13) Les femmes sont plus intelligentes que les hommes.

The use of the definite article is summarized below:

---

### Use of the Definite Article

---

Use the definite article (**le, la, l', les**) when

1. you wish to refer to a specific object that your addressee can easily identify because
   a. it has been previously (recently) mentioned in the conversation;
   b. it is physically present in the immediate context (may be seen, heard, or perceived otherwise by the senses);
   c. it is shared common knowledge (common ground);

or

2. you wish to refer to all members of a given group in a generic sense (often used for stereotyping).

---

### The Indefinite Article

In contrast to the definite article, the indefinite article is used when the speaker does not think that his addressee can identify the entity to which he is referring. In (14), for example, the presence of the indefinite article indicates that the speaker assumes that his addressee cannot or need not identify the particular entity in question:

(14) Je vois un train.                    (*I see a train.*)

Example (14) would be appropriate in the following context: Two people are about to cross the tracks at a railroad crossing, and they are checking to be sure that the coast is clear. They begin to cross, and then suddenly one exclaims, in a panic:

(14) Je vois un train!                    (*I see a train!*)

It would be pragmatically odd for him to exclaim:

(15) Je vois le train!                    (*I see the train!*)

unless both participants are well aware that there is a particular train about to appear somewhere, thus making the train identifiable. It is important to note that both (14) and (15) are grammatical sentences. The question is whether one or the other is pragmatically acceptable in a given discourse setting.

Lambrecht (1994) explains that there are two types of indefinite articles: *specific* and *non-specific* (80). He provides examples (16) and (17) to differentiate between the two (translated here into French):

(16) Je cherche un livre mais je ne l'ai pas trouvé.
     (*I'm looking for a book, but I haven't found it.*)

(17) Je cherche un livre, mais je n'en ai pas trouvé.
     (*I'm looking for a book, but I haven't found one.*)

Imagine the following scenario. An aunt has gone to a bookstore to look for a particular book as a gift for her nephew. She is unable to locate it and thus goes to the information desk to inquire if the store has it. She may initiate her conversation with the clerk using an utterance such as (16). In (16), the speaker clearly has a specific book in mind, which she demonstrates through using the direct-object pronoun **le** in the second clause.

Now consider another discourse setting. The aunt has no children of her own and is uncertain as to what kind of book a child of her nephew's age might like. She has gone up and down the children's aisle at the bookstore but has found nothing interesting. This time when she goes to the information desk asking for advice, using utterance (17) would be a logical way to begin her conversation with the clerk. In (17), the use of the pronoun **en** shows that there is no particular book in the speaker's mind. She is simply looking for a book. This differentiation is not vital for students to understand, since the phenomenon corresponds to what one finds in English. It clearly demonstrates, however, why it is incorrect to say that definite articles refer to "specific" entities and indefinite articles to "unspecific" ones.

Conversely, the definite article may be used instead of the indefinite article in (16), if the communicative goal is different. In (18), the speaker assumes that her addressee is able to identify the book in question, which was not the case in (16):

(18) Je cherche le livre mais je ne l'ai pas trouvé.
     (I'm looking for the book, but I haven't found it.)

She presupposes that her addressee already knows that she is looking for a particular book, which the addressee can identify. As Lambrecht has pointed out, however, it would be impossible to find a definite article in (17), as shown in (19), because the pronoun **en,** which is indefinite, requires that its referent be indefinite and unidentifiable:

(19) *Je cherche le livre mais je n'en ai pas trouvé.
     (*I am looking for the book, but I haven't found one.)

Like the definite articles **le/la/les,** the direct-object pronouns **le/la/les** refer to identifiable or generic nouns. The pronoun **en** is used to refer to unidentifiable nouns, whether they are specific or unspecific.

## Synthesis: Definite and Indefinite Articles

In order to master the concepts presented in the sections above, students should be encouraged to analyze the differences among various examples of article usage, such as those found in (20), (21), and (22):

(20) Ma sœur a un chat. J'aime **les chats.**
     (My sister has a cat. I like cats.)

(21) On est entrés dans la maison et on a vu **des chats** dans le salon.
     (We went into the house and saw (some) cats in the living room.)

(22) Mon voisin a trois chats et deux chiens. On a vu **les chats** dans le salon.
     (My neighbor has three cats and two dogs. We saw the cats in the living room.)

Note that although these examples are not authentic snippets of discourse, the input is structured very carefully in order to focus students' attention on the pragmatic properties of the articles. Each example above contains a specific context, even if it is not particularly developed. In (20), it is clear that the entire class of cats is being considered. **Les chats** cannot be translated as *the cats*, since only one cat has already been mentioned as a referent in the current context. In (21), it is not the entire class of cats to which one is referring, but merely to a particular subset of the cats that exist in the world. In (22), the definite article is used, since these cats have been mentioned in the preceding discourse and are identifiable.

In cases where students are not sure which article is appropriate, they should ask themselves if the group in question represents all the members of a particular group or simply a subset. If it is indeed a subset, they should decide whether this group has already been introduced into the discourse (either through words or through the physical setting in which the discourse takes place) and is therefore identifiable. Then they can choose the proper articles accordingly. Consciousness-raising activities of this type are included in the Classroom Applications section of this chapter.

Herschensohn (1988) correctly notes that when explaining the difference between definite and indefinite articles, "the terms 'specific' and 'general' are used in most of the texts in inaccurate or even contradictory ways" (410). The examples given in (20)–(22) illustrate some of the problems that can arise due to the use of these terms. The cats that were seen in the living room in (21) were indeed "specific" cats, which according to many textbooks would mean the definite article should be used. We have seen above in the section on the Indefinite Article that this is not the case. The real reason why the indefinite article is used in (21) is that these cats cannot be identified by the addressee. Likewise, in an utterance such as (23), one sees the problem of asserting that the definite article is used to describe a particular group "in general."

(23) Je n'aime pas entrer dans une maison où il y a des chats, parce que j'ai des allergies.
    (*I don't like going into a house where there are cats, because I have allergies.*)

In this case the speaker appears to be referring to cats in general, yet he has used the indefinite article. The reason that the definite article is not a possibility in this case is that the speaker is not referring to all the members of the group; instead, he has in mind a subset of "cats that exist in the world" that might be present in a living room on a given day.

In (24), Fox (1993, 324) gives an example of a type of student mistake that illustrates the difficulty students have in differentiating between the generic definite article and the unspecific indefinite article:

(24) Teacher: Quelle sorte de film est-ce que vous préférez?
         (*What kind of movies do you prefer?*)
     Student: ! Je préfère un western.
         (*! I prefer a western.*)

Native speakers will unequivocally agree that a response using the plural definite article is much more natural in this context, as seen in (25):

(25) Teacher: Quelle sorte de film est-ce que vous préférez?
         (*What kind of movies do you prefer?*)
     Student: Je préfère les westerns.
         (*I prefer westerns.*)

The reason (25) is better formed pragmatically than (24) is that the student wishes to refer to the whole category of films, that is, westerns, which is in fact generic. If, however, the adjective **bon** is inserted before **western** in the student's original response, the utterance becomes much more acceptable:

(26) Teacher: Quelle sorte de film est-ce que vous préférez?
         (*What kind of movies do you prefer?*)
     Student: Je préfère un bon western.
         (*I prefer a good western.*)

In fact, it would sound rather odd if one were to use the definite article before an adjective describing **les westerns:**

(27) Teacher: Quelle sorte de film est-ce que vous préférez?
         (*What kind of movies do you prefer?*)
     Student: ! Je préfère les bons westerns.
         (*! I prefer good westerns.*)

As Knud Lambrecht has pointed out (personal correspondence), the exchange in (26) sounds more acceptable than what one finds in (27), because it is difficult to conceive of a generic category of **bons westerns;** the notion is simply too subjective and undefined. In fact, adjectives often change what might be considered a generic category into a subset of a generic group that may be too difficult to categorize. Speakers are unable to come up with such a category. **Un bon western** is appropriate in the context above because it is just that: one good non-specific western, which remains unidentifiable and ungeneric. The following chart summarizes the process students should go through when choosing whether to use a definite or indefinite article.

### Definite or Indefinite Article?

Does the noun in question . . .

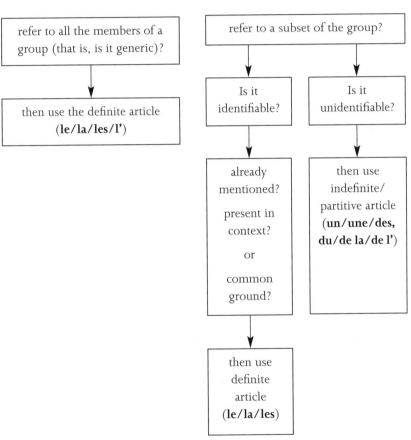

## The Partitive

It is important to note that indefinite and partitive articles have the same basic function in discourse. Unlike the case of the definite article, they refer to unidentifiable entities that are not generic.[2] Students often have difficulty choosing between indefinite and partitive articles, because there is no such distinction in English. Both **Je voudrais du vin** (*I'd like some wine*) and **Je voudrais des pistaches** (*I'd like some pistachios*) may be translated using the article *some* in English. The simplest and most effective way to explain the difference between the two ways of saying *some* in French is by pointing out that indefinite articles are used exclusively with count nouns. Count nouns can be defined quite simply as entities that can be enumerated—any noun that can have both singular and plural forms (with the exception of certain nouns that are always in the plural form, such as **gens**). Mass nouns, on the other hand, are entities that contain an uncountable mass, such as **du sucre** or **de l'eau.** The particles that compose a mass noun are often too small to be counted, and it is the entire mass that is being considered, not the individual parts.[3]

The appropriate article to precede unidentifiable specific or non-specific mass nouns is the partitive: **du, de la,** and **de l'.** Many textbooks present **des** as a partitive article, but we disagree with this assessment. In our analysis, partitive articles can precede only mass nouns. Nouns that represent an idea are also considered mass nouns, such as **de la patience,** or **du charme.** Sports are mass nouns as well, because one thinks of a particular sport in abstract terms. Therefore, **on fait du tennis,** but **on joue un match de tennis,** since individual games may be counted.

The situation is further complicated by the fact that some nouns may be either count or mass, and thus may require the indefinite or partitive article, based on the mental image in the speaker's (and, in an accommodating fashion, the addressee's) mind. For example, it is possible to find both **du thé** and **un thé,** the difference being that the first refers to the mass of tea flowing from a pot. **Un thé,** on the other hand, denotes a cup of tea within its container.

It is important to note that students often make errors not only when choosing between the indefinite and partitive articles, but also when deciding between the definite and partitive articles. Fox (1993, 324) gives another example of a student grammar mistake that her teaching assistants were able to correct, but unable to explain, as in (28):

(28) Teacher: Qu'est-ce que vous prenez le matin, en général?
                   (*What do you usually have in the morning?*)
        Student: ! Je prends le thé.
                   (! *I drink the tea.*)

Fox explains that many of the teaching assistants incorrectly attributed this error to a mass/count misunderstanding (318). She also states that: "The remaining seventy-six percent . . . stated that the student was claiming to be drinking 'all of the tea in the world.' . . . This last statement is not surprising to anyone teaching French; in discussions of the partitive, 'you can't x all of the y in the world' is a stock phrase. However, like the plurality of the TA responses, this response confuses the notion of mass noun with that of generic or non-referential use" (318). Based on our analysis above, Fox's TAs are not completely off base. They are, in fact, correct in pointing out that it is not appropriate to use an article denoting genericness in this context. The verb **prendre** simply does not elicit a generic direct object (note that this is also the case for most verbs that denote ingestion or acquisition of food or beverages, such as **boire, manger, goûter, acheter,** etc.). The student who has made this error needs to understand that it is more likely that she wishes to assert that she drinks an unidentifiable and non-specific cup of tea each morning. She can express this point using the indefinite article, as in (29):

(29) Teacher: Qu'est-ce que vous prenez le matin, en général?
        (*What do you usually have in the morning?*)
     Student: Je prends un thé/une tasse de thé.
        (*I drink tea/a cup of tea.*)

The partitive would also be acceptable, as in (30):

(30) Teacher: Qu'est-ce que vous prenez le matin, en général?
        (*What do you usually have in the morning?*)
     Student: Je prends du thé.
        (*I drink some tea.*)

The partitive would represent a mass of non-specific tea.

If the student had replied as in (31), changing the verb **prendre** (*to take*) to **aimer** (*to like*), the use of the definite article would have been appropriate; in this case **thé** (*tea*) would be generic:

(31) Teacher: Qu'est-ce que vous prenez le matin, en général?
        (*What do you usually have in the morning?*)
     Student: J'aime le thé.
        (*I like tea.*)

One can in principle like "all the tea in the world" (all that is "tea," in a generic sense), but one cannot realistically drink all the tea in the world.

What one likes (at an abstract level) and what one actually drinks are two very different things, which is reflected by the use of the different verbs and the different articles.

It is interesting to note that the verb **aimer** requires a generic noun as its direct object when the verb is conjugated in most forms of the indicative. When **aimer** is found in the conditional, however, it requires a direct object that is not generic, since the speaker is in fact asking for a particular item. For example, one can say **J'aime le thé** (I like tea), but if one would like to order a cup of tea, one would say **J'aimerais un thé, du thé,** or **une tasse de thé.** Students are often bewildered by this distinction, and it is helpful to present the verb **aimer** (to like) in both discourse environments to illustrate theses differences, as in (32):

(32) Je ne commande jamais de café. J'aime le thé. Alors, monsieur, s'il vous plaît, j'aimerais un thé.
(*I don't ever order coffee. I like tea. So, sir, I would like a tea please.*)

The following chart expands upon the one provided above (although the generic section is not included).

### Definite Article, Indefinite Article, or Partitive?

Does the noun in question refer to a subset of the group?

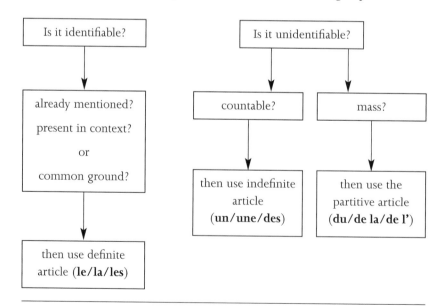

## Zero Article

Contrary to what learners of French are often taught, French nouns are not always preceded by an article. Consider the examples given in (33)–(38):

(33) Vous aimez Miami. (*You like Miami.*)
(34) Je vais à la gym lundi. (*I'm going to work out on Monday.*)
(35) Elle est professeur. (*She is a professor.*)
(36) Elle ne boit pas de vin. (*She doesn't drink wine.*)
(37) Il commande une carafe d'eau. (*He is ordering a carafe of water.*)
(38) Elle est dans la salle de classe. (*She is in the classroom.*)

In this section, we discuss the phenomena responsible for this absence (or perceived absence) of the article. Each example above corresponds to a particular category:

• Proper Nouns (33)
• Days of the Week (34)
• Predicate Nominatives (35)
• Negation/Deletion (36)
• Expressions of Quantity/Absorption (37)
• Compound Nouns (38)

Each type is explained and illustrated below.

### Proper Nouns

As in English, proper nouns in French are not usually preceded by an article. Therefore, one finds utterances such as (39)–(41):

(39) Tout le monde aime **Olivier.**
(40) Elle est étudiante à **Yale.**
(41) Vous aimez **Miami.**

The only complicated case is (41), because cities (and some islands) are the only geographical entities in French that are not preceded by an article. States, regions, countries, and continents usually have a definite article preceding them:

(42) Vous aimez **la Floride.**
(43) Vous aimez **les États-Unis.**
(44) Vous aimez **l'Amérique du Nord.**

### Days of the Week

Taken out of context, it is unclear why there is no article in (45), a definite article in (46) and an indefinite article in (47):

(45) Je dîne chez ma grand-mère lundi.
    (*I'm having dinner Monday at my grandmother's.*)
(46) Je dîne chez ma grand-mère le lundi.
    (*I have dinner at my grandmother's on Mondays.*)
(47) Je dînerai chez ma grand-mère un lundi.
    (*I'll have dinner at my grandmother's on a Monday.*)

Including the discourse environments in which these articles are found, however, clears up any misunderstandings, as shown in (48):

(48) En général je dîne chez ma grand-mère **le lundi,** mais cette semaine j'y vais **mardi,** à cause de la grève du métro **lundi.** Si jamais tu es disponible **un lundi,** tu devrais venir avec moi; c'est une très bonne cuisinière.
    (*In general, I eat dinner at my grandmother's on **Mondays,** but this week, I'm going on **Tuesday,** because of the subway strike **Monday.** If you are ever free on **a Monday,** you should come with me. She's a great cook.*)

The definite article is used when one is speaking about Mondays in general, which is logical since the definite article is used for generic entities. **Lundi** by itself refers to a particular Monday, and it is used without an article because it functions like a proper name. **Un lundi** refers to an unidentifiable Monday. Note that the indefinite article may refer to an unspecific entity, as in (48), or a specific one, as in (49):

(49) Un lundi après-midi, elle est allée chez sa grand-mère,
    (*One Monday afternoon, she went to her grandmother's.*)

### Predicate Nominatives

Predicate nominatives are nouns that function as adjectives in French. Consider the following example:

(50) Elle est professeur.    (*She is a professor.*)

In this case, the absence of an article before **professeur** shows that **professeur** is being used as an adjective. One can demonstrate its adjectival properties by attempting to modify **professeur** with an adjective:

(51) *Elle est professeur préféré.    (*She is a favorite professor.)

The impossibility of modifying **professeur** shows that it is no longer functioning as a noun. On the other hand, in (52), **professeur** is clearly a noun, because there is an article preceding it:

(52) Mme Jones est mon professeur.    (Mrs. Jones is my professor.)

In this case it is possible to modify **professeur:**

(53) Mme Jones est mon professeur    (Mrs. Jones is my favorite professor.)
     préféré.

Many adjectives may also function as nouns, if they are preceded by a determiner:

(54) Il est malade.    (He's sick.)
(55) C'est un malade.    (He's a sick person.)
(56) Il est américain.    (He's American.)
(57) C'est un Américain.    (He's an American.)

The adjectives **malade** and **américain** differ from the predicate nominative **professeur,** because **professeur** may not be used as an adjective to modify another noun, as demonstrated in (58):

(58) *C'est un Américain professeur.    (*He's a professor American.)

**Malade** or **américain,** on the other hand, can be used to modify another noun without any difficulty:

(59) C'est un professeur malade.    (He's a sick professor.)
(60) C'est un professeur américain.    (He's an American professor.)

### Negation/Deletion

Deletion occurs when an indefinite or partitive article is deleted and replaced by **de** following a negative expression (**ne ... pas, ne ... jamais, ne ... personne, ne ... rien,** etc.), as in examples (61)–(63):[4]

(61) Elle ne boit pas **de** vin.    (She doesn't drink wine.)
(62) Je ne prends jamais **de** sucre    (I don't ever put sugar in my coffee.)
     dans mon café.
(63) Elle n'a pas **de** frère.    (She doesn't have any brothers.)

The definite article, on the other hand, does not change following negation:

(64) Je n'aime pas **la** pluie.                    (*I don't like [the] rain.*)

The definite article is not deleted and replaced by **de** because, despite the negation, the noun phrase still represents either a particular identifiable entity or all the members of a given class.

### Expressions of Quantity / Absorption

Absorption looks a bit like deletion, but it is in fact another phenomenon. It often occurs with expressions of quantity, such as **beaucoup de, trop de, assez de, une tranche de, une bouteille de, une carafe de,** etc. Absorption occurs when the preposition **de** absorbs the partitive (**du, de la, de l'**) or plural indefinite article (**des**) that follows it, as in example (65):

(65) Elle boit beaucoup d'eau.                 (*She drinks a lot of water.*)

Had absorption not occurred, the utterance would be as in (66):

(66) *Elle boit beaucoup de de l'eau.         (*\*She drinks a lot of some water.*)

As Lambrecht has pointed out to us, however (personal correspondence), the French language rejects the presence of two identical items in succession. Therefore, it is not possible to have **beaucoup de** followed by **de.** In addition, if only the particle **de** were absorbed into the preposition, the resulting utterance would become indistinguishable from an already well-formed utterance that means something else, as provided in (67):

(67) Elle boit beaucoup de l'eau.

Example (67) is best translated as "She is drinking a lot of the water." This utterance would be perfectly acceptable in a context such as the following: two people are walking their Labrador retrievers, and one has brought a bottle of water for the dogs. At one point, the individual with the water puts all the water into a big bowl for the dogs. The first dog then begins drinking all the water. The other person exclaims: "Hey, Emma's drinking a lot of the water! There won't be any left for Floyd!" In this context, "Emma's drinking a lot of water" would be acceptable, but it would have a different communicative goal. Instead it would be a simple comment on Emma's general consumption of water. In this discourse setting, Emma is drinking a lot of a specific, identifiable amount of water, which is meant to be shared. Therefore, in order to eliminate the ambiguity, the partitive article is absorbed into the preposition **de** in the case where the water is not identifiable.

When a verb or other expression contains a preposition other than **de,** absorption does not take place, because there are not two identical elements in succession, as one can see in (68):

(68) Elle pense à du vin.

Example (68) may be translated as "She is thinking about some wine," whereas (69) may be translated as either "She is thinking about the wine," or "She is thinking about wine" (that is, wine generically):

(69) Elle pense au vin.

Finally, it is important to note that the indefinite articles **un** and **une** are not absorbed, because they do not begin with **de.** Therefore, one finds utterances such as those in (70) and (71):

(70) J'ai besoin d'une serviette.          (*I need a napkin.*)

(71) Je parle d'un chien que je connais.    (*I'm talking about a dog that I know.*)

### Compound Nouns

Though compound nouns may sometimes prove difficult for students, they are in reality rather straightforward. The rule is as follows: when one noun modifies another, insert the preposition **de** between the modified noun and the modifier, as in (72):

(72) Elle est dans la salle de classe.      (*She is in the classroom.*)

Words that can be either nouns or adjectives can sometimes confuse students. Consider example (73):

(73) Elle suit un cours de français.        (*She is taking a French class.*)

In this case **français** is a noun, but it also can be an adjective, as in (74):

(74) Elle achète un livre français.         (*She is buying a French book.*)

This distinction is subtle but important, and students' attention should be drawn to the difference between the use of **français** in these two examples. If one compares (73) and (74) to (75) and (76), where the noun and corresponding adjective do not have the same form, the distinction may be clearer:

(75) Elle suit un cours de biologie.          (*She is taking a biology class.*)
(76) Elle fait une expérience                 (*She is doing a biological experiment.*)
     biologique.

## GOING BEYOND: FOR THE ADVANCED LEARNER

### Retention of the Indefinite or Partitive Article

Despite what one learns in most textbooks, there are cases where the indefinite or partitive article is retained after negation. For example, consider the difference between (77) and (78):

(77) Je (n')ai pas de sœur.                   (*I don't have any sisters.*)
(78) Je (n')ai pas une sœur.                  (*I don't have one sister.*)

In (77), it is implied that the speaker has no sister at all. In (78), however, one finds an instance of metalinguistic stress; the speaker wishes to highlight **une** (*one*) to bring attention to the word itself. The speaker's goal is to emphasize that she does not have *one* sister, but more than one. The indefinite article **une,** which is really being used more as a quantifier than as an article in this case, is contrasted with the actual number of sisters. The plural indefinite article **des** may be retained after negation for the same reason, as shown in (79) and (80):

(79) Je (n')ai pas d'amis.                    (*I don't have [any] friends.*)
(80) Je (n')ai pas des amis; j'en            (*I don't have friends; I have one*
     ai un.                                   *[friend].*)

It is important to note that utterances such as (78) and (80) are rather rare in French. It would be more likely for a French speaker to use a cleft construction (which will be presented in Chapter 6) instead of the utterances in (78) or (80):

(78a) Ce (n')est pas une sœur que j'ai. J'en ai trois.
(80a) Ce (n')est pas des amis que j'ai. J'en ai un.

Sometimes the scope of negation is not well defined to native speakers of French. For example, some French speakers are unsure whether (81) or (82) is "correct":

(81) Il (ne) veut pas boire du vin.  (*He doesn't want to drink any of the wine.*)

(82) Il (ne) veut pas boire de vin.  (*He doesn't want to drink any wine.*)

Since the noun **vin** follows the verb **boire** and not the verb **vouloir,** it is not clear whether the partitive article should be deleted and replaced by **de.** Most grammar books avoid this topic entirely; in fact, one is hard-pressed to find any discussion of this phenomenon at all. Grevisse (1993, 874) gives the following sentence as an example of this phenomenon:

(83) Il ne faudrait pas perdre DE  (*One must not waste time.*)
   temps (Proust).

Example (84) would probably be acceptable as well:

(84) Il ne faudrait pas perdre DU  (*One must not waste any of the time.*)
   temps.

However, it is important to note that it is impossible to determine which utterances are better formed—(81) vs. (82) or (83) vs. (84)—without considering their discourse environments. According to Knud Lambrecht, (personal correspondence), (81) and (82) are both grammatically correct but would be found in different contexts. (81) would probably be used when the wine in question is being contrasted with another drink possibility. Consider the context given in (85):

(85) Speaker 1: Vas-y, donne-lui du blanc.
   (*Go ahead, give him some of the white.*)
   Speaker 2: Mais, non, il ne veut pas boire du vin; il veut de la bière.
   (*But he doesn't want to drink any of the wine; he wants some beer.*)

Note that in (85) it would be much more natural to find Speaker 2's answer in the form of a cleft construction, as in (86):

(86) Speaker 1: Vas-y, donne-lui du blanc.
   (*Go ahead, give him some of the white.*)
   Speaker 2: Mais, non, ce (n')est pas **du** vin qu'il veut; il veut de la bière.
   (*No, no, it's not wine that he wants; he wants some beer.*)

In contexts (85) and (86), the partitive article is maintained after the negation in order to contrast two different referents: **du vin** et **de la bière.** In (87), however, there is no such contrast. Speaker 2 asserts that Jean does not ever want wine. He does not drink alcohol:

(87) Speaker 1: Je vais acheter une bouteille de vin pour Jean.
    (*I'm going to buy a bottle of wine for John.*)
  Speaker 2: Mais non, il ne veut pas boire de vin. Il est alcoolique, et
    il ne boit pas.
    (*But he doesn't want to drink any wine. He's an alcoholic, and he doesn't
    drink.*)

Although this explanation goes beyond the scope of undergraduate French grammar or stylistics classes, it does help to exemplify the retention of the partitive or indefinite article following negation in specific contexts.

### Equivalents of *some*

Another topic that goes beyond what is usually taught in French language classes is the various ways to say *some*. As mentioned above, the word *some* is usually expressed in French by either the partitive article or the indefinite article **des.** There are, however, other ways to say *some*, some of which are more appropriate than others in various discourse situations.

Consider the following three examples, which all can be translated as "I saw some dogs in their yard":

(88) J'ai vu des chiens dans leur jardin.
(89) J'ai vu quelques chiens dans leur jardin.
(90) J'ai vu certains chiens dans leur jardin.

The choice of determiner depends on the presupposition of the speaker. **Certains,** which agrees in number and gender with the plural noun it precedes, is clearly different from **des** and **quelques.** It is used in a particular pragmatic situation, namely when one wishes to contrast a particular element of an utterance (the noun that follows it) with another entity. Utterance (90) implies that there are other dogs that were not seen in the yard, and in its English equivalent, the word *some* would receive a pitch accent to denote its contrastive quality:

(91) *I saw SOME dogs in the yard.* (implied: *but not others*)

The difference between **quelques** and **des** is less obvious, and sometimes the two can be used interchangeably. There are three main differences between them. First, whereas **des** can never be preceded by another determiner, **quelques** can:

(92) Ils se sont brouillés pour les quelques hectares de vignobles de leur
    père. (Rosenberg et al. 1991, 281)
    (*They had a falling out over their father's few hectares of vineyards.*)

It can be argued that in (92), however, **quelques** is not a determiner, but
an adjective. It does not mean *some* in this context, but *few*.

The second difference between **quelques** and **des** is that it is unusual
to find a sentence that begins with **des,** especially in the spoken language.
**Quelques** seems more grammatical in sentence-initial position, although
other constructions would likely be used to avoid this word order.
Whereas sentence (93) is acceptable, especially in the written language,
many French speakers would prefer sentence (94), which uses an **avoir-**
cleft (see Chapter 6), because it is more natural-sounding French:

(93) J'étais dans ma maison. Quelques chiens jouaient dans le jardin de
    mon voisin.
    (*I was in my house. Some dogs were playing in my neighbor's yard.*)
(94) J'étais dans ma maison. Il y avait quelques chiens qui jouaient dans
    le jardin de mon voisin.
    (*I was in my house. There were some dogs playing in my neighbor's yard.*)

Finally, the third major difference between **des** and **quelques** is that
**quelques** may be in the singular form (**quelque**) and still mean *some*, as
in the following example:

(95) Quelque chien errant a dû pénétrer dans le jardin la nuit dernière.
    (Dubos 1990, 174)
    (*Some wandering dog must have gotten into the yard last night.*)

In this case **quelque** is a determiner meaning *some*, not an adjective. It is,
however, in the singular and followed by a count noun, which distinguishes it from **des** and **certains** (as a determiner), which can only be
followed by plural nouns.

## CLASSROOM APPLICATIONS

This chapter contains a great deal of material, and the thought of im-
parting such information to students may seem daunting. Most important, instructors need to keep in mind the following guidelines:

- Do not present too much to students at one time, especially at the early levels of instruction.
- Have students discover and make their own hypotheses regarding the pragmatic properties of the various categories (in other words, do not simply provide students with the rules).
- Supplement each point with a good number of consciousness-raising activities, moving from input/analysis exercises to output (in other words, do not have students produce output immediately).

In addition, the concepts of identifiability and genericness and the mass/count distinction may be taught as early as the first semester. Teachers will need to gauge their students' readiness for more advanced concepts.

Below are some suggestions for teaching some of the topics in this chapter, along with accompanying exercises. We have tried to follow the order in which concepts have been presented in the chapter.

### Grammar Point 1: *L'article défini*

We suggest that instructors begin teaching articles by leading students to induce the rules for the use of definite articles. An overhead such as Overhead 1 provides students with three discourse settings where the definite article is used. Teachers should ask students why **le/la/les** is used in each case. The goal is for students to hypothesize that the nouns in question are identifiable. In example 1, the noun is identifiable because it has been mentioned previously; in 2, the object is physically present; and in 3, the speakers share some common ground (the existence of a particular train for which someone is waiting is part of a normal situation at a train station).

---

**Overhead 1: L'article défini**

**le   la   les**

1. Devant une maison qui brûle [drawing: a woman speaking to a fireman]:
   «J'ai deux chiens et deux chats. Les chiens sont dans la cave, et les chats sont dans le salon.»
2. À la pâtisserie [drawing: a mother and her child are in a bakery.

---

The child is looking in the display cases and pointing at a strawberry pie, saying]:

«Je veux la tarte aux fraises!»

3. À la gare [drawing: a woman impatiently looking at her watch]:

«Mais où est le train???»

The goal of Overhead 2 is to lead students to hypothesize the concept of genericness:

---

**Overhead 2: L'article défini: la généricité**

**le    la    les**

*Context:* A young child is being interviewed for the school newspaper about his likes and dislikes.

Quel animal aimes-tu?

    J'aime les chiens.

Quel dessert préfères-tu?

    Je préfère la glace.

Qu'est-ce que tu n'aimes pas à l'école?

    Je déteste les devoirs.

---

Instructors should begin by asking students whether the dogs, ice cream, and homework assignments mentioned here are identifiable (the obvious answer is that they are not). Next, instructors should ask students to therefore hypothesize a rule for the use of the definite article in these sentences. Once students have figured out that these are generic categories, they could be asked to add to these lists, including their own likes and dislikes. Instructors should explain to students that verbs of liking and disliking (**aimer, adorer, préférer, détester,** etc.) are often followed by the definite article because what is liked or disliked is usually generic. For example, one can generally dislike the generic category of cats but like certain individual cats. Still, one would say: **Je n'aime pas les chats,** in principle.

The purpose of Overhead 3 is to contrast the use of the definite and indefinite article and to show that the definite article, when refering to generic entities, represents all the members of the group, while the indefinite article refers to a subset of the group:

---

### Overhead 3: L'article défini et l'article indéfini

*Step 1*: Comparez les deux phrases suivantes:

Les chiens sont des animaux.

Les serpents sont des reptiles.

[*Note to instructors*: Ask students why one would not find **les animaux** or **les reptiles** in these contexts.]

*Step 2*: Étudiez le tableau suivant et complétez les phrases.

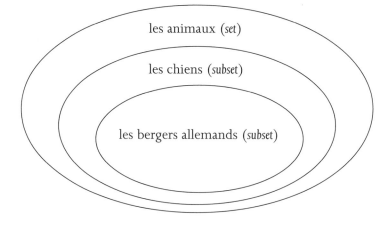

Les chiens sont des _____.

Les bergers allemands _____.

*Step 3*: Complétez les phrases suivantes:

Les tartes sont des _____. [*likely answer*: desserts]

Les Québécois sont des _____. [*likely answer*: Canadiens]

Les pommes sont des _____. [*likely answer*: fruits]

---

Note that these overheads are neither complicated nor long. They are designed to raise students' consciousness of the points at hand and lead them to make hypotheses. The following exercises, to be done after the initial grammar exploration, will allow students to focus on and master these concepts in context. Note that the activities given in the early sections of this chapter are not based on authentic discourse, yet they still take place within meaningful contexts. For lower-level students, authentic materials could prove to be overwhelming and distracting. It is better to structure the input carefully to meet their needs. Toward the end of this chapter, however, we provide activities for more advanced students that contain passages of authentic discourse. Note that these activities must be carefully structured as well. Activity 4.1, a consciousness-raising exercise, allows students to analyze snippets of discourse and to review the use of the definite article in various situations.

● ● ● ● ●

**Activity 4.1: Pourquoi l'article défini?** (consciousness-raising)

Choose the reason for the use of the definite article in each case:

a. Identifiable (discours)      (Identifiable due to the discourse—
                                 already mentioned)
b. Identifiable (présence)      (Identifiable due to physical
                                 presence)
c. Identifiable (le fond commun)  (Identifiable due to common
                                   ground)
d. Générique                    (Generic)

1. Louise a deux lapins, Thomas et Pierre. J'aime **les** lapins, mais pas Thomas et Pierre.
2. Louise a des lapins et des hamsters. **Les** lapins sont noirs, et **les** hamsters sont bruns.
3. Hier j'ai fait du shopping. J'aime regarder **les** soldes. J'ai acheté un blouson et des chaussettes. **Le** blouson, je l'ai acheté au Bon Marché et **les** chaussettes au Printemps. J'aime **les** grands magasins. Regarde **la** couleur de ce blouson! C'est chic, non?

Activity 4.2 is also designed to help students master the definite article. The concept of genericness is often tied to the notion of stereotyping, and using stereotypes to reinforce the use of the definite article with generic nouns is an effective teaching tool. In this activity, students are asked to create their own stereotypes about groups, using the definite article. Note that the first two sections contain structured input, as students are not asked to produce the articles in question. The last section, however, includes some structured output; it pushes students to combine the stereotyping use of the definite article with the liking/disliking function.

• • • • •

**Activity 4.2: Les stéréotypes.** (structured input and output)

*Step* 1: Select the best answer(s) from the list given for each stereotype, or provide your own answer.

En général, on pense que...
1. les Américains sont...
    a. gros                c. sportifs
    b. cultivés            d. (à vous)
2. les Français sont...
    a. snobs               c. ivres
    b. cultivés            d. (à vous)
3. les Anglais sont...
    a. raffinés            c. obèses
    b. très sexy           d. (à vous)
4. les Allemands sont...
    a. organisés           c. sauvages
    b. bruns               d. (à vous)

*Step* 2: Now provide your own stereotypes:

En général, je pense que...
1. les professeurs sont...
2. les étudiants de cette université sont...
3. les hommes sont...
4. les femmes sont...
5. les exercices comme celui-ci sont...

En général,  ...
1. les New Yorkais aiment...
2. les Texans détestent...
3. les terroristes préfèrent...
4. les chiens adorent...

### Grammar Point 2: *L'article indéfini et l'article partitif*

Overhead 4 is designed to focus students' attention on the differences between the indefinite article and the partitive. The goal is for students to realize that the partitive is used with mass nouns and the indefinite article with count nouns:

---

### Overhead 4: L'article indéfini et l'article partitif

### un, une, des vs. du, de la, de l'

*Step* 1: Comparez les deux listes suivantes:

| Liste A | Liste B |
|---|---|
| une carotte/des carottes | du riz |
| une baguette/des baguettes | du pain |
| une bouteille/des bouteilles | de l'eau |
| un steak/des steaks | de la viande |

[Note to instructors: Ask students to generalize: what are the differences between the nouns in List A and the nouns in List B? Goal: Students come up with count vs. mass noun distinction.]

*Step* 2: Décidez lesquels des noms suivants sont nombrables:
Modèle: sandwich → *des sandwichs*

petit pois
vin
tomate
croissant
beurre
sel
poulet

[Note to instructors: **Poulet** can be both a count noun and a mass noun: for example, it could be **un poulet** if one were to buy an entire uncooked chicken at the supermarket.]

---

At this point, structured-input activities such as the following would be appropriate:

● ● ● ● ●

#### Activity 4.3: Les récipients. (structured input)

Decide whether each noun represents a quantity inside a container or an unspecified mass of a given substance.

1. Elle a pris une salade.                container    mass
2. Nous mangeons de la soupe.            container    mass
3. J'aimerais du sel.                     container    mass
4. Vous buvez du café.                    container    mass
5. Elle a pris une bière.                 container    mass
6. Veux-tu de l'eau?                      container    mass
7. Il a commandé une omelette.           container    mass
8. Vous avez de la patience.             container    mass

• • • • •

### Activity 4.4: C'est vous le chef. (structured input)

Select the ingredient that one does not usually find in each of the following dishes.

Une omelette: des oignons, du fromage, des champignons, du chocolat
Une tarte: de la farine, du sel, du beurre, du poivre
Un sandwich: de la mayonnaise, du maïs, du pain, de la salade
Une salade: des tomates, des pâtes, du pâté, des pommes de terre
Une salade de fruits: des cerises, du raisin, des oranges, des haricots

Activity 4.5 is a consciousness-raising exercise. Note that students need not produce any structures; their goal is to analyze facts and come up with hypotheses.

• • • • •

### Activity 4.5: Les contextes. (consciousness-raising)

In each of the following situations, your task is to decide whether the noun in question is countable or not. Then determine whether the indefinite or partitive article should be used, and supply the correct form.

[Note to instructors: The questions could be asked either in English or in French; both are provided below.]

1. Vous êtes dans un restaurant, et vous commandez votre repas. La serveuse demande si vous voulez une salade. Pourquoi pas «de la salade»? Quand est-ce que l'expression «de la salade» serait appropriée? Donnez un contexte.
   (You are in a restaurant, and you are ordering your meal. The waitress asks if you would like "**une** salade" (a salad). Why not "**de la** salade"

(some salad)? When would "de la salade" (some salad) be appropriate? Give a particular discourse environment.)

2. Vous êtes chez vous et votre mère vous demande si vous voulez «un coca». Décrivez l'image de la boisson que vous avez dans votre tête. Est-ce qu'on pourrait avoir cette conversation à table?
(You are at home, and your mother asks if you would like "**un** coca" (a cola). Describe the image of the drink that you have in your head. Could this conversation take place at the dinner table?)

3. Expliquez la différence entre les deux paires de mots de chaque groupe, en donnant un contexte différent pour chacun:
(Explain the difference between the following pairs of words, giving appropriate discourse environments for each:)

du café / un café
de la glace / une glace
du sandwich / un sandwich

After the consciousness-raising and structured-input activities, students are ready for structured-output exercises, such as Activity 4.6:

• • • • •

**Activity 4.6: Votre frigo.** (structured output)

Step 1: Make a list of everything that is currently in your refrigerator. Be sure to include the appropriate indefinite or partitive article:
Example: du beurre.

Step 2: Make lists of what you would get rid of and what you would buy if your parents were coming to stay with you.

Step 3: Find someone in the class who seems different from you in some way (personality, sex, taste in clothing, etc.). Compare your lists, and then report back to class what you have in common and what each of you has that is unique. Is there something in particular that your partner has that you find bizarre? Is there something bizarre that you both have?

Step 4: Finally, make a list of things that you do not have but would like to have.
Example: Je n'ai pas de bon vin.

Activity 4.7 serves to reinforce some of the concepts presented above. Students are asked to choose possible responses to various questions. Afterward, they should explain their choices.

$\bullet\ \bullet\ \bullet\ \bullet\ \bullet$

**Activity 4.7: La bonne réponse.** (structured input)

For each interaction, which of the answers sound correct to you?[5]

1. *Contexte:* Vous commandez dans un restaurant.
   SERVEUR: Vous désirez?
   VOUS:    Je voudrais un café.
             Je voudrais le café.
             Je voudrais du café.
             Je voudrais le café du jour.

2. *Contexte:* Une amie vous invite au dîner.
   AMIE:    Est-ce qu'il y a quelque chose que tu ne manges pas?
            (*Is there anything that you don't eat?*)
   VOUS:    Je n'aime pas la viande.
             Je ne mange pas de viande.
             Je ne mange pas la viande.

3. *Contexte:* Chez le psy.
   LE PSY:   Qu'est-ce qui ne va pas?
   VOUS:    Je n'ai pas d'amis.
             Je n'ai pas des amis.
             Je n'aime pas les amis.
             Je n'aime pas les amis que j'ai.
             Je n'ai pas beaucoup d'amis.

Activity 4.8 is developed to help students grasp the difference between specific and non-specific indefinite articles. Note that this topic may be too advanced for first- or second-year students. Before doing Activity 4.8, teachers should ask students why the utterance **Elle cherche un homme** is ambiguous. The answer is that **un homme** may be either a specific man or an unspecific one, depending on the context.

$\bullet\ \bullet\ \bullet\ \bullet\ \bullet$

**Activity 4.8: Spécifique ou pas spécifique?** (consciousness-raising)

The passage below contains several indefinite articles, which are bold-faced. Your task is to decide for each indefinite article whether it refers to a specific or non-specific entity, or whether it could be either. Remember that for specific indefinite articles, the speaker has a representation in her mind of the exact entity to which she refers; in the non-specific case, there is no such representation.

> Dominique cherche (1) **un** homme. Ça fait trop longtemps qu'elle est célibataire. Il faut que cet homme soit gentil, intelligent et beau. (2) **Un** jour, elle a décidé de mettre (3) **une** petite annonce dans (4) **un** journal. Elle sait qu'il y a (5) **des** hommes de qualité qui eux aussi cherchent (6) **une** femme. Ses amis pensent que c'est (7) **une** bonne idée.

1. spécifique     pas spécifique     ambigu
   etc.

Before teaching students about all the cases where there is no article, it is a good idea to start with the days of the week. Using Overhead 5, have students analyze the various cases of zero-article use based on the discourse environments in which they are found. Then Activity 4.9 gives students the opportunity to test their knowledge and understanding of these concepts.

---

**Overhead 5: L'article zéro et les jours de la semaine**

1. Marie est très fidèle à sa grand-mère. Elle va la voir le dimanche, même si elle est malade de temps en temps.
2. Marie a un concert dimanche, alors, elle va arriver en retard chez sa grand-mère cette semaine.
3. Si jamais tu es disponible un dimanche, tu devrais y aller avec elle. Sa grand-mère est une très bonne cuisinière.

[Note to instructors: In item 1, the definite article is used because it is a generic Sunday. In item 2, there is no article, because it refers to a specific (identifiable) day. In item 3, it is an unspecific, unidentifiable Sunday.]

---

• • • • •

**Activity 4.9: Les jours de la semaine.** (consciousness-raising)

Decide in each case whether the day of the week in question is:

a. generic     b. a specific (identifiable) day     c. unidentifiable

Then, provide the proper form of the corresponding article (**le, un,** or **ø**):

1. Mary likes to go see her grandmother on Tuesdays.

                        a        b        c        _____ mardi

2. If ever you are free on a Saturday night, give me a call.

                        a        b        c        _____ samedi soir

3. If you are free on Saturday night, I'd like to take you to a movie.

                        a        b        c        _____ samedi soir

4. Monday is a very difficult day for me in general. I never get enough
   sleep on Sunday night.

   Monday               a        b        c        _____ lundi

   Sunday night     a        b        c        _____ dimanche soir

5. Monday is a very difficult day for me this week. I have to get my hair
   cut at 7 A.M.

                        a        b        c        _____ lundi

Overhead 6 presents all the cases of the zero article presented in this
chapter.

---

**Overhead 6: L'article zéro**

[Note to instructors: Ask students to formulate the rules for the missing
articles.]

| | |
|---|---|
| Vous aimez Miami. | [Compare with: Vous aimez la Floride.] |
| Je vais à la gym lundi. | [Compare with: Je vais à la gym le lundi.] |
| Elle est professeur. | [Compare with: C'est un professeur.] |
| Elle ne boit pas de vin. | [Compare with: Elle boit du vin.] |
| Il commande une carafe d'eau. | |
| Elle est dans la salle de classe. | |

---

Activity 4.10 may follow Overhead 6:

• • • • •

**Activity 4.10: Le cas de l'article qui manque.** (consciousness-raising)

Decide why each of the highlighted nouns in the passage below does not
have an article preceding it. Choose the reason from the following list:

| a. Les noms propres | (Proper Nouns) |
| b. Les jours de la semaine | (Days of the Week) |
| c. Le nominatif prédicat | (Predicate Nominative) |
| d. Les noms composés | (Compound Nouns) |
| e. La négation/l'effacement | (Negation/Deletion) |
| f. L'absorption/expression de quantité | (Absorption/Quantity Expression) |

Dans notre salle de (1) classe, il n'y a pas de (2) cours (3) mardi à cause de (4) visiteurs de (5) Reims qui viennent nous parler de (6) cinéma. Monsieur Renard, qui est (7) professeur d'(8) anglais dans une université française, veut établir beaucoup de (9) contacts avec des élèves américains pour qu'il n'y ait plus de (10) malentendus entre les jeunes des deux pays.

It is beneficial to give more advanced students the opportunity to work with longer passages of naturally occurring French, as in excerpts from a corpus or film clips. Structuring the input in this way and focusing students' attention on the articles allows learners to analyze the grammatical function of the articles in a meaningful manner. Activity 4.11 is an example of this type of activity:

● ● ● ● ●

### Activity 4.11: Jeu de mémoire. (dictogloss)

Listen to your teacher read the following excerpt about how to choose a menu for a wedding. Don't take any notes. Then, in groups, try to reconstruct the recommendations of the text, making a list of the food items that were mentioned.

### Comment choisir un menu? Lequel choisir?

Nous vous conseillons tout d'abord de faire une sélection de traiteurs de votre région, de les appeler, et de vous faire envoyer leurs menus type ainsi que leurs tarifs. Il va vous falloir alors potasser un à un les menus reçus et faire un premier choix, l'idéal étant d'avoir déjà des idées de plats en tête. Ensuite, prenez rendez-vous chez les traiteurs ou restaurateurs sélectionnés et qui semblent vous correspondre le mieux, afin de vous faire préciser l'élaboration de leurs plats et de leur cuisine, de voir ou goûter ce qu'ils font, et de comparer leurs tarifs. Pensez à communiquer bien entendu au traiteur le nombre exact de convives.

Les traiteurs, comme les restaurateurs, vous proposeront un vaste choix de menus, à des prix divers. Composé par le traiteur ou par vous-même, le menu a pour base en général une entrée, une viande ou un poisson, un féculent, un légume et un dessert.

Du Foie Gras, des Noix de Saint-Jacques, de la Lotte, une Pièce de Bœuf? autant de produits synonymes de fête. Le Foie Gras de Canard est bien souvent la grande star des repas de mariage. Vous ne surprendrez personne en le choisissant et vous aurez la certitude de faire plaisir à tout le monde. Que vous optiez pour la simplicité ou le raffinement, la tradition ou le classicisme? surtout choisissez un menu qui s'intègre parfaitement au style de votre mariage.

Vous accompagnerez votre repas de champagne ou d'un vin coordonné aux saveurs des plats. Demandez conseil à un caviste, il saura vous conseiller. Pensez à organiser une dégustation avec des amis connaisseurs pour être vraiment sûr de votre choix.

Source: http://www.mariage.fr/article/feter/intro_feter.cfm

Activity 4.12, a discourse-analysis exercise, gives students the opportunity to make hypotheses based on actually occurring discourse.

● ● ● ● ●

**Activity 4.12: Les Français aux États-Unis.** (discourse analysis)

Below you will find an excerpt from the Minnesota Corpus of Spoken French (Kerr 1983), which is a lengthy transcription of conversations among educated native speakers of French. First read through the dialogue, paying attention to the boldfaced articles. Then, answer the questions that follow the dialogue.

Context: Three French women are discussing a soup that one of them has eaten for the first time in the United States.

E: Alors c'est une sorte **de** soupe avec **des** betteraves rouges! Alors ta soupe, elle arrive rose!

M: Ah ha!

C: Ouais.

E: La première fois que j'ai vu ça, j'ai dit oh la la! Qu'est-ce que ça, non mais **la** couleur tu sais, pour **un** Français, **une** soupe rose comme ça.

M: Rose pâle, oui.

E: Tu te dis, qu'est-ce que ça va être, mais c'est excellent! Avec **de la** crème, et aussi **des** petites pommes de terre et **du** lard, c'est vraiment bon.

M: Ah ça doit être bon, hein!

E: Ah oui, c'est vraiment vraiment bon!

M: Mais **du** lard, **du** lard,

E: **Du** lard entier **du** lard ah oui parce qu'il l'achète pas ici, il l'achète à Kramarczuk, qui est **une**

(...)

E: qui est une charcuterie et une boucherie polonaise et y a

M: y a **le** vrai lard, parce que

E: Et y a **du** vrai lard,

(...)

E: Et on y va de temps en temps, et y a aussi **des** saucisses, excellentes, **des** saucisses polonaises vraiment très très bonnes.

M: Non mais, tu sais **le** lard ça m'intéresse.

Reprinted with permission from Betsy Kerr, University of Minnesota.

Questions:

1. For each article that is boldfaced, define it as either a definite article, an indefinite article, a partitive, or the particle **de.**
2. Next, give the reason why each article is used:
   • definite article:
   a. generic
   b. identifiable due to
      i. prior mention
      ii. presence
      iii. common ground
   • indefinite article: unidentifiable count noun
   • partitive: unidentifiable mass noun
   • **de:** due to
      a. its following negation
      b. its being an expression of quantity
      c. its being a compound noun
3. Near the end of the conversation, the speakers go back and forth between saying **du lard** and **le lard.** Hypothesize why both articles are used and why the speakers seem to hesitate between the two. Which article seems more appropriate to you? Why?
4. With a partner, describe a dish or a meal that you have eaten which Americans might consider a bit odd. What ingredients are included? What is not included that Americans might consider lacking? Did you enjoy the dish/meal? Why or why not? If you cannot think of a dish that fits into this category, invent your own, describing its ingredients and giving your assessment of it.

In Activity 4.13, students work with two film clips to test their knowledge of the use of articles in discourse.[6] They are given a sheet with the transcript of a film dialogue in which the articles are missing. First, the students work in groups, deciding which articles are the most appropriate for each blank. Then they watch the film to see if they were correct. Finally, as a class, they discuss the reasons for each article in each situation.

• • • • •

**Activity 4.13: Les scènes sans articles.** (discourse analysis)

Fill in the missing articles.

Film 1: *La Cage aux folles*

Context: Albin is going shopping. Laurent, his partner's son, has just arrived the night before, and Albin has not seen him yet. Albin wants to prepare a special meal for Laurent. In this scene he is chatting with some shopkeepers.

c = Shopkeeper, a = Albin

c: Tiens, bonjour, Monsieur Albin.

a: Bonjour, Monsieur Lefèvre. (1) _____ petit est arrivé.

c: Je vous mets (2) _____ bon rôti, alors?

a: Je passe le prendre tout à l'heure.

c: D'accord.

---

c: Ça va, Monsieur Albin?

a: Très bien, Monsieur Leprise. (3) _____ pâtes fraîches et (4) _____ parmesan.

c: Alors (5) _____ petit est arrivé?

a: Oui, il est arrivé. Je me dépêche . . . ça ne sera jamais prêt.

---

a: Bonjour Monsieur Lafaille.

c: Bonjour Monsieur Albin. Comme d'habitude?

a: Oui. (6) _____ nougatine et vous écrivez . . .

c: À mon lolo, sa tatie.

a: À mon lolo, sa tatie. Merci pour (7) _____ pain. Je me sauve parce qu'il va se réveiller.

c: Je vous la livrerai, (8) _____ nougatine?

A: Non, laissez ... ben non ... Jacob viendra la chercher. Je prends
(9) _____ chocolat, hein? Au revoir.

Answers:
1. Le 2. un 3. Des 4. du 5. le 6. Une 7. le 8. la 9. un

Film 2: *Au Revoir les enfants*
Context: This film takes place in the South of France during World War II. In this scene Mme Quentin, the mother of Julien and François, comes to their school to visit them. She takes them out to eat. They go to a good restaurant, but because of the war the restaurant is limited as to what it can serve. She asks the waiter what he suggests.
s = Waiter, M = Mme Quentin, F = François

s: Je vous recommande (1) _____ lapin chasseur. (2) _____ demi-ticket (3) _____ viande par portion.
F: C'est (4) _____ lapin ou (5) _____ chat?
M: François!
s: (6) _____ lapin, monsieur. Avec (7) _____ pommes rissolées.
M: Elles sont au beurre, vos pommes (8) _____ terre?
s: À la margarine, madame. Sans ticket.
s: Bon, on va pour (9) _____ lapin chasseur. Et (10) _____ bouteille (11) _____ bordeaux, s'il vous plaît.

Answers:
1. le 2. Un 3. de 4. du 5. du 6. Du 7. des 8. de 9. le 10. une 11. de

Reprinted with permission from the *French Review.*

## CONSOLIDATION EXERCISES

1. Explain why the following sentences are ambiguous, giving two translations, as well as appropriate discourse environments, for each:
    a. Fréd n'aime pas les Américains.
    b. Il n'aime pas le café.
2. Early in this chapter, we give contexts where what seem to be grammatically incorrect sentences are in fact correct in certain discourse settings (**Je préfère des chiens,** and **Jacques a commandé une bouteille**

**du vin**). Try to come up with contexts where the other four pragmatically odd utterances (repeated here) would be acceptable:

! J'ai pris les tomates et les oignons.

! J'aimerais le sucre.

! Super! Mais je ne mange pas des olives.

! Je sais que les éléphants sont les animaux.

3. Consider the following statement, made by a young woman who lives in Neuilly and has attended a party in Paris:

Samedi soir je suis allée à une soirée chez des amis. J'ai pris **le bus** pour y aller, mais j'ai pris **le taxi** pour rentrer.

Imagine two discourse environments, one in which the article **le** preceding the word **taxi** is pragmatically odd, and one in which it would be acceptable. Why is it usually acceptable to say **le bus** (the bus) but not **le taxi** (the taxi)?

4. Can you imagine a context in which the following utterance[7] would be possible?

**Quelle horreur! Il y avait du chat partout sur la route.**

5. French speakers are sometimes not sure whether it is preferable to say

a. En général, j'aime manger des frites avec un steak.

or

b. En général, j'aime manger les frites avec un steak.

(Both mean: In general, I like to eat French fries with a steak.)

Why do you think that native speakers hesitate between the use of **les** or **des**? Using the concepts discussed in this chapter, decide which utterance is better formed.

6. The following utterance is ambiguous in English:

Monday is a very difficult day for me. I have to get up very early.

Give two different translations into French that elucidate the two possible meanings of the utterance.

7. The utterances in each of the groups below differ in their either retaining or losing the indefinite or partitive article. For each set, give two distinctly different discourse environments in which they could be found:

1a. Elle parle de chiens.

1b. Elle parle des chiens.

2a. Elle a besoin d'aide.

2b. Elle a besoin de l'aide.

3a. Nous aimons parler de philosophie.

3b. Nous aimons parler de la philosophie.

8. Unlike in English, the French definite article is often required instead of the possessive determiner to denote a body part. Therefore, one finds utterances such as **Elle s'est lavé les cheveux** (*she washed her hair*) or **Elle lui a cassé le nez** (*she broke his nose*) instead of (!) **Elle a lavé ses mains** or (!) **Elle a cassé sa figure.** On the other hand, it is acceptable to say **Elle a regardé sa figure** (*she looked at his face*). Hypothesize why this distinction exists and how it should be explained to advanced students.

9. It is acceptable to say both **Elle a les cheveux bruns** and **Elle a des cheveux bruns.** However, while one can say **Elle a de(s) jolis cheveux,** (!) **Elle a les jolis cheveux** is pragmatically odd. Based on the discussions in this chapter, can you come up with a rule or an explanation for this discrepancy?

## TYPICAL STUDENT ERRORS

Imagine that your students have made the mistakes provided below. Each sentence is either grammatically or pragmatically ill-formed. A grammatically ill-formed sentence is simply wrong (it would never be acceptable, in any context), whereas a pragmatically ill-formed sentence might be possible in another context. Decide which is the case for each. Finally, come up with an explanation for your students as to why each utterance is "wrong." Note: This activity could also be done with students. They could be asked to find and correct the mistakes.

1. *Context:* Students are asked what they like to eat.
   J'aime manger le chocolat.
2. *Context:* Students are asked what they like to do in their free time.
   J'aime faire des sports, et aussi faire du camping et la pêche.
3. *Context:* Student is apologizing for his lack of proficiency in French.
   J'ai beaucoup oublié mon français, je crois. Je n'ai pas suivi les cours français depuis longtemps.
4. *Context:* Student is asked what kind of vegetable she prefers.
   Comme légume, je préfère des frites.
5. *Context:* Student is asked why he didn't argue with his friend about an unreasonable request.
   Je ne voulais pas des problèmes.
6. *Context:* Student is asked what she did after seeing a movie.
   Alors, on est allés au restaurant, et j'ai commandé une carafe de l'eau.

7. *Context:* Student is asked what he likes to do in his free time.
   Qu'est-ce que j'aime faire? Je lis les journaux.
8. *Context:* At the dinner table, where there is a large salad bowl in the middle of the table.
   «Pourrais-je avoir une salade?»
9. *Context:* Students are asked about their familial situation.
   J'habite seul. Je n'ai même pas des poissons rouges.

## Corrections of Student Errors (answers may vary)

1. J'aime manger du chocolat. (*pragmatically ill-formed*)
2. Et finalement, j'aime faire du sport, et aussi faire du camping et de la pêche. (*grammatically ill-formed*)
3. J'ai beaucoup oublié de mon français, je crois. Je n'ai pas suivi de cours de français depuis longtemps. (*grammatically ill-formed*)
4. Comme légume, je préfère les frites. (*pragmatically ill-formed*)
5. Je ne voulais pas de problèmes. (*pragmatically ill-formed*)
6. Alors, on est allés au restaurant, et j'ai commandé une carafe d'eau. (*pragmatically ill-formed*)
7. Je lis des journaux. (*pragmatically ill-formed*)
8. «Pourrais-je avoir de la salade?» (*pragmatically ill-formed*)
9. J'habite seul. Je n'ai même pas de poissons rouges. (*pragmatically ill-formed*)

## DISCUSSION TOPICS/PROJECTS

1. Some textbooks refer to various types of determiners as adjectives. For example, the possessive determiners **mon, ma, mes,** etc., are sometimes called possessive adjectives. Do you agree with this analysis? Why or why not?
2. Some languages do not have articles at all. Do you think that it would be easier or more difficult to teach native speakers of these languages about the French article system? Why?
3. Imagine that you are teaching an English as a Second Language class. A student asks you when one should use the verb "make" and when one should use "do." Using your native speaker intuitions (or asking a native speaker of English, if you are not a native speaker), create a list of

various sentences that contain each expression in discourse. Can you posit a rule for their use?

4. Compile a list of French movie titles, and analyze their use of determiners. Consider, for example, the following: *La vie n'est pas un long fleuve tranquille; Le dîner de cons; La haine; La règle du jeu; À bout de souffle.*

5. Based on the discussion in Chapter 3 about methods for teaching various types of grammar points, how might you teach possessive determiners as vocabulary items? What kinds of activities would you use?

6. Go through two or three textbooks and compare the grammar explanations and exercises for any aspect of teaching articles. Do you see any problems, flaws, or confusing terminology? Make a list of undefined terms or erroneous explanations, and try to correct or rework them.

## FURTHER READING

### On Articles in French

Herschensohn, Julia. "The Predictability of the Article in French." In *Contemporary Studies in Romance Linguistics*, edited by Margarita Suñer, 176–193. Washington, DC: Georgetown University Press, 1977.

Katz, Stacey. "Teaching Articles: How Students Can Master the French Determiner System." *French Review* 75 (2001): 290–304.

### On Articles in English

Master, Peter. "Consciousness Raising and Article Pedagogy." In *Academic Writing in a Second Language*, edited by Diane Belcher and George Braine, 183-204. Norwood, NJ: Ablex, 1995.

———. "The Effect of Systematic Instruction on Learning the English Article System." In *Perspectives on Pedagogical Grammar*, edited by Terence Odlin, 229–249. Cambridge: Cambridge University Press, 1994.

### On the Treatment of Articles in Textbooks

Herschensohn, Julia. "Linguistic Accuracy of Textbook Grammar." *Modern Language Journal* 72 (1988): 409–414.

# 5 · Narrative Past Tenses

## OVERVIEW / KEY CONSIDERATIONS

The following grammatical topics are covered in this chapter:

• Passé composé
• Imparfait
• Plus-que-parfait
• The concept of narrativity: what makes a text a narrative
• The concept of aspect: perfectivity vs. imperfectivity
• Grammatical aspect vs. lexical aspect
• Pragmatic functions of narrative tenses

## DIFFICULTIES FOR THE LEARNER

If Marcel Proust, one of the greatest writers in the French literary canon, struggled with the difficulties of past tenses, what hope is there for our students? Narrative past tenses can be tricky, but the situation is not as bleak as Proust would lead us to believe. After all, Proust had a notorious penchant for drama and melancholy. In this chapter, we will show teachers what they can do to help their students grasp the differences between the following sentences:

- Elle était fâchée. (**imparfait**)
- Elle a été fâchée. (**passé composé**)
- Elle avait été fâchée. (**plus-que-parfait**)

Kaplan (1987, 53) states that teachers find the choice between the **passé composé** and the **imparfait** "particularly problematic for English-speaking learners of French." The widespread perception of the problematic nature of this particular grammar point in teaching circles is largely corroborated by data-based studies of learner performance. In a review of the findings on the efficacy of the Canadian French immersion schools, Harley (1992) notes that advanced students who had received 6000 hours of instruction still had difficulty choosing the correct past tenses in narrative discourse. In addition to performance problems, students themselves frequently mention how daunting past-tense selection seems when presented in a confusing terminology of seemingly contradictory rules (Dansereau 1987; Blyth 1997).

One of the reasons that students have difficulty employing past tenses to construct a narrative is that they often fail to think about narrative as a distinct genre with specific conventions. Students would be wise to consider what constitutes a narrative before trying to learn the so-called narrative tenses. So what is a narrative? Defining the set of features common to all narratives is a central concern of the field called *narratology*. Within this area of research, the term *narrativity* is used for the sum of special qualities that constitute narrative. Prince (1982, 1991) argues that a text's narrativity is based on four features:

1. Events must have clearly defined beginnings and ends, and they must be non-trivial, specific, and relevant to humans.
2. There must be conflict between two opposites or adversaries.
3. There must be a discernible beginning, a middle, and an end.
4. The audience must recognize the text as a narrative.

Polanyi (1981) suggests that spontaneous oral narrative deserves special attention from narratologists since it may hold the key to a more profound understanding of narrativity. She explains that: "oral storytelling in conversational contexts constitutes the primary site for understanding narrative structure. Once we understand what every competent speaker is doing when s(he) recounts the experiences in his/her life or the lives of other people, we will be in a somewhat better position to understand the transformation of the 'story' into written, fictional, and literary artifact" (316). Polanyi's arguments reflect the stance of many linguists who contend that speech is more basic than writing because humans always learn to speak before they learn to write.

The so-called Labovian narrative model, outlined in Labov and Waletsky (1967) and later refined in Labov (1972), was soon recognized as a breakthrough in narrative studies. In particular, sociolinguists have found it a useful model for analyzing naturally-occurring conversational narratives. Toolan (1988, 146) contends that the Labovian model illuminates a wide range of data because the model is based on structural and functional properties common to all oral narratives: "Labov and Waletsky's hypothesis is that fundamental narrative structures are to be found in oral versions of personal experience—the ordinary narratives of ordinary speakers. They wish, by looking at many narratives, to identify and relate formal linguistic properties of narrative to their functions." According to Labov (1972, 363), "fully-formed" narratives exhibit a typical structure that may be described in terms of the communicative function a clause serves in context and in terms of the clause's relative freedom of movement within the narrative. Labov argues that the beginnings, middles, and ends of fully-formed stories perform different communicative functions that are important for the effective telling of a story. He lists six basic components that comprise the prototypical oral story. Fleischman (1990, 135) notes that the various components answer different questions on the part of the listener:

1. Abstract: what will this be about?
2. Orientation: who, what, when, where?
3. Complicating Action: what happened?
4. Narrator Evaluation of Events: so what?
5. Resolution: what finally happened?
6. Coda: what is the relation to the present context?

We show in later sections how past tenses (the formal linguistic properties of narrative) map onto these narrative components in order to form a story with a discernible plot and crucial supporting detail.

In addition to the complexity of narrative structure, there are many reasons why students have difficulty mastering narrative past tenses in French. One of the most obvious difficulties is the linguistic complexity of French past tenses themselves. Linguistic complexity is comprised of two categories—*formal complexity* and *functional complexity*. French past tenses are formally complex, because there are many different forms to learn in order to use French past tenses with any mastery (e.g., **passé composé/simple, imparfait, plus-que-parfait**). Moreover, the **passé composé** and the **plus-que-parfait** require the learner not only to select the correct auxiliaries (**avoir** vs. **être**) but also to make the past participle agree according to a set of complex rules. Perhaps even more problematic is the extent to which the same tense has multiple semantic meanings or discourse functions, a phenomenon referred to as *functional complexity*. For example, the French **imparfait** comprises three distinct meanings: *imperfective* (ongoing action in the past with out-of-focus endpoints), *iterative* (habitual events as well as repeated events), and *durative* (states of being).

Textbook rules that lead learners to make incorrect hypotheses are another well-known problem. Dansereau (1987, 35) blames "vague, incomplete, contradictory, and generally poor explanations found in most beginning textbooks" for much of the learner's confusion surrounding this grammar point. In particular, she argues that much of the problem stems from a misunderstanding of the terminology traditionally employed in textbooks, for example, *descriptive event, action, continuing event*, etc. Using the following examples taken from her own classroom experience teaching college-level French, Dansereau illustrates the difficulty that students encounter when trying to apply typical textbook rules:

(1) Le roi a régné pendant soixante ans.
(2) À huit heures, j'étais dans mon bureau.
(3) Il est souvent venu me voir.
(4) Cet été-là, il ne mangeait que deux fois par jour.

When encountering (1), the student may wonder why an event that continued for sixty years is encoded in the **passé composé** and not the **imparfait,** since the textbook prescribes the **imparfait** for continuing events. The student could reason that a reign of sixty years constitutes an excellent example of a continuing event. In (2), the student may be puzzled by the use of the **imparfait** which, according to the textbook, is supposedly reserved for situations without reference to an exact moment of

time. In (3), the student finds the **passé composé** used with an event repeated an undefined number of times (**souvent**), even though the textbook rule states that the **passé composé** encodes an event repeated a
defined number of times. In (4), the **imparfait** is used despite the fact
that the number of times is clearly stated (**deux fois par jour**), a contra-
diction of the rule prescribing the **imparfait** for an event repeated an
undefined number of times.

It appears that much of the difficulty students have with this grammar
item arises from the confusing terminology used by teachers and textbook writers to describe tense usage. Writing a pedagogical rule, however, is not an easy task. On the one hand, if teachers use technical linguistic jargon when explaining grammar, the flood of unfamiliar terms
may confuse students. On the other hand, if teachers rely on the traditional terminology, the resulting rules are unreliable and frustrating.
Below, we suggest replacing the confusing linguistic terminology with
more transparent language borrowed from cinematography and visual
perception studies.

Another difficulty for learners is the mismatch between the French and
English past tense system. Beginning learners overwhelmingly look for
one-to-one correspondences between a linguistic form and a given
meaning in the target language. This strategy works well much of the
time but also leads to overgeneralizations and the formation of erroneous
hypotheses. For example, Anglophones correctly learn rather quickly that
a verb in English with the -ing ending (the progressive form) and the *used
to* form (the habitual form) are successfully translated into French using
the **imparfait,** as shown in (5) and (6):

(5) I was watching  =  Je regard**ais**
(6) I *used to* watch  =  Je regard**ais**

Unfortunately, learners also overgeneralize and equate the English simple
past tense ending -*ed* with the **passé composé** as in (7):

(7) I watched  =  J'ai regard**é**

While this strategy of matching an English form to a French form may
produce felicitous results much of the time, it also leads students to posit
an erroneous hypothesis about the French tense system that proves hard
to correct in later stages. For example, students operating with this hy-

pothesis must learn that the English simple past tense can, depending on the context and on the semantics of the verb, be translated by using the **imparfait** as in (8):

(8) She seemed nervous.   >   Elle semblait nerveuse.

We show in later sections how to develop classroom activities to direct learners to attend to these differences in both languages in order to avoid positing these common erroneous hypotheses.

One of the most basic difficulties for students is that narrative discourse rarely occurs in classroom settings, and as a consequence, students receive little exposure to the **passé composé/imparfait** contrast (Liskin-Gasparro, 2000). Other grammar points, such as determiners or interrogative expressions, are frequent in French discourse, thus giving students many opportunities to hear the grammar item in context. Unfortunately, even learners living in a francophone country who are surrounded by native speaker input may not receive enough exposure to past tenses used in narrative discourse. Studies of naturally-occurring conversational narrative demonstrate that native speakers often replace both the **passé composé** and **imparfait** with the present tense (Fleischman 1990). Apparently, once the narrative time frame has been established at the story's outset, past tenses become redundant. To remedy the low frequency of narrative tenses in classroom input, we suggest ways for teachers to recycle this grammar point throughout the semester.

And finally, narrative tenses present a perceptual difficulty for anglophone learners. Harley (1986) argues that Anglophones often have difficulty distinguishing the phonetic differences between the **passé composé** and the **imparfait:** for example, **J'ai regardé** vs. **Je regardais.** Moreover, careful studies of spoken French have revealed that the ending of the past participle and the ending of the **imparfait** form, for example, **regardé** and **regardais,** are often pronounced the same by native speakers in rapid, informal conversation.

In summary, French past tenses are formally and functionally complex, mismatched with their English near-equivalents, infrequent in the input, and difficult to perceive. To make matters worse, they are typically explained using confusing terminology and captured in textbook rules that prove difficult to apply. If teaching methods are to be effective, they must find concrete ways of overcoming each of these problems.

## BASIC FORMS AND MEANINGS

In order to understand narrative past tenses in French, it is important to distinguish the grammatical categories *tense* and *aspect*. Tense is the grammatical term that refers to the time when the action of the verb occurs: past, present, or future. The time frame of an action is established by referring to the present moment of speaking; for example, the **passé composé** and the **imparfait** are both in the past in relation to the present moment of speaking. Some verbs establish their time frame by referring to other actions in the past or in the future. For example, the **plus-que-parfait** indicates a past action that occurred prior to the completion of another past action.

Aspect, unlike tense, is not concerned with placing events on a time line. Rather, aspect is concerned with making distinctions among the kinds of actions that are described by verbs, as in the following examples:

• A habitual action
  (**Quand j'avais 16 ans, je me comportais comme une adolescente typique.**)
• An action that is ongoing throughout the entirety of a story
  (**Il faisait très froid cette nuit-là.**)
• An action that occurs all at once
  (**Elle a brisé la glace.**)

Comrie (1976, 3) defines aspect as the "way of viewing the internal temporal constituency of a situation." Linguists claim that French has two aspects, that is, two different ways of viewing a situation: *perfective* and *imperfective*. The word *perfective* comes from the past participle **perfectum** of the Latin verb **perficere** (*to bring to completion*). The modern French infinitive **parfaire** and the modern English infinitive *to perfect* have the same sense (to make perfect and to complete). Although most English speakers are familiar with the evaluative sense of the verb, to improve something to the point of perfection, they are frequently unaware of the second sense intended by linguists, to do something to the point of completion. The perfective aspect is used when the speaker or storyteller views the action as completed, that is, with a beginning and an end in focus. In contrast, the imperfective aspect is used when the action is seen as incomplete, that is, with no apparent beginning or end.

Linguists further distinguish between *grammatical aspect* and *lexical aspect*.

Grammatical aspect refers to how the two aspects (perfective and imperfective) are encoded in French grammar by the two different past tense forms (**passé composé** and **imparfait**). In contrast, lexical aspect does not refer to grammar at all but rather to the dictionary meaning of the verb. For example, the verb **s'apercevoir** (to notice) is used for a so-called punctual action, that is, an action that occurs instantaneously. The punctual nature of the verb, its lexical aspect, is simply part of the definition of the verb itself. Lexical aspect is best understood by observing the various classes of lexical aspect. Following Vendler (1957), linguists typically recognize four different classes of verbs according to their lexical aspect:

• States
• Activities
• Accomplishments
• Achievements

States are typically long-lasting and do not require any input of energy. Activities are processes without well-defined endpoints. Accomplishments are processes with distinct endpoints. And achievements are actions that occur quickly with inherent endpoints. The following table provides some typical examples of the various verb classes based on lexical aspect.

### Classifications Based on Lexical Aspectual Class

| States | Activities | Accomplishments | Achievements |
|---|---|---|---|
| have | run | paint a picture | recognize (something) |
| possess | walk | make a chair | realize (something) |
| desire | swim | build a house | find (something) |
| like | breathe | write a novel | win the race |
| want | pull | grow up | lose (something) |

Source: Andersen 1991

Linguists have noted that there is a strong correlation between lexical aspect and grammatical aspect in language use. States and activities are typically encoded in the imperfective aspect (**imparfait**), whereas accomplishments and achievements are typically encoded in the perfective aspect (**passé composé**). These patterns of frequencies and distributions in naturally occurring discourse are commonly referred to as *distributional biases of the input* by researchers in second language acquisition. The acquisition of grammatical aspect (perfective vs. imperfective) is thought to be largely dependent on the lexical aspect of the verb. Andersen (1986, 1990, 1991) claims that learners pass through stages in the acquisition of the past tenses; first learners master the present tense, then the perfective aspect (**passé composé),** and finally the imperfective aspect (**imparfait).** Andersen also notes, however, that when learners first begin to employ the **passé composé** and the **imparfait,** they do so according to lexical aspect, using the **passé composé** for prototypical punctual events and the **imparfait** for prototypical states.

As noted above, the **passé composé** has one basic meaning: *perfective* or completed action. The **imparfait,** however, is semantically more complex, as it has three possible meanings: *imperfective* (ongoing action in the past with out-of-focus endpoints), *iterative* (habitual events as well as repeated events), and *durative* (states of being). In (9a) and (9b), reading the paper, an accomplishment, is construed as both a completed and an uncompleted action.

(9a) **J'ai lu** le journal.     *I read the paper.* (perfective accomplishment)
(9b) **Je lisais** le journal.     *I was reading the paper.* (imperfective accomplishment)

In (9a) the action of reading the paper came to an end, while it was ongoing in (9b). The iterative meaning refers to a habitual action as in (10):

(10) Le samedi, **je prenais** le petit déjeuner au lit.
      *On Saturdays, I used to have breakfast in bed.*
      *On Saturdays, I would have breakfast in bed.*

Finally, the durative meaning refers to states or activities that are ongoing, as in (11):

(11) **Je savais** bien qu'**il n'était pas au courant** de la situation.
      *I knew very well that he wasn't aware of the situation.*

The **plus-que-parfait** refers to a completed action that occurs prior to another past action. The relationship between the **plus-que-parfait** and the **passé composé** in French is the same as the relationship between the English pluperfect (for example, *she had left*) and the English simple past (for example, *he arrived*) as shown in (12) and (13).

(12) Quand il est arrivé, **sa femme était (déjà) partie.**
*When he arrived, his wife had (already) left.*

(13) Il s'est souvenu de la réponse, mais **il avait (déjà) rendu** son examen.
*He remembered the answer, but he had (already) turned in his test.*

Linguists note that the simple past is often used in informal English where prescriptive grammars call for the pluperfect. For example, (12) and (13) could be translated in informal English as (12a) and (13a):

(12a) *When he arrived, his wife already left.*

(13a) *He remembered the answer, but he already turned in his test.*

In French, the **plus-que-parfait** remains a robust marker of anteriority and is not to be confused with the **passé composé.** Thus, anglophone students may be confused because French does not allow both options.

And finally, the conditional may be used in past narratives in instances of indirect discourse in which a character (or narrator) reports what someone says will occur. This usage of the conditional is commonly referred to as the "future in the past." Note that in (14) and (15), the conditional is used in a subordinate clause introduced by a main clause that contains a speech act verb (**promettre, dire**).

(14) **Mon professeur m'a promis** au début du semestre **que je recevrais** une bonne note.

(15) **Elle a dit** hier matin **qu'il neigerait** le soir.

The following table summarizes the basic meanings of the narrative tenses.

**Basic Meanings of Narrative Past Tenses**

| Tense | Meaning | Example |
|---|---|---|
| **Passé composé**[1] | perfective (completed) | J'ai mangé...<br>*I ate, I did eat, I have eaten* |
| **Imparfait** | imperfective (ongoing) | Je mangeais...<br>*I was eating . . .* |
| | iterative (habitual) | Le samedi, je mangeais...<br>*Saturdays, I would/used to eat . . .* |
| | durative (state) | Je n'avais plus faim...<br>*I wasn't hungry anymore. . .* |

| Plus-que-parfait | perfective/anterior | J'avais déjà mangé quand... |
| | | *I had already eaten when . . .* |
| Conditionnel | future-in-the-past | Il m'a dit qu'elle viendrait... |
| | | *He told me that she would come . . .* |

## MEANINGS IN CONTEXT

While most textbooks attempt to adopt a discourse-based approach when explaining the **passé composé/imparfait** distinction, in our opinion they simply do not go far enough. For example, most textbooks give a rather bare-bones account of narrative structure, rarely mentioning the important differences between spoken and written narratives. Furthermore, textbooks do little to raise learners' consciousness about the process of narration. In this section, we explore how past tenses commonly function in narrative discourses of various types.

Narrative is typically divided into two main parts—the foreground (**le premier plan**) and the background (**l'arrière-plan**). In French, the foreground correlates with the **passé composé** and the background with the **imparfait.** Foreground events are chronologically ordered and move the story forward through time. Background events are not chronologically ordered and often suspend narrative movement. These tenses allow storytellers to present events from different perspectives. Note the following two sentences in (16).

(16) ———— (1) ————————————— (2) ———→

Le père **a fermé** la porte.          Le pauvre bébé **a pleuré.**
*The father closed the door.*          *The poor baby cried.*

Here, two consecutive actions in the **passé composé** are interpreted as being in chronological sequence. Listeners infer that the order of telling mirrors the order in which the events actually occurred in reality (or in the fictional world). Furthermore, listeners infer that the baby cried *because* the father closed the door. In other words, sequenced events in the **passé composé** are often interpreted as causally linked. Notice how we interpret the narrative events differently when the second event is in the **imparfait** as shown in (17).

(17) ———— (1) ————————→              (?)

Le père **a fermé** la porte.          Le pauvre bébé **pleurait.**
*The father closed the door.*          *The poor baby was crying.*

When did the baby begin to cry? Since the two events are no longer in sequence, it is hard to say with precision. The **imparfait (pleurait)** represents the action as ongoing and thus overlapping the **passé composé** event of the plotline (**a fermé**). Listeners may infer that the baby was already crying when the father closed the door. They may also infer that the baby continued to cry after the door was closed. The question mark represents the fact that the event does not belong to a strict chronological sequence, because the exact beginning and end of the baby's crying is not given and not known to the listener.

Narrators often use adverbs to make the foreground and background more explicit. Adverbs associated with the **passé composé** emphasize the punctual or sequential nature of an event and thus indicate the foreground. In contrast, adverbs associated with the **imparfait** are correlated with the background because they emphasize the ongoing or habitual or stative aspect of the event. Common adverbs typically associated with the **passé composé** and the **imparfait** are listed below:

---

### Adverbs Associated with the Foreground (*passé composé*)

| | |
|---|---|
| un jour, un matin, un soir . . . | soudain, brusquement, brutalement . . . |
| tout d'un coup, tout à coup . . . | tout de suite, immédiatement . . . |
| puis, ensuite . . . | |

### Adverbs Associated with the Background (*imparfait*)

| | |
|---|---|
| tous les jours, tous les matins . . . | chaque jour, chaque mois . . . |
| en général, généralement, d'habitude . . . | |
| | autrefois, à l'époque . . . |
| toujours, souvent . . . | rarement . . . |

---

The foreground/background distinction is typically represented in textbooks with a short narrative. This narrative begins with scene-setting information that contextualizes the series of plotline events, as in (18).

(18) Tous les après-midis, après une longue journée au bureau, Sophie s'installait à la terrasse de son café préféré pour regarder le monde. Et, comme toujours, elle était de bonne humeur cet après-midi parce qu'il y avait beaucoup de beaux garçons qui passaient dans la rue. Pourtant, quelque chose manquait . . . une cigarette! Tout de suite, elle a sorti une cigarette de son paquet. Elle l'a allumée et elle a tiré une grande bouffée. Mmm . . . extase!

Students usually have little difficulty understanding the so-called *décor* or scene-setting function of the background. This function is easily apprehended by students because it essentially corresponds to the opening paragraph of a story. What students find more problematic is the background information used throughout a narrative to contextualize the plot. For beginning students, it is important to emphasize the basic difference in *sequentiality* between the foreground and the background: the sequential foreground versus the non-sequential background.

Given that this distinction is a universal property of narrative regardless of the language, beginning students find it more accessible to learn this distinction by analyzing short narratives in English, such as (19):

(19) Joe *felt* grumpy and in need of company. He *marched* straight for the bar where he *used to go* after work. As usual, the regulars *were* already there. Joe quickly *surveyed* the nearly empty room and *chose* a seat at the bar. Next, he *stuck* his hand in his jacket, *pulled* out a piece of paper, and *dropped* it on the counter in front of the owner who *was feigning* interest in the baseball game on TV. The paper *contained* the key to Joe's future.

By examining a simple English narrative text of this sort, anglophone learners are able not only to understand the concept of sequentiality, but also to become aware of the correspondences they tend to make between English and French verbal forms, for example: *used to* + verb = **imparfait; -ing** verbs = **imparfait; -ed** verbs = **passé composé.** By posing a few incisive questions, teachers can help students become aware that some English verbs that may "look like actions" are actually stative. Consider the last verb *contained*. At what point in the story did the paper contain Joe's future? Many students mistake this non-sequenced background verb for a sequenced foreground action because of the *-ed* ending. The background events and the foreground events of this brief narrative are categorized as follows:

- Background (non-sequenced events): *felt, used to go, were, was feigning, contained*
- Foreground (sequenced events): (1) *marched,* (2) *surveyed,* (3) *chose,* (4) *stuck,* (5) *pulled out,* (6) *dropped*

When students have mastered distinguishing the background from the foreground in English narrative, they are ready to perform a similar analysis on a short French narrative, such as (20):

(20) Il avait un studio de répète à l'Hôpital Ephémère. Je faisais des photos sur l'endroit. Je n'arrêtais pas de le croiser avec sa petite baguette sous le bras, à l'heure du déjeuner. Un jour je lui ai dit «bon appétit», et on est partis discuter dans un café.[2]

The background events and the foreground events of (18) are categorized as follows:

- Background: **avait, faisais, n'arrêtais pas**
- Foreground: (1) **je lui ai dit**, (2) **on est partis**

Given that the foreground in French is always indicated by the **passé composé** and the background by the **imparfait,** this task may seem trivial. Yet, this deceptively simple activity of categorizing verbs according to the foreground/background distinction helps students grasp how the French and English past tense systems map differently onto the two opposing narrative functions.

It should be obvious from the above discussion that the narrative past tenses in French can be understood only in opposition to one another. By encountering many examples of past tenses in narrative contexts, students begin to understand that the foreground and the background actually *depend* on each other for their meaning. In other words, it is impossible to comprehend fully the functions of the **passé composé** in narrative without also grasping the functions of the **imparfait.** Below we suggest pedagogical principles and techniques to help students achieve a fuller understanding of the functional interdependency of narrative tenses.

## CLASSROOM APPLICATIONS

Based on empirical studies on the acquisition of tense and aspect in Romance languages, Blyth (2005, 218) contends that all classroom applications for the teaching of narrative tenses should take into account the following three research findings:

1. Learners acquire the past tenses in gradual, developmental stages that reflect associations between lexical aspect, grammatical aspect, and narrative structure (as discussed in previous sections).
2. Past tense selection is based on how a narrator sees an event and therefore requires pedagogical techniques that emphasize the visual.
3. Past tense usage varies widely depending on contextual factors such as spoken vs. written norms.

Blyth (2005, 218) goes on to translate these three research findings into pedagogical principles that help teachers construct materials and devise lessons that are more consonant with current research:

1. Design pedagogical interventions to enhance the input in keeping with students' developmental readiness.
2. Base grammatical explanations and activities on the students' own visual perception of events.
3. Choose appropriate narrative texts and tasks that take into account cognitive and linguistic complexity as well as native speaker norms.

Studies on the acquisition of narrative past tenses in Romance languages have examined both tutored and untutored learners as well as a host of possible factors that might explain various learning trajectories. The main finding of the early research on untutored learners was that tense/aspect morphology was acquired in rather predictable stages (Kumpf 1984; Andersen 1986; Flashner 1989). Next, researchers turned their attention to instructed learners and discovered similar developmental stages (Robison 1990; Bardovi-Harlig 1992, 1995; Bergström 1995; Salaberry 1998, 1999). Bardovi-Harlig (1998, 2000) argued that the line of research on the developmental stages of both tutored and untutored learners pointed to two "conspiring factors"—lexical aspect and narrative structure.

While most researchers agree that lexical aspect and narrative structure are important factors in understanding the acquisition of narrative past tenses, not all agree on the exact nature and duration of the developmental stages that learners pass through. More recent studies point to the existence of three distinct developmental stages (see Salaberry 1999, 2000, 2005; Schell 2000). In the brief initial stage, learners commit many transfer errors due to an overreliance on their first language (L1), and they tend to overgeneralize the **passé composé,** using it in contexts where native norms call for the **imparfait.** During the second phase, learners become increasingly sensitive to lexical aspect (see Basic Forms and Meanings section). During this protracted stage, learners slowly begin to acquire the non-prototypical uses of the **passé composé** and **imparfait,** for example, the **passé composé** for change of states (**Il a été malade**) and the **imparfait** for accomplishments and achievements (**Au cours de l'année, il se rendait compte de la gravité de la situation**). The third and final stage has been reached when learners are able to employ both the **passé composé** and the **imparfait** with all four lexical aspectual classes (states, activities, accomplishments, achievements) in keeping with their communicative intent.

In light of the developmental stages described above, it seems reasonable that one of the instructional goals of first-year college French courses should be to help learners with their overreliance on the **passé composé.** Teachers should assist beginning learners to acquire the prototypical uses of the **passé composé** (= past achievement verbs, for example, **J'ai trouvé, J'ai fini**) and **imparfait** (= past states of being, for example, **J'avais, J'étais**). Teachers should also maintain realistic expectations for learner production. Beginning learners are usually limited to verbs conjugated with the **avoir** auxiliary and a few high-frequency verbs conjugated with **être** (intransitive verbs of coming and going, for example, **aller, venir, partir**). And finally, it is important for teachers to keep in mind the kind of narrative input that most beginning learners are likely to find comprehensible: prototypical narratives with a clearly demarcated foreground and a handful of background events used at the beginning of the story to set the scene. According to the Labovian model, scene-setting events of this sort belong to the orientation section of a narrative and typically have scope over the entire narrative (**Il faisait un sale temps dehors. Il y avait du monde à l'intérieur du café**).

Narrative person (first person vs. third person) is another important factor to consider in the beginning stage. It is typically easier for beginners to produce first-person narratives based on real, lived experience rather than fictional, third-person narratives. Oller (1993) argues that fictional narratives and third-person narratives are best avoided in the beginning stages of language instruction because of their inherent ambiguity, that is, they require the learner to reconstruct somebody else's perspective on the narrative events.

The second stage coincides with the second and third years of college foreign language study. At this stage, students should be exposed to a wider array of past tense uses and, in particular, should be encouraged to begin exploring non-prototypical uses. Teachers would be wise to choose narratives that flood learners with examples of sudden changes of states encoded in the **passé composé** (for example, **Elle a eu 18 ans** / *She turned 18 years old*), and achievement verbs encoded in the **imparfait** (for example, **Elle découvrait petit à petit la différence entre son mari et son amant** / *She discovered little by little the difference between her husband and her lover*). Teachers should also target the use of the **passé composé** with the auxiliary **être** at this intermediate stage.

In addition to choosing texts with many examples of non-prototypical uses of narrative tenses, teachers should also introduce stories that have a more complex structure with background **imparfait** clauses interspersed throughout the text rather than limited to the orientation section, as is often the case in beginners' narratives. Furthermore, the uses of the **imparfait** in these texts should exemplify all three aspectual values (imperfective, durative, iterative). Students in the second and third year can greatly benefit from consciousness-raising activities about the act of narration itself. Students who have difficulty grasping the differences between the narrative tenses are often helped by activities that emphasize the fluidity of perspective-taking. For example, students could read differing eyewitness reports of the "same events" as found in courtroom testimony or in newspaper articles. Such an exercise helps students realize the agency of the narrator in constructing the narrative. A follow-up step would be to have students discuss how the different narratives lead to different visualizations of the events.

By the final stage, roughly equivalent to the fourth year of college, students have mastered the uses of the **passé composé** but are still having difficulties with the **imparfait.** In particular, the use of the **imparfait** is typically restricted to a small subset of high-frequency stative verbs (**avoir, être, sembler**). Teachers should try to include many more tokens of non-prototypical uses of the **imparfait** (for example, with achievement verbs) as well as a greater variety of verbs.

Linguists seem to agree that aspectual choice is related to the perspective of the narrator. As such, visual metaphors abound in descriptions of aspect (Terry 1981; Thogmartin 1984; Andrews 1992; Connor 1992; Cox 1994; Blyth 1997). Lunn (1985) maintains that "the existence and comprehensibility of metaphors linking aspect and perception are meant to be taken as evidence that the aspect-perception link is real" (52). Andersen (1993) extends Lunn's reasoning by arguing that aspect arises from human visual perception: "the perceptual systems of humans and other animals allow or perhaps we might say force us to distinguish an important or foregrounded entity or event from all the unimportant events . . . According to this basic notion of distinguishing figure from ground, we would say that the learner perceives the punctual or telic events as key, important, foreground, and learns to mark them as such and to not mark the background events of situations" (328). Andersen's basic claim is that some events are more perceptually salient than others and appear in the visual foreground against a background of less salient events.

Applied linguists have developed various pedagogical techniques that emphasize the link between visual perception and aspectual choice. Connor (1992, 323) describes a technique for helping students visualize events in their mind's eye before attempting to verbalize them in narrative form. The technique amounts to having students create a movie in their head that they can refer to while making aspectual choices. Connor contends that such a technique avoids contradictory rules and confusing grammatical terminology by giving students "one concrete visualizable template in which . . . plot vs. background equals **passé composé** vs. **imparfait.**"

In a similar vein, Blyth (1997) describes several techniques using video in the teaching of aspect. In one exercise, students watch a short video several times, preferably a thirty-second commercial with a clear narrative structure. After the students have seen the video enough times to be able to recall it with ease, they retell the commercial in writing. Next, students compare their retellings in small groups, paying close attention to any differences they may encounter: choice of verbs, order of events, aspectual choices, etc. According to Blyth, the main point of this activity is to help students realize that "a narrative is the creation of a narrator who intentionally, although largely unconsciously, chooses what to attend to when perceiving the 'seamless web of history'" (61). This may seem like a trivial point, but it isn't. The paradox of most pedagogical approaches to narrative past tenses is that the speech act of narration is usually given little attention. And yet, tense usage cannot be fully grasped until students understand what is at stake when narrators attempt to tell a story.

Once students have compared their different versions of the retelling task, they should categorize all the verbs into the two opposing narrative categories: foreground and background. Next, the students should view the video again with an eye for how each scene is represented in terms of cinematography. In such a manner, students can be led to discover the correlations between cinematic choices and aspectual choices: in-focus, close-up shots typically signal foreground events (**passé composé**), while wide-angle or out-of-focus shots usually indicate background events (**imparfait**). As a final consciousness-raising activity in this sequence, students read retellings of the same commercial written by native speakers and note how the cinematic events are narrated. Do the native speaker retellings differ from the non-native retellings? Do the correlations between cinematic technique and aspectual choice hold for the native speaker retellings? These activities guide students to apprehend for themselves the different ways of grounding events, that is, packaging them as either foreground or background. When students watch the same video several times, read several retellings of the video, and then analyze the video in terms of cinematic technique, they come to understand more fully that aspectual choices are always the prerogative of the narrator, who simply verbalizes the perspective in his or her mind's eye.

That aspectual distinctions are related to visual perception should also be obvious from the common teaching practice of representing the narrative past tenses with visual mnemonics on the blackboard: staccato dots or dashes for the **passé composé** events and lines for the events encoded in the **imparfait.** Westfall and Foerster (1996) maintain that because these kinds of visual cues are immediately transparent to students, they should be used in various ways to reinforce form-meaning connections during reading. For example, they advocate having students draw an arrow (→) above all verbs in a narrative text that move the plot forward in time and a circle above all verbs that do not advance the time line. Blyth (1997, 61) advocates another technique that requires students to represent narrative events in a visual fashion. After students have read a narrative, they are asked to number all foreground events (all events encoded in the **passé composé**). Students indicate forward chronological movement by putting an arrow after each numbered event. Next, students indicate the background events (all events in the **imparfait**) by tracing a line above the foregrounded events. The background events should not be numbered since they are not in a strict chronological sequence. By drawing these lines, students can see exactly where the ongoing or habitual background events overlap the punctual foreground events—a graphic representation of the notion of scope or simultaneity. Students should use question marks to indicate that the exact beginning and end of a background event may be impossible to discern from a narrative text. In fact, unlike the strictly ordered foreground events, background events are never numbered since their chronological order is not a distinguishing feature. A reader or listener needs to know only that the background event is in progress at the point of the relevant foreground events. The result of this visual technique is greater awareness of the *relation* between narrative foreground and background. This technique is demonstrated below, using the narrative text in (20), reprinted here as (21).

(21) Il avait un studio de répète à l'Hôpital Ephémère. Je faisais des photos sur l'endroit. Je n'arrêtais pas de le croiser avec sa petite baguette sous le bras, à l'heure du déjeuner. Un jour je lui ai dit «bon appétit», et on est partis discuter dans un café.

**Representing the Foreground and the Background of a Narrative Text**

| | |
|---|---|
| ?_____? | [Il avait] |
| ?_____? | [Je faisais] |
| ?_____? | [Je n'arrêtais pas] |

[1] j'ai dit  →  [2] on est partis

From the graphic representation of this brief narrative, students can clearly see the simultaneity of all three **imparfait** events. Despite the impossibility of establishing the precise beginning and end of the background events, students can nevertheless envision that the background events have scope over the foreground events.

While these activities and techniques are helpful to those who wish to give their students a better understanding of past tense usage, teachers need to know what kinds of narrative production are reasonable at different proficiency levels in order to make informed pedagogical choices. Unfortunately, the *ACTFL Proficiency Guidelines* (1986) are of little help in developing a pedagogical norm in this area, since they list narration as an Advanced-level skill. This is misleading, since speakers with beginning or intermediate proficiencies are capable of producing recognizable narratives. Apparently, what the ACTFL guidelines mean by narration is more accurately referred to as a "fully-formed" narrative following the Labovian method for narrative analysis (see Difficulties for the Learner). In light of the ACTFL guidelines' deficiencies, it would be helpful for teachers to have some guidelines to help them choose appropriate narrative texts and formulate realistic expectations for narrative production. In other words, teachers need to know in what ways a narrative produced by a student with Novice-level proficiency will differ from a student with Beginning-level or Intermediate-level proficiency. Teachers may wonder which narrative structures (abstract, orientation, complicating action, etc.) learners are likely to produce at different proficiency levels.

Blyth (2002, 245) attempts to catalogue some of the most important parameters of narrative variation for teachers to consider: genre (fiction vs. non-fiction), narrative person (first person vs. third person), modality (oral vs. written), narrative tone (formal vs. informal), etc. Based on these parameters as well as on research on narrative production in children and adults (Berman and Slobin 1994) and on the prototypical Western narrative as proposed by Fleishman (1990), Blyth (2002, 262) claims that narrative texts can be arranged along a continuum of cognitive and linguistic difficulty, with narrative texts that are the easiest to produce and comprehend at one end of the continuum and those that are the most difficult at the other end. The cognitively "easy" or "simple" narratives for second language learners to produce and comprehend would all have the following criteria:

1. They refer to specific past experiences.
2. They contain a foreground but no background.
3. They follow the chronological order of events.
4. They require no narrator evaluation.

At the opposite end of the continuum would be the most linguistically and cognitively challenging narratives. These narratives would all have the following distinguishing features:

1. They refer to generic experiences that are difficult to individuate.
2. They contain a mutually contextualizing foreground and background with multiple episodes.

3. They include flashbacks and flash-forwards.

4. They require extensive evaluation by the narrator.

By keeping these various elements in mind, teachers can better gauge the linguistic and cognitive complexity of narrative tasks and texts. For example, using the criteria mentioned above, Blyth (2002) describes five narrative genres, from the simplest to the most complex: routine, report, fairy tale, conversational story, short story. The simplest of the five is appropriately called a *routine* because it is entirely made up of mundane events that form a recognizable sequence (for example, getting ready for work in the morning or getting ready for bed). While these events are usually trivial, they have the cognitive advantage of being shared cultural knowledge and therefore highly predictable as noted by reading specialists and psychologists. The structural simplicity of the routine is obvious in (22), which consists only of a narrative foreground with no background or evaluative information.

(22) À la fin de la journée, j'ai quitté le bureau et j'ai pris l'autobus pour rentrer. À la maison, j'ai préparé mon dîner. Après le repas, j'ai regardé un peu de télé. Enfin, j'ai pris une longue douche et je me suis couché tôt.

As evident from (22), the routine is distinguished by its utter ordinariness—nothing unusual happens. While the lack of drama makes for a boring story, it does facilitate the narrative task for beginning second language learners struggling to remember many different pieces of linguistic information: vocabulary, syntax, conjugation, pronunciation. As such, teachers should consider the routine as the **degré zéro** of narrative production, appropriate for learners with minimal proficiency. Of course, even routines may hold potential difficulties, especially routines that have a preponderance of pronominal and intransitive verbs conjugated with **être.**

A *report* is only slightly more structurally complex than a routine. Reports are cognitively more complex than routines because they contain some background information, usually limited to the opening orientation. More dramatic and less predictable than routines, reports are basically plot summaries of movies or television programs, usually recounted in the present tense in authentic discourse. Students in first-year classes are capable of producing coherent reports, although the background events of these narratives are typically limited to state-of-being verbs (**avoir** and **être**) clustered in the opening orientation paragraph. Teachers should expose students to a wider range of verbs in the **imparfait** at this stage. They should also draw students' attention to the use of background events that are found throughout a narrative and not simply those that form the beginning orientation section. For example, students at this stage can benefit from discovering how subordinate relative clauses are used to create the narrative background by introducing important descriptive details (J'ai vu la femme **qui portait des lunettes de soleil**).

Next on the continuum is the *fairy tale*. Fairy tales contain a foreground, a background of imagined events, and some narrator evaluation. They are typically comprised of several episodes or scenes and are thus more complex than simple routines or reports. Despite genre-specific constructions (**Il était une fois...** ) and a more difficult episodic structure, most fairy tales are made easier to tell and comprehend by the familiar plotlines and stylistic repetition (Cook 2000).

Further along the continuum of complexity is the *conversational story*. Conversational stories differ crucially from routines, reports, and fairy tales because they arise spontaneously from the local dynamics of a conversation ("Oh, that reminds me of a funny incident yesterday . . ."). In addition to their foreground and background sections, conversational narratives are usually more heavily evaluated than simpler genres. Due to the evaluative content and its unplanned nature, the conversational story is beyond the proficiency of students in the first two years of foreign language study. Linguistic anthropologists and sociolinguists have noted that a story told in a conversation often triggers interlocutors to follow up with subsequent stories of similar situations, a phenomenon they refer to as story rounds. Given their locally-occasioned nature, conversational stories would appear to be more appropriate for advanced conversation classes where students could practice telling stories in rounds, as naturally occurs in spontaneous discourse. Such a course would also be an ideal time to have students ponder the sociolinguistic context of storytelling. Who tells what kinds of stories, to whom, and for what reasons? Liskin-Gasparro (1996) offers several consciousness-raising techniques for improving storytelling skills at the Advanced level. For example, she advocates having students record themselves telling a story in their native language in order to discover what rhetorical devices they tend to favor, for example direct speech ("And I'm like, 'Careful, it's gonna fall!'") or expressive intonation and phonology ("It was HUGE!"). Once students discover their particular storytelling style in their native language, they can make a conscious effort to transfer those patterns or devices to their second language narratives to create more drama or interest.

At the far end of the continuum of cognitive and linguistic difficulty is the *short story*. A short story typically has an episodic structure with a foreground, a background, and lots of narrator evaluation. In addition to those basic parts, a short story often contains complex, embedded syntax and literary language that make it more challenging to comprehend and to produce. The following table summarizes some of the variations in narrative genre described above:

### Summary of Narrative Genres

| | |
|---|---|
| Routine: | minimal narrative of highly predictable foreground events; no background or narrator evaluation of events; conforms to cultural schema ("the daily grind") |
| Report: | plot summary that contains a simple foreground accompanied by minimal background information; no evaluation of events |
| Fairy Tale: | well-known fictional stories with foreground, background, and evaluation; repetitions and simple episodic structure make it easier to remember and recount |
| Conversational Story: | foreground and background, heavily evaluated, embedded in ongoing talk; difficult to produce because it is locally occasioned and unplanned |
| Short Story: | complex episodic structure; may contain flashbacks and flash-forwards; planned discourse |

### Activities

As a means of demonstrating how to combine the ideas and techniques discussed throughout this chapter, a lesson for first-year college students focused on narrative past tenses will be sketched below with actual activities from the French curricula at the University of Chicago and the University of Texas at Austin.[3] The lesson includes five suggested design principles for teaching narrative past tenses gleaned from current research as proposed by Blyth (2005, 246):

- Learners are encouraged to discover grammar rules for themselves, including grammatical differences between English and French.
- Learners watch videos before attempting to narrate in order to circumvent the well-known tendency to focus on the sentence instead of the entire story when selecting past tenses.
- Learners are encouraged to process several input activities before attempting to produce past tenses.
- Learners are instructed with the aid of transparent visual mnemonics in order to avoid confusing grammatical jargon.
- Learners are carefully guided through a series of output tasks.

This lesson is aimed at beginning students in the second semester of the first year of study. By this time in the semester, students will have already been introduced to both the **passé composé** and the **imparfait** and will have studied them separately. Consequently, it is expected that the students will already know the formation rules and basic meanings of both tenses. However, students at this stage are usually unclear about how to use these tenses in narration, since they have yet to encounter them together in a narrative text. Therefore, the primary goal of this lesson is to demonstrate the relation between the tenses in narration and to help students select the appropriate tense in the production of their own stories.

Activity 5.1 aims to introduce essential concepts for understanding and analyzing narrative discourse (for example, *foreground, background, chronological order*). Note that this consciousness-raising activity is written entirely in English. There are several reasons that motivate the use of English as the point of departure for this lesson. First, the main goal of the activity is to draw students' attention to *universal* properties of narrative structure; the foreground/background distinction is found in both the L1 and the L2. Second, the use of English allows students to focus all their attention on the new concepts without getting bogged down in unknown French vocabulary. And third, the contrastive analysis of the English and French narrative tense systems alerts students to potential mismatches between the two languages at the outset of the lesson. For example, this exercise helps students learn that the English simple past tense (*I saw*) can be used to translate *both* the **passé composé** (**j'ai vu**) and the **imparfait** (**je voyais**). As such, this activity should help students circumvent a common false hypothesis that the English simple past tense is always translated in French by employing the **passé composé.**

• • • • •

## Activity 5.1: Comparing French and English Past Tenses.

(consciousness-raising)

**A.** Read the following text and decide if each underlined verb serves as the foreground or the background of the story. Confirm your choices by organizing your foreground verbs on the timeline given below. Remember that only foreground events can be placed in chronological order. Background events usually overlap some or all the foregrounded events.

| | | | |
|---|---|---|---|
| "Every night after dinner, my mother and I <u>would sit</u> at the Formica kitchen table. She <u>would present</u> new tests, taking her examples from stories of amazing children she had read in *Ripley's Believe It or Not*, or *Good Housekeeping*, *Reader's Digest*, and a dozen other magazines she <u>kept</u> in a pile in our bathroom. She <u>would look</u> through them all, searching for stories about remarkable children. | would sit | F | B |
| | would present | F | B |
| | kept | F | B |
| | would look | F | B |
| The first night she <u>brought out</u> a story about a three-year-old boy who <u>knew</u> the capitals of all the states and even most of the European countries. A teacher <u>was quoted</u> as saying the little boy <u>could</u> also pronounce the names of the foreign cities correctly. | brought out | F | B |
| | knew | F | B |
| | was quoted | F | B |
| | could | F | B |
| "What's the capital of Finland?" my mother <u>asked</u> me, looking at the magazine story. | asked | F | B |

Source: *Two Kinds*, by Amy Tan

**B.** Now place the foreground verbs on this time line:

Time Line ——————————————————————————————

**C.** Observe. Look at the following table of past tenses in French and in English and answer the following questions:

1. What English tense may be used to refer either to the foreground or to the background of the story (i.e., might be translated by the verb in the **passé composé** or the **imparfait**)?

2. What English verbal phrases will always be used to refer to the background of the story (i.e., will always correspond to an **imparfait** in French)?

### Table of English and French Past Tenses

| Foreground | Background |
|---|---|
| Passé Composé | Imparfait |
| **j'ai fait/j'ai vu/je suis allé** | **je faisais/je voyais/j'allais** |
| | |
| Simple Past | Simple Past |
| I did/I saw/I went | I did/I saw/I went |
| | |
| | Past Progressive |
| | I was doing/seeing/going |
| | |
| | Habitual Past |
| | I used to do/I would do |
| | I used to see/I would see |
| | I used to go/I would go |

Source: University of Chicago, French 103

Activity 5.2 requires students to perform a similar task as in the first activity, but this time to do it in French. Note that this activity subtly teaches students about the use of the **passé composé** to preview the story by collapsing the entire plot into a single event, referred to as the *abstract* in the Labovian model. This activity also gives students much-needed French vocabulary for analyzing narrative structure (**circonstances, événements chronologiques**).

· · · · ·

**Activity 5.2: Comment raconter une histoire.** (How to tell a story.)
(consciousness-raising)

Observez et analysez. Lisez le texte et répondez aux questions suivantes.

#### Je quitte la maison!

Je **suis parti** de la maison! J'**étais** en train de jouer dans le salon et j'**étais** bien sage, et puis simplement parce que j'**ai renversé** une bouteille d'encre (ink) sur le tapis neuf (new rug), maman **est venue** et elle **m'a grondé** (chewed me out). Alors, **je me suis mis** à pleurer et je lui **ai dit** que je m'en irais (would go away) et qu'on me regretterait beaucoup (would miss me) . . .

Excerpted from *Le petit Nicolas*, Jean-Jacques Sempé and René Goscinny.

- Souvent la première phrase d'une narration fait une sorte de résumé de toute l'histoire. C'est le cas ici? _____

- Quelles étaient les circonstances? _____

- Et quels événements chronologiques ont provoqué son départ?

    1. _____

    2. _____

    3. _____

    4. _____

    5. _____

Source: University of Chicago, French 103

Activity 5.3, an input-processing activity, requires students to focus on targeted forms but to do so in a meaningful context. Note that as an input activity, this does not ask students to produce any of the targeted forms. In this activity, students must first watch a short television commercial (approximately thirty seconds). Next, students must order the sentences to match the chronological events of the video. Finally, students are asked to schematize the narrative events according to the visual techniques described above. Again, the main point of these initial activities is to help students grasp the relational, discursive meanings of the narrative tenses. The use of video is extremely important here since it allows students to see the story for themselves and thus form a visual perspective of the events. Pedagogical activities that ignore this step place students in a difficult situation of analyzing narratives without having a clear picture in their mind's eye of the events.

● ● ● ● ●

### Activity 5.3: Qu'est-ce qui s'est passé dans la publicité de Renault?
(structured input)

Vous allez regarder une publicité de Renault.

**A.** Puis, vous allez mettre les phrases dans l'ordre de l'action dans la pub (1–21).

**B.** Après, vous allez mettre les phrases au tableau pour montrer l'ordre chronologique des actions. Sur une ligne horizontale, mettez un petit point pour les actions au passé composé et numérotez-les. Ensuite, indiquez la durée des événements à l'imparfait avec des flèches (>>>).

Modèle: [Il pleuvait] >>>>>>>>>>>>>>>>>>>>>>>>>>>>>>>>>>

_____._____._____

[Il l'a regardée.]     [La femme s'est fâchée.]

_____ A. La femme s'est fâchée.

_____ B. Il l'a regardée.

_____ C. Elle a fermé la porte de la voiture violemment.

_____ D. Il a baissé sa vitre.

_____ E. Il pleuvait.

_____ F. Il regardait dans l'eau.

_____ G. Elle est montée dans la voiture.

_____ H. Elle a frappé sur la vitre (window).

_____ I. L'homme conduisait sa voiture et chantait.

_____ J. Il est resté tout seul.

_____ K. Elle a pris les clés de la voiture.

_____ L. Un couple rentrait d'une soirée élégante.

_____ M. Elle a trouvé une barrette dans la voiture.

_____ N. Il est sorti de la voiture pour chercher ses clés.

_____ O. Il y avait un cheveu blond dans la barrette.

_____ P. Elle est sortie de la voiture furieuse.

_____ Q. Elle a fait semblant (pretended) de jeter les clés dans la Seine.

_____ R. C'était une nuit d'hiver.

_____ S. Elle a rayé (scratched) la voiture avec la barrette.

_____ T. Ils étaient très bien habillés.

_____ U. Elle est partie toute seule avec la voiture.

Source: *Français Interactif*, © University of Texas, http://www.laits.utexas.edu/fi/index .html.

Activity 5.4 takes the same task as in the previous activity—watch a video and reconstruct the story—although this time the students are asked to produce the targeted forms. Again, the use of a short commercial is key here, since without any visual input (as is the case in cloze activities) tense selection is often highly ambiguous. For example, in the context of the video, the stative event in line 7 (**être triste**) is best represented as a sudden change of state, a good example of a non-prototypical use of the **passé composé.** This sudden change of state is clearly indicated by the wife's facial reaction in the video. Her expectant smile immediately dissolves into a frown as soon as her husband slams the car door and walks away without saying good-bye. Similarly, in the context of the video, the activity verb (**penser à sa femme**) in line 9 is unambiguously shown to be a punctual event. Running to his meeting, the husband passes a billboard that suddenly makes him think of his wife. Again, an activity verb encoded in the **passé composé** represents a nonprototypical use of the tense and would undoubtedly prove problematic for students without the video support. Furthermore, the video shows the link between visual perception and tense selection, with the choice of tense correlating strongly to camera angle and focus. Panoramic shots are used for scene-setting purposes, that is, to give circumstantial details such as weather or traffic conditions best verbalized in the **imparfait.** In contrast, when the camera zooms in for a close-up of the couple, the cinematic action should invariably be captured by using the **passé composé.**

· · · · ·

### Activity 5.4: Qu'est-ce qui s'est passé dans la publicité de Fiat?
(structured output)

Regardez la publicité de Fiat. Ensuite, conjuguez les verbes donnés au passé composé ou à l'imparfait.

1. Il _____ (pleuvoir).

2. Il y _____ (avoir) un couple dans une voiture.

3. La voiture _____ (être) rouge.

4. Ils _____ (se disputer).

5. L'homme _____ (sortir) de la voiture.

6. Il _____ (ne pas parler) à sa femme.

7. La femme _____ (être) triste.

8. Il _____ (a. marcher) sous la

pluie, quand il _____ (b. voir)
une affiche publicitaire.

9. Il _____ (penser) à sa femme.

10. Il _____ (se dépêcher) pour la
retrouver.

11. Il _____ (voir) la voiture.

12. Sa femme _____ (être) dans un
embouteillage (traffic jam).

13. Elle _____ (être) surprise de le
voir.

14. Il _____ (embrasser = to kiss) sa
femme.

Source: *Français Interactif*, © University of Texas, http://www.laits.utexas.edu/fi/index
.html.

Activity 5.5 increases the cognitive load substantially from the preceding activities. As a dictogloss, a guided production exercise, students must first listen to the teacher read a short text that contains the targeted forms. Next they must recall the text as best they can and reconstruct it as a group. Not only must students remember the events, but they must also remember in which tense the events were narrated. The point of this activity is to promote productive metatalk about tense selection. According to the literature on the dictogloss task, teachers must choose texts with care in order to elicit the intended metatalk. Teachers should also keep in mind the predictability and prototypicality of the events. The more predictable/prototypical the event, the easier it will be for students to correctly recall.

• • • • •

**Activity 5.5: Le week-end pluvieux d'Émilie.** (dictogloss)

Écoutez le récit. Votre professeur va lire l'histoire deux fois. Ensuite récrivez l'histoire avec un partenaire.

[Teacher's script:] «Samedi après-midi, ma mère et moi, nous voulions aller faire une promenade et peut-être aussi faire les boutiques, mais il a commencé à pleuvoir. Comme il y avait heureusement de bonnes émissions à la télé, ma mère et moi, nous sommes restées à la maison et nous avons regardé la télé. Samedi soir, nous ne sommes pas sorties parce qu'il pleuvait toujours. Nous avons préparé un bon dîner à la maison. Dimanche, le temps était toujours pluvieux. Le matin, je suis allée à la salle de sports pour faire un peu d'exercice. Ensuite, je suis rentrée déjeuner avec ma famille et l'après-midi, j'ai fait mes devoirs pour la fac.»

Source: *Français Interactif*, © University of Texas, http://www.laits.utexas.edu/fi/index.html.

Activity 5.6 requires students to develop their own personal narrative in a step-by-step fashion (first, elaborate the plotline events; second, add descriptive background details; finally . . .). Note that the goal of the activity is for students to create a fully-formed narrative in the Labovian sense (abstract, orientation, complicating action, narrator evaluation, summary/coda). This is the most difficult activity of the lesson, in large part because it is the most open-ended. Students are given full communicative freedom to choose verbs and tenses as they wish. Of course, such communicative freedom means that they may choose to avoid verbs and tenses that they have not yet mastered. Teachers should be careful to monitor any apparent avoidance. The activity could be made interactive by having students exchange their personal narratives with a partner who must read the story and give feedback or respond to the content in some way.

● ● ● ● ●

**Activity 5.6: L'événement le plus mémorable de votre vie.**
(structured output)

Écrivez un bon récit avec au moins 15 verbes différents au passé composé ou à l'imparfait. Suivez les étapes pour écrire une histoire complète.

**A.** Écrivez une phrase qui résume votre histoire.
   Par exemple:
   Ma maison a été détruite par une tornade.
**B.** Puis, écrivez l'intrigue de l'histoire (*the plot*). N'oubliez pas que les événements de l'intrigue doivent être en séquence chronologique.
   Par exemple:
   [1] Tout d'un coup j'ai entendu un bruit terrible dehors. [2] Tout de suite après, les murs ont commencé à trembler.
**C.** Ajoutez les détails descriptifs qui donnent les conditions et les états

d'âme (*states of being*) des personnages. Parfois, ces détails importants clarifient la causalité pour le lecteur.

Par exemple:

Ma mère avait l'air inquiète parce que mon père n'était pas encore rentré du bureau.

**D.** Ensuite, ajoutez vos réactions personnelles aux événements si nécessaire.

Par exemple:

Je me suis dit: «Ça y est! On va mourir!» C'était absolument terrifiant.

**E.** Finalement, terminez votre histoire avec une phrase qui résume l'histoire tout en ajoutant une évaluation.

Par exemple:

Cela a été un véritable désastre pour toute ma famille.

As noted above, studies of classroom discourse have shown that past narration is relatively infrequent. The real challenge for teachers is to recycle this grammar point throughout the semester. One simple way for teachers to include more past narrative tenses in classroom input is to tell more stories themselves. The stories need not be elaborate or literary or even particularly dramatic. Rather, teachers could tell stories about everyday goings-on around the college (**«Avez-vous entendu les nouvelles? Il y a eu un vol sur le campus ce week-end.»**) Similarly, teachers could also tell more personal experience stories that are so common to conversational discourse (**«Quelque chose d'amusant m'est arrivé hier...»**). Teachers could also elicit short narratives from their students. Asking students what they did during the weekend usually results in a single sentence response (**«Je suis allé au match de football ce week-end.»**). To elicit a more fully-formed narrative, teachers must be willing to ask less predictable questions that generate more drama.

Beginning students are usually incapable of producing spontaneous oral narrative discourse by themselves. They need much assistance and linguistic scaffolding. Teachers could elicit a narrative in English from a willing student ("Did anybody have something unusual happen this weekend?"). As soon as the student recounts the story in English to the class, the teacher should ask the class to reconstruct the narrative in French. As students dictate the narrative events as best they can, the teacher should make any necessary corrections on the board.

## CONSOLIDATION EXERCISES

1. Using key examples, explain the difference between *perfectivity* and *imperfectivity*, the important aspectual distinction that distinguishes the **passé composé** from the **imparfait.**

2. Create appropriate narrative contexts for the following sentences:
   a. Elle avait 21 ans.
   b. Elle a eu 21 ans.

3. Explain why perfectivity (viewing an action as completed, that is, with a clear beginning and end) is a necessary condition for sequentiality. Can narrative events in the **imparfait** ever be sequenced?

4. Give three examples of French verbs for each of the categories of lexical aspect: states, activities, accomplishments, and achievements.

5. Why is the verb **fumer** categorized as an activity, while the phrase **fumer une cigarette** is categorized as an accomplishment? Explain why the addition of a direct object changes the lexical aspect.

6. Give a brief explanation of the so-called distributional bias of past tenses in native discourse. In other words, why are states typically in the **imparfait,** and punctual actions typically in the **passé composé?**

7. Beginning students typically associate the English simple past with the **passé composé,** an example of overgeneralizing a rule or pattern in language learning. Show how the English simple past *I knew* may be translated as either the **passé composé** or the **imparfait** depending on the context.

8. Exemplify the three meanings of the **imparfait** (imperfective, iterative, and durative) with appropriate sentences and contexts.

9. List as many factors as you can think of that might influence narrative production for learners, such as modality (spoken vs. written), genre, topic or theme, etc.

## TYPICAL STUDENT ERRORS

As stated throughout this chapter, tense selection in narrative depends on the global structure of a story. All too often, students make mistakes because they do not take the entire narrative into account when selecting past tenses. Similarly, teachers would be wise to read through a student's entire narrative text before making corrections.

In the narrative cited below, produced by a fifth-semester student, all problematic verbs are boldfaced. Note that most errors involve the selection of the two main narrative tenses: **passé composé** and **imparfait.** Nevertheless, auxiliary selection (**avoir** and **être**), past participle agreement, and anteriority of past events (**plus-que-parfait**) are also quite troublesome. Two verbs in particular prove problematic in this student's composition: **savoir** and **pouvoir. Savoir** in the **passé composé** means *to discover* or *find out* a piece of information. In the context of this story, that meaning does not make much sense. Rather, the narrator intends to refer to her state of not knowing, that is, her state of amnesia. As such, the narrator should employ the **imparfait** of **savoir.** In similar fashion, the verb **pouvoir** in the **passé composé** implies that an attempt was made. Again, the narrator intends to refer to her inability to remember her name, or the names of her parents. In the context of this story, the inability to remember should be properly expressed as a state of being. While there are many things that may be improved upon besides tense usage in this student's essay, they receive no comment here since they are not the focus of this chapter.

### «Crise d'amnésie» (version originale)

Pour célébrer mon anniversaire, mes amies et moi avons décidé d'aller à la Martinique. Pendant le vol, j'ai eu un mauvais pressentiment parce que l'hôtesse de l'air **a semblé** un peu nerveuse.

Et tout à coup, au milieu du vol, l'avion **commençait à plonger** à toute vitesse. Puis, j'**ai réveillé** quelques heures plus tard dans une chambre d'hôpital. Je **ne n'ai pas su** ce qui s'était passé. Quelques minutes plus tard, une femme est rentrée dans la chambre et m'a demandé si je me sentais mieux. Je lui ai dit que je **préfère** parler au docteur. Elle m'a répondu: «Mais je suis ta mère! Ne te souviens-tu pas de moi?» C'était bizarre. Elle **n'a pas eu** l'air de ma mère mais elle disait que j'étais sa fille. Je me suis rendu compte que je **n'ai pas pu** me souvenir de mon nom. J'**ai oublié** les noms de mes amies, et de mes parents. Je **n'ai pas su** où j'**ai habité,** ni quand je **suis née.** Je n'avais jamais été si terrifiée.

Le docteur est enfin arrivé. Il m'a dit que j'**ai perdu** ma mémoire à cause de mon accident d'avion. Il m'a assuré que je **regagnerai** ma mémoire dans une semaine. Trois jours **passaient** mais rien ne changeait. Tous les jours mes parents me montraient des photos de mon passé et me racontaient des histoires de mon enfance. J'avais toujours mal à la tête et je m'ennuyais beaucoup à l'hôpital. Je me fâchais parce que mon progrès était lent.

Un jour, en sortant de la douche, j'ai glissé sur le savon et j'ai frappé mon front. J'**ai réveillé** dans mon lit et j'ai vu ma mère qui **est** assise à côté de moi. Je lui ai demandé ce que je faisais à l'hôpital. Elle a souri et m'a dit, «Enfin, tu as retrouvé ta mémoire.»

Source: Student in fifth-semester course

## Correction of Student Errors

«**Crise d'amnésie**» (version corrigée)

Pour célébrer mon anniversaire, mes amies et moi avons décidé d'aller à la Martinique. Pendant le vol, j'ai eu un mauvais pressentiment parce que l'hôtesse de l'air **semblait** un peu nerveuse.

Et tout à coup, au milieu du vol, l'avion **a commencé à plonger** à toute vitesse. Puis, je **me suis réveillée** quelques heures plus tard dans une chambre d'hôpital. Je **ne savais pas** ce qui s'était passé. Quelques minutes plus tard, une femme est rentrée dans la chambre et m'a demandé si je me sentais mieux. Je lui ai dit que je **préférerais** parler au docteur. Elle m'a répondu: «Mais je suis ta mère! Ne te souviens-tu pas de moi?» C'était bizarre. Elle **n'avait pas** l'air de ma mère mais elle **disait/a dit** que j'étais sa fille. Je me suis rendu compte que je **ne pouvais pas** me souvenir de mon nom. J'**avais oublié** aussi les noms de mes amies, et de mes parents. Je **ne savais pas** où j'**habitais,** ni quand j'**étais née.** Je n'avais jamais été si ter-rifiée.

Le docteur est enfin arrivé. Il m'a dit que j'**avais perdu** ma mémoire à cause de mon accident d'avion. Il m'a assuré que je **regagnerais** ma mé-moire dans une semaine. Trois jours **ont passé** mais rien **ne changeait/n'a changé.** Tous les jours mes parents me montraient des photos de mon passé et me racontaient des histoires de mon enfance. J'avais toujours mal à la tête et je m'ennuyais beaucoup à l'hôpital. Je me fâchais parce que mon progrès était lent.

Un jour, en sortant de la douche, j'ai glissé sur le savon et j'ai frappé mon front. Je **me suis réveillée** dans mon lit et j'ai vu ma mère qui **était** assise à côté de moi. Je lui ai demandé ce que je faisais à l'hôpital. Elle a souri et m'a dit: «Enfin, tu as retrouvé ta mémoire!»

## DISCUSSION TOPICS / PROJECTS

1. In this chapter, we argue against the use of cloze passages (fill-in-the-blank) for beginners because they unwittingly reinforce erroneous hy-potheses. Do you think that cloze passages might be useful under cer-tain circumstances for certain students?

2. Linguists and narratologists have described how narrative may vary ac-cording to different parameters: spoken vs. written, first person vs. third person, fiction vs. non-fiction, etc. What kinds of narratives do you find most appropriate for language learning at different levels? Can you give specific examples? What kinds of narratives do you remem-ber from your language learning days?

3. In this chapter, we contend that video should be used to teach narrative past tenses because this particular grammar item is grounded in visual perception. But what kinds of videos work best? What length video is optimal for pedagogical purposes? Should videos contain dialogue and sounds, or do silent videos work best? And what about comic strips? Might still images work just as well as videos? Try to find a television commercial or scene from a movie that has a well-delineated narrative structure, and then discuss its advantages and disadvantages as a teaching tool.

4. Many teachers use a well-known mnemonic device called **La Maison d'Être** to help their students remember which verbs are conjugated with the auxiliary **être.** Essentially, this device is an image of a house with a person or persons performing the different actions of the intransitive **être** verbs (**aller, venir, monter, descendre,** etc.). Beginning students typically overgeneralize the auxiliary **avoir,** frequently replacing **être** altogether in their narrative discourse. Based on **La Maison d'Être,** write a short narrative using as many intransitive **être** verbs for the plotline as possible (**La semaine dernière, elle est rentrée chez sa famille. Quand elle est entrée dans la maison . . .** ).

5. Metaphors are important teaching tools. A well-chosen metaphor can often help students to understand a difficult concept. In this chapter, we employ several metaphors to describe the **passé composé/imparfait** distinction: foreground vs. background, scene-setting vs. action, etc. Some authors have suggested the metaphor of a skeleton and flesh for narrative structure. The skeleton or backbone represents the plot, and the flesh represents the descriptive detail of the background. This metaphor also illustrates how plots are the essential bones of a story (another metaphor!) on which "hangs" the less essential material. Can you think of other metaphors for highlighting various aspects of narration or of narrative structure?

6. Tense usage is closely tied to narrative genre. For example, plot summaries of movies are typically told in the present tense in French and English. To see if this holds true, ask a few of your friends to recommend a movie that they have recently seen. When they tell you the movie, ask them what the story is about (but do not tell them that you are monitoring their tense usage!). Do they summarize the plot in the present tense or do they switch their tenses? Is there a discernible pattern to the switches? Why do you think that speakers conventionally recount movie plots in the present tense?

7. Spoken narratives are usually unplanned and thus very loosely organized, compared to written narratives that allow for more planning. In order to examine the differences between spoken and written narratives, show a short video to several individuals. Immediately following the video, record people as they recount the video as faithfully as possible. Remind them to use the past tense, since otherwise they might summarize the story in the present tense (see project 6 above!). As soon as they have finished with the oral task, give them a piece of paper and ask them to write out the story. After you have collected stories from several people, transcribe the recordings and compare the oral versions with the written versions. You may do this in either French or in English. Are there linguistic items (words or phrases or grammatical constructions) that appear in one version but not in the other? Do the oral and written versions differ in overall structure?

### FURTHER READING

#### Aspect

Comrie, Bernard. *Aspect*. Cambridge: Cambridge University Press, 1976.

#### Development of Narrative Past Tenses in Second Language Learning

Ayoun, Dalila, and M. Rafael Salaberry, eds. *Tense and Aspect in Romance Languages: Theoretical and Applied Perspectives*. Amsterdam: John Benjamins, 2005.

Bardovi-Harlig, Kathleen. *Tense and Aspect in Second Language Acquisition: Form, Meaning and Use*. Oxford: Basil Blackwell, 2000.

Kaplan, Marsha. "Developmental Patterns of Past Tense Acquisition Among Foreign Language Learners of French." In *Foreign Language Learning: A Research Perspective*, edited by Bill Van-Patten, Trisha Dvorak, and James Lee, 52–60. Cambridge, MA: Newbury House, 1987.

Salaberry, Maximo Rafael. "The Development of Aspectual Distinctions in L2 French Classroom Learning." *Canadian Modern Language Review* 54 (1998): 508–542.

#### Narrative Structure

Fleischman, Suzanne. *Tense and Narrativity: From Medieval Performance to Modern Fiction*. Austin, TX: University of Texas Press, 1990.

Labov, William. "The Transformation of Experience in Narrative Syntax." In *Language in the Inner City: Studies in Black English Vernacular*, edited by William Labov, 354–396. Philadelphia: University of Pennsylvania Press, 1972.

#### Pedagogical Approaches to Narrative Past Tenses

Blyth, Carl. "A Constructivist Approach to Grammar: Teaching Teachers to Teach Aspect." *Modern Language Journal* 81 (1997): 50–66.

————. "Between Orality and Literacy: Developing a Pedagogical Norm for Narrative Discourse." In *Pedagogical Norms for Second and Foreign Language Learning and Teaching*, edited by Susan Gass, Kathleen Bardovi-Harlig, Sally Magnan, and Joel Walz, 241–274. Amsterdam: John Benjamins, 2002.

————. "From Empirical Findings to the Teaching of Aspectual Distinctions." In *Tense and Aspect in Romance Languages: Theoretical and Applied Perspectives*, edited by Dalila Ayoun and M. Rafael Salaberry, 211–252. Amsterdam: John Benjamins, 2005.

Cox, Thomas J. "How to See What to Say in French." *French Review* 68 (1994): 203–208.

Dansereau, Diane. "A Discussion of Techniques Used in the Teaching of the Passé Composé/Imparfait Distinction in French." *French Review* 61 (1987): 33–38.

Di Vito, Nadine O'Connor. "Using Native Speech to Formulate Past-Tense Rules in French." *Georgetown University Roundtable on Languages and Linguistics* (1995): 188–197.

# 6 · Word-Order Constructions in the Spoken and Written Languages

The following grammatical topics are covered in this chapter:

- Left dislocations
- Right dislocations
- The Presentational/**Il y a** cleft construction
- The **C'est**-cleft construction

### DIFFICULTIES FOR THE LEARNER

Unlike most other languages, written and spoken French have diverged to the extent that some linguists contend that they are actually two separate languages. This is not a recent development. As Vendryès pointed out in 1923, the French insistence on maintaining the purity of the French language in its written form has led to a discernable break between how French speakers express themselves orally and in written form. He explains that:

> l'écart entre la langue écrite et la langue parlée est de plus en plus grand. Ni la syntaxe, ni le vocabulaire ne sont les mêmes. Même la morphologie présente des différences: le passé défini, l'imparfait du subjonctif ne sont plus employés dans la langue parlée. Surtout la différence des vocabulaires éclate à tous les yeux. Nous écrivons une langue morte, cette langue qui remonte aux écrivains du XVIIe siècle... Un homme qui parle comme il écrit nous fait l'effet d'un être artificiel, anormal... Nous écrivons une langue morte... On peut prévoir qu'il en sera du français littéraire comme du latin; il se conservera à l'état de langue morte, avec ses règles et son vocabulaire fixés une fois pour toutes. La langue vivante se développera indépendamment de lui, comme ont fait les langues romanes. Tout au plus servira-t-il de réservoir pour alimenter le vocabulaire du parler vivant... Il y aura un français littéraire qui s'opposera au français vulgaire. (303–305)[1]

Unfortunately, the reality is that many of today's instructors of French, especially if they rely on their textbooks, may be teaching their students to speak a dead language. Most textbooks do not adequately distinguish between written and spoken French or even acknowledge their differences with rigor or consistency. The end result is that students are often taught a sort of hybrid language that is composed of both written and spoken elements.

At the same time, the situation has improved over the years. Many American instructors of French "d'un certain âge" remember well the conversations they were expected to parrot from their own elementary French textbooks, which they assumed were accurate representations of actually occurring discourse. Consider the following excerpt from Harris and Lévêque's (1978) *Basic Conversational French*:

MARIE:  Connaissez-vous Louise Bedel?

JEAN:   Non, je ne la connais pas.

MARIE:  Mais si. Vous avez fait sa connaissance chez Suzanne samedi dernier.

JEAN:   Est-ce une petite jeune fille brune?

MARIE:  Pas du tout. C'est une grande blonde. (76)

Even though most native speakers of French would deem this conversation "correct," very few people actually speak, or spoke, like this, even in the 1970s. A more natural-sounding version of this exchange might be something along the lines of the following:

MARIE: Vous connaissez Louise Bedel?

JEAN: Non, (je) (la) connais pas.

MARIE: Mais si, vous avez fait sa connaissance chez Suzanne samedi dernier.

JEAN: C'est une petite (jeune fille) brune?

MARIE: Pas du tout. C'est une grande blonde.

(Note: Words in parentheses may be omitted.)

Unfortunately, students in the 1970s did not realize that the conversations in their textbooks were stilted and unnatural. They learned French believing, for example, that **nous** was commonly used as a subject pronoun, that **ne** was needed for negation, and that inversion was standardly used in conversations. These assumptions, among others, are false, as we discuss in this chapter and in Chapter 7.

Although modern textbook writers and publishers try to produce materials that accurately reflect how French speakers converse, most textbooks still fall short. Linguists have long lamented the discrepancies between the French presented in textbooks and the actual spoken language (see Bonin 1978; Walz 1986; Herschensohn 1988; and Joseph 1988). Blyth (1999) points out that "relatively few foreign language materials make extensive use of authentic interaction; scripted dialogues and scripted videos still rule the day. . . . How is one supposed to teach the spoken language with materials that do not reliably reflect typical speech patterns? In fact, textbooks frequently fail to even mention or exemplify constructions that are prevalent in the spoken language" (186–187).

Because students usually receive little or no explicit instruction about the differences between spoken and written forms (note that we are referring specifically to grammatical structures, not to lexical items, which, of course, play a significant role in distinguishing between the spoken and written codes), when they are asked to produce spoken discourse they end up sounding obviously foreign, even if they have excellent pronunciation. They may not make any "mistakes" (in other words, they speak "grammatically"), yet somehow native speakers immediately know that they are not francophone. Often, the reason they are exposed as non-native is that learners use constructions that are pragmatically odd or sociolinguistically inappropriate in particular discourse contexts.[2]

The goal of this chapter is to elucidate the use of various French word-order constructions so that instructors can teach their students to use the correct structures when speaking and writing. There are two major reasons why, when speaking, students choose inappropriate word-order constructions. First, they are not aware of the differences between the structures that are used in various contexts (spoken vs. written French, formal vs. informal speech, etc.). Second, learners often make what are called *transfer errors*, which means that they mistakenly assume that structures that are appropriate in their native language are also suitable in the language they are learning.

The choice of appropriate word-order constructions is the skill at the core of Canale's (1983) definition of discourse competence. He explains that discourse competence "concerns mastery of how to combine grammatical forms and meanings to achieve a unified spoken or written text in different genres" (9). He provides the following example to illustrate a lapse in discourse competence, noting that "discourse knowledge and skill can be distinguished from grammatical competence and sociolinguistic competence":

SPEAKER A:  What did the rain do?

SPEAKER B:  (!) The crops were destroyed by the rain. (10)

There is nothing grammatically or sociolinguistically odd about Speaker B's response, and Speaker A undoubtedly understands what Speaker B means. Still, Speaker A is struck by the awkwardness of the grammatical construction Speaker B has chosen and must reformulate Speaker B's utterance as "The rain destroyed the crops" in order to parse the utterance properly.

Due to their own transfer errors, native French speakers who are learning English often make mistakes that reflect the structures that are preferred or required in French. Consider examples (1)–(4), all of which contain pragmatically odd utterances that are typical or have actually been attested in the English of native French speakers:

(1) What a lovely hat. Where did you get it?
    ! It's my mother who gave it to me.
    [*Correct answer*: My mother gave it to me.]
(2) What's wrong? Why are you so upset?
    ! I have my dog that died.
    [*Correct answer*: My dog died.]
(3) What would y'all like to eat?

! Me, I like salads, but my brother, he would probably prefer a hamburger.

[*More natural answer*: I like salads, but my brother would probably prefer a hamburger.]

(4) What are you going to do? They're going to be speaking Spanish tonight.

! I speak Spanish, me.

[*More natural answer*: I speak Spanish.]

These transfer errors are particularly revealing of the structure of spoken French. In French, not only would the responses above be pragmatically well-formed, but in (1) and (2), these constructions would be required, and in (3) and (4), they make the spoken French sound more natural.

Unfortunately, anglophone learners of French are often exposed primarily to what is called the *canonical* form of French sentences. Canonical sentences consist of the subject followed by the verb and then (if required) an object. Thus, they are referred to as *SVO* (Subject Verb Object) sentences. Lambrecht (1987) has demonstrated, however, that SVO sentences are rare in spoken French. Conversely, they are quite common in English. Due to transfer errors, anglophone learners of French might respond to the French equivalents of the questions given above (and repeated below in French) in the following manner:

(5) Quel joli chapeau! Où est-ce que tu l'as acheté?

! Ma mère me l'a offert.

[*Correct answer*: C'est ma mère qui me l'a offert.]

(6) Qu'est-ce qui ne va pas? Pourquoi tu es si bouleversé?

! Mon chien est mort.

[*Correct answer*: J'ai mon chien qui est mort.]

(7) Qu'est-ce que vous aimeriez manger?

! J'aime les salades, mais mon frère aimerait probablement un hamburger.

[*More natural answer*: Moi, j'aime les salades, mais mon frère, il aimerait probablement un hamburger.]

(8) Qu'est-ce que tu vas faire? Ils vont parler espagnol ce soir.

! Je parle espagnol.

[*More natural answer*: Je parle espagnol, moi.]

In this chapter, we concentrate on the pragmatic properties of the word-order constructions presented in the exchanges above, highlighting the differences between spoken and written French forms. We then provide suggestions for making these variations accessible to learners.

## BASIC FORMS AND MEANINGS

We introduced above the concept of the *canonical form* (SVO) of an utterance. Take, for example, the following SVO sentence: **Marie déteste Jean.** There are many ways to express the same idea contained in this sentence using various types of constructions. Below is a partial list of different ways to express what semanticists call the same "truth conditions" (meaning) as those contained in the canonical sentence:

1. Marie, elle déteste Jean.
2. Jean, Marie le déteste.
3. Elle déteste Jean, Marie.
4. Marie le déteste, Jean.
5. Il y a Marie qui déteste Jean.
6. Il y a Jean que Marie déteste.
7. C'est Marie qui déteste Jean.
8. C'est Jean que Marie déteste.

These eight utterances represent particular types of word-order constructions that are each used in specific discourse environments. Utterances 1 and 2 are examples of *left dislocations*. Utterances 3 and 4 are *right dislocations*.[3] Sentences 5 through 8 are called *cleft constructions*, with 5 and 6 being examples of the *presentational* or **il y a** *cleft* and 7 and 8 of the **c'est**-*cleft*.

Barnes (1990) explains that dislocations are formed when "un nom ou on pronom qui 'double' un pronom dans la proposition est 'détaché' à gauche ou à droite de la proposition" (96). Left dislocations occur when a noun or pronoun is dislocated before the rest of the proposition, as in **Marie$_i$, elle$_i$ déteste Jean.**[4] The following are attested examples of left dislocations, taken from French films:

- Mais ce chiEN$_i$, qu'est-ce qu'il$_i$ peut être crétin! (*Tatie Danièle*)
- Ton café est franchement dégueulasse. VOUS$_i$, les FranÇAIS$_i$, vous$_i$ faites un café de merde. (*La Cage aux folles*)
- Ce moufFLET$_i$, elle$_i$ s'appelle Marie. (*Trois Hommes et un couffin*)
- Et MOI$_i$, je$_i$ l'aime et elle s'en fout. (*Le Péril jeune*)

The intonation of left dislocations is significant, as the dislocated noun always receives a rising intonation, otherwise known as a "pitch accent."

Note that pitch accents (when relevant to the discussion at hand) are indicated with capital letters in the examples throughout this chapter.

In right dislocations, the dislocated element *follows* the proposition, as in **Elle$_i$ déteste Jean, Marie$_i$.** Again, here are some examples from French films that exemplify this phenomenon:

- Je les$_i$ trouve où, les 7300 balles$_i$? (*Tatie Danièle*)
- J$_i$'suis pas très chien, moi$_i$. (*Tatie Danièle*)
- Vous savez bien qu'elle$_i$ est pourrie, ma bagnole$_i$. (*Tatie Danièle*)
- Il$_i$ se drogue, votre fils$_i$? (*Les Compères*)
- C$_i$'est drôle, (ce que tu viens de me dire)$_i$, parce qu'il y a quoi huit jours, j'ai rêvé qu'il$_{ii}$ se mariait, le petit$_{ii}$. (*La Cage aux folles*)

Right dislocations differ slightly in their syntactic structure from left dislocations in that it is possible, although not obligatory, for them to be preceded by a preposition if they are indirect objects or objects of a preposition. Therefore, the left-dislocated form of (9) would be (10):

(9)  On m'a téléphoné.
(10)  Moi, on m'a téléphoné.

whereas one may find either (11) or (12) for the corresponding right dislocation:

(11)  On m'a téléphoné, moi.
(12)  On m'a téléphoné, à moi.

The prosody of right dislocations differs from that of left dislocations in that the right-dislocated noun has a falling intonation, unless, of course, the utterance is a yes-no question, as in **Il$_i$ se drogue, votre fils$_i$?**

Cleft constructions differ from typical canonical sentences and from dislocations because they consist of two clauses instead of one.[5] Jespersen (1937) coined the term "cleft construction" and defined it as a sentence construction consisting of a main clause and a subordinate clause that together express a proposition that could otherwise be conveyed in one single clause. In fact, one of the requirements of a cleft construction is that it can be "unclefted" into one clause that contains the same meaning. For example, a cleft such as **C'est elle qui parle français** may be "unclefted" into **Elle parle français.** The presentational cleft and the **c'est-**cleft are the two cleft constructions that are found the most frequently in French.

The presentational cleft construction, also referred to sometimes as the **il y a** or the **avoir** cleft, consists of a presentational expression, such as **(Il) y a,** the verb **avoir,** the verb **voir,** or the expression **voilà,** followed by a noun and then a relative clause beginning with **qui** or **que.** Here are some examples of the presentational cleft from Lambrecht (2002, 171):

- (Il) y a le téléPHONE qui SONNE.
- J'ai eu mon beau-FRÈRE qui a fait Paris-NICE.
- Je vois le facTEUR qui arRIVE.
- Voilà le facTEUR qui arRIVE.

The intonation of the presentational cleft, as indicated above, contains a rising intonation on the last syllable of the noun that follows the presentational expression, followed by another pitch accent on the last syllable within the relative clause.

Like the presentational cleft, the **c'est**-cleft consists of a main clause (this time containing **c'est**[6] and a phrase), followed by a relative clause beginning with either **qui** or **que.** The phrase following **c'est,** which is referred to in linguistic terms as an *argument*, is more varied than what one finds in the presentational cleft (which is always a noun phrase); it may be either a noun phrase, a prepositional phrase, an adverbial phrase, or a verb phrase containing **en** followed by a present participle. The following are attested **c'est**-clefts found in corpora of spoken French (see Katz 1997), each representing a different grammatical category following **c'est:**

- C'est les FEMMES qui dominent. (*noun phrase*—Giacomi 1980)
- C'est à leurs MUScles qu'on reconnaît les linguistes. (*prepositional phrase*—Moreau 1976)
- C'est LÀ qu'on se comprend le plus. (*adverbial phrase*—Giacomi 1980)
- C'est en faisant des errEURS qu'ils apprennent. (*verb phrase*—*personal correspondence*)

Note that the majority of **c'est**-clefts contain noun phrases and prepositional phrases following **c'est.** In addition, the argument that follows **c'est** almost always receives a strong pitch accent, significantly stronger than what one finds in the presentational cleft.[7]

The following table contains a summary of the basic forms of these four grammatical constructions.

### Basic Forms of Dislocations and Cleft Constructions

*Canonical sentence:* SVO (subject verb object)

**Marie déteste Jean.**

*Left Dislocations:* Left-dislocated noun/pronoun followed by a sentence that includes a pronoun that is co-referential with the dislocated noun or pronoun.

**Marie$_i$, elle$_i$ déteste Jean.**

*Right Dislocations:* Sentence that includes a pronoun that is co-referential with a right dislocated noun or pronoun.

**Elle$_i$ déteste Jean, Marie$_i$.**

*Presentational cleft construction:* Sentence that begins with a presentational expression followed by a noun phrase and a relative clause that begins with **qui** or **que**.

**Il y a Jean que Marie déteste.**
**On a Jean que Marie déteste.**
**On voit Marie qui déteste Jean.**
**Voilà Marie qui déteste Jean.**

***C'est**-cleft construction:* Sentence that begins with **C'est** followed by an argument (either a noun phrase, a prepositional phrase, an adverbial phrase, or a verb phrase) and a relative clause that begins with **qui** or **que**.

**C'est Marie qui déteste Jean.** (noun phrase)
**C'est à cause de son égoïsme que Marie déteste Jean.** (prepositional phrase)
**C'est sans pitié que Marie déteste Jean.** (adverbial phrase)
**C'est en le regardant manger que Marie commence à détester Jean.** (verb phrase)

---

### MEANINGS IN CONTEXT

Before examining the functions of dislocations and clefts in discourse, one must recognize that there is not just one form of spoken French, just as there are many different varieties of written French. First, one must understand the concepts of *register* and *sociolinguistic variation* and their role in creating discourse-appropriate utterances. Unfortunately most text-books either omit or only briefly touch upon these topics. Ball (2000, 1) stresses the importance of distinguishing three dimensions of linguistic variation:

• Speech versus writing
• Formality/informality of the situation
• Social level of the speaker

He points out that a great deal of overlapping occurs and that forms can pass back and forth between categories depending on the precise com-municative situation. For example, he explains: "Spoken language is not inevitably more informal than written language. Someone speaking in public, for example, might well feel it appropriate to use features which would otherwise give a 'bookish' effect. Conversely, there are many nov-elists and journalists whose writing is characterized by its deliberately colloquial flavour" (1). Thus, a professor delivering a lecture in a French university might purposely include the **ne** particle when expressing ne-gation or use inversion to form questions. These choices reflect the issue of *register*, which is linked to the perceived formality of a given situation.

Batchelor and Offord (2000) describe register as being concerned with "the relationship of formality/information existing between the two par-ticipants in a conversation or any other situation in which language is used" (5). They contend that register depends on four variable factors: sex, age, status, and intimacy. All linguists agree that some degree of artificiality is involved when determining how many registers exist since the factors involved are not rigidly defined. For instance, Batchelor and Of-ford describe three distinct registers for French as being most practical for learners (although scholars often prefer more finely nuanced categories): R1 "informal," R2 "neutral" and R3 "formal." They describe R1 as "very informal, casual, colloquial, familiar, careless, admitting new terms almost indiscriminately, certain terms short-lived, at times truncated, elliptical, incorrect grammatically, prone to redundant expressions, includes slang expressions and vulgarisms, likely to include regional variations." R2 is "standard, polite, educated, equivalent of 'BBC English,' compromise be-tween the two extremes," and R3 is "formal, literary, official, with archaic ring, language of scholars and purists, meticulously correct, reluctant to admit new terms" (6). Batchelor and Offord explain, however, that these classifications represent more of a continuum than three discrete categories: "It must be stressed once more that these sections are the result of an artificial division and that the reality behind them consists of subtle, imperceptible shifts, not of rigidly defined categories"(6).

Sanders (1993) argues that while register is recognized as playing an important role in sociosituational variation, it has received relatively little attention compared to other sociolinguistic constructs (28). As a result, linguists and grammarians employ a confusing and idiosyncratic lexicon to refer to various register differences. The result is that different terms are frequently used to classify the same linguistic phenomenon. Nevertheless, Sanders gives the following terms in French for five different levels of increasing formality: **populaire, familier, courant, soutenu, académique/littéraire** (29). She illustrates these registers with interrogative forms as shown below:

### Register Differences

| | | |
|---|---|---|
| Populaire: | Interrogative particle **-ti** | **Tu viens-ti?** |
| Familier: | No inversion | **Tu peux?** |
| Courant: | **Est-ce que +** subject + verb | **Est-ce que tu peux?** |
| Soutenu: | Inversion of subject + verb | **Peux-tu?** |
| Académique: | Certain formulae | **Puis-je . . . ?** |

Source: Adapted from Sanders 1993.

As mentioned, linguists frequently disagree over the use of descriptive terms for different registers, since the terms may carry unintended negative or prescriptive evaluations. For example, Ball (2000) stresses that one should not confuse **le français familier,** a distinction of register (formal vs. informal) with **le français populaire,** which is a distinction of class and education: "'Popular' forms (**le livre que tu as besoin,** for example) should be distinguished from 'familiar' ones (**je comprends pas,** for example), which are usable by all speakers, irrespective of their backgrounds. So **familiar/familier,** unlike **popular/populaire,** is a formality-related not a class-related term; it need not imply 'used exclusively by upper-class and middle-class speakers'" (2).

It is also important to recognize that a standard form of spoken French has emerged that differs considerably from what is acceptable in written French. Dislocations fall into this category, as does the presentational cleft construction. Without these structures, spoken French sounds stilted, **soigné,** and perhaps a bit pretentious. It would be odd, however, to find these constructions in the written language, except, as mentioned above, to create a particular effect (to imitate the spoken language, etc.). As we discuss below, it is essential to be aware that, unlike the other word-order constructions presented in this chapter, the **c'est-**cleft is not exclusively a spoken construction. It is regularly used and often required in written French. For this reason, we devote a considerable amount of attention to the **c'est-**cleft.

The following table summarizes some of the main properties of spoken French that will be found throughout the examples given in this chapter. It is important to note that most of these structures are not found in the written language, unless its purpose is to imitate authentic speech.

### Elements of Spoken French

1. Use of disolations and presentational clefts

    written French:  **Jacques est parti.**

    spoken French:  left dislocation: **Jacques, il est parti.**

     right dislocation: **Il est parti, Jacques.**

     presentational cleft: **Il y a Jacques qui est parti.**

2. Deletion of negation marker **ne**

    written French: **Jacques n'est pas parti.**

    spoken French: **Jacques est pas parti.**

3. Lack of inversion in interrogatives (see Chapter 7)

    written French: **Jacques est-il parti?**

    spoken French: **Jacques est parti?**

4. Use of **on** instead of **nous** as a subject pronoun

    written French: **Nous partons.**

    spoken French: **On part.**

5. Elision with second-person singular subject pronoun

    written French: **Tu as faim.**

    spoken French: **T'as faim.**

6. **C'est** instead of **Ce sont**

    written French: **Ce sont mes parents.**

    spoken French: **C'est mes parents.**

## Dislocations

Left dislocations are one of the most common grammatical constructions found in spoken French. According to Lambrecht (1981, 1987), Ashby (1988), and Barnes (1990), left dislocations are used primarily as a "topic-shifting" or "topic-creating" device. In other words, by isolating a particular noun or pronoun and putting it into the left-dislocated position, the speaker is indicating to his addressee that this entity will be the topic for discussion in the ensuing discourse. Therefore, if someone begins a clause with **Mon chien,** one knows that the dog has been selected as the topic for discussion in the assertion that will follow. Sometimes there may be more than one topic within a given utterance, as in Ashby's (1988) example: "Alors je sais que mon frère, son C.A.P., il l'a pas eu" (205), where both the brother and his exam are the topics for discussion.

It is important to note that not just any noun can be put into left dislocation within a conversation. In order for a noun to be left-dislocated, it must somehow be relevant to the discussion at hand and accessible to the addressee. This is why it is nearly impossible to find a noun beginning with an indefinite article in left-dislocated position; it simply is not accessible to the addressee.[8] The speaker assumes that his addressee will accept a given entity as a topic for discussion because of one of the following factors:

- It has already been mentioned in the preceding discourse.
- It is somehow linked to the preceding discourse (the interlocutor is able to infer its existence due to the situation at hand).
- It is present in the physical surroundings that the speakers share.

Linguists (see Ashby 1988 and Barnes 1990) concur that left dislocations are generally used to indicate a contrast, the reintroduction of an earlier topic back into the discourse, a topic shift, or turn-taking.

Finally, when analyzing the topic construction, one should realize that the subject pronoun **nous** has been virtually replaced by **on** in the spoken language. At the same time, the emphatic **nous, on** is found with great frequency. Note that **nous** is always accessible as a topic for discussion, since one of the referents is physically present in the discourse. Obviously, the same is true for any first- or second-person pronoun as well (**moi, je; toi, tu; vous, vous**).

Right dislocations are also used to introduce or reaffirm a topic for dis-

cussion, and most linguists concur that there are times when left dislocations and right dislocations can be employed in similar situations. Sometimes speakers go so far as to include both in the same utterance, as seen
in (13):

(13) Moi, je suis normande, mais je ne mange pas de crème, moi. (per-
    sonal correspondence)

Ashby makes a further distinction between left and right dislocations:
"My data confirm the conclusion of Barnes, Lambrecht and others that
LD [left dislocation] is essentially a mechanism for topicalizing and fore-
grounding the referent. We have seen that RDs [right dislocations] in my
corpus are also used for this purpose. But RDs seem to code other discourse functions that LDs do not. They are also used to clarify or to give
additional information about the referent, to fill discourse space, and to
close discourse" (224). In addition, only nouns (not pronouns) should
appear in the right-dislocated position in order to clarify the referent of
an earlier pronoun, as in (14):

(14) Elle est très jolie, ta mère.

A right-dislocated pronoun, however, "may be part of a strategy for filling
discourse space as the speaker formulates his thoughts" (222). In addition, a right-dislocated pronoun often "[signals] to the interlocutor that
discourse space is momentarily being ceded" (222), which was probably
the case in (13). Thus, left dislocations are used mostly to introduce or
to "open" one's turn speaking, while right dislocations are employed to
reiterate or clarify a topic or to "close" one's turn.

There are a few right-dislocated structures that are found with great
frequency in spoken French. It is worth noting that demonstratives often
occur in right dislocations, as in Astérix's famous example: "Ils sont fous,
ces Romains." This phenomenon may be attributed to the fact that the information that is found in right dislocations is often redundant (unlike in
left dislocations). Right dislocations can also be evaluative, as in (14a) and
(14b):

(14a) Context: One member of a dining party whispers to another while a
    third carefully calculates his portion of a restaurant bill:
    **«Il est radin, ce petit con.»**
(14b) Context: A couple looking at homes for sale walks into a living room

whose walls are painted bright yellow. The woman exclaims: «**Mon Dieu, c'est jaunâtre, ces murs!**»

In spoken discourse, evaluative comments are usually made once the topic has already been established or is easily recoverable from the given context. The following table summarizes the functions of left and right dislocations in discourse.

### Functions of Right and Left Dislocations

Left Dislocations
1. Introduce a topic for discussion (note: the topic must be accessible to the addressee because of its having been mentioned, its being present in the discourse environment, or its being inferable due to the discussion at hand)
2. Indicate a contrast
3. Reintroduce an earlier topic back into the discourse
4. Designate a topic shift
5. Indicate turn-taking

Right Dislocations
1. Introduce a topic for discussion
2. Reaffirm a topic for discussion
3. Clarify a referent
4. Give additional information about or an evaluation of a referent
5. Fill discourse space
6. Close discourse

### Cleft Constructions

Cleft constructions are a bit more complicated than dislocations syntactically, and they have a different function in discourse. In constrast to dislocations, which introduce or remind the addressee of a topic for discussion, cleft constructions serve to put a particular part of a sentence into what is called *focus* position. Lambrecht (1994) explains that the *focus* of a sentence is the part of an utterance that makes it informative. In other words, the focus combines with what is already known (the knowledge that the speaker presupposes his listener already possesses) to produce whatever assertion the speaker wishes to convey.

The presentational cleft is an example of what Lambrecht (1994) calls *sentence focus.* This cleft construction is a component of the spoken language only; it is considered bad form to write it. In the presentational cleft, everything that the speaker says after the introductory presentational expression (**il y a, j'ai, je vois, voilà,** etc.) is considered to be new information to the addressee. Therefore, in an utterance such as (15), the speaker does not presuppose that the addressee is aware that something is ringing:

(15) Il y a le téléphone qui sonne.

 Everything that the speaker says is new to the addressee; the entire sentence is in "focus." Similarly, in the exchange in (16), Speaker A knows that something is wrong but does not know that someone has died until Speaker B has told him:

(16) SPEAKER A: Mais qu'est-ce qu'il y a? Tu fais une tête, toi.
  SPEAKER B: J'ai mon chien qui est mort.

When one does not choose the correct word-order construction, the result is often a request for a clarification. Consider the following exchange from the film *La Cage aux folles.* Albin returns home from grocery shopping to find Renato (his partner) in a terrible mood. The night before, Renato's son had come home for a visit:

(17) ALBIN:    Tu aurais pu me prévenir que Laurent arrivait . . . [diatribe about how Renato does not want to share his son with Albin] . . . Mais tu en fais une tête, toi, ce matin. Qu'est-ce que tu as, hein?
  RENATO: Il se marie.
  ALBIN:    Comment?
  RENATO: Mon fils, il se marie.
  ALBIN:    Oh (rire) tu es bête . . .

Renato's response to **Qu'est-ce que tu as?** is incomprehensible on various levels. Had he replied using the presentational construction, as in **J'ai mon fils qui se marie,** it is still possible that Albin's reaction would have been one of confusion, due to the bizarre and troubling content of the message. This cleft, however, would have been a more appropriate construction in this context, since all the information is new. The other problem is that Renato uses the subject pronoun **il** when its referent is not clearly identifiable to Albin. Even though Laurent had been mentioned in the preceding discourse, he needed to be reintroduced into the discourse, because the topic for conversation had shifted to Renato and his grouchiness. It is revealing that Renato reframes the utterance using a left dislocation (**Mon fils, il se marie**). He introduces his son as a topic for conversation and then repeats the news that Laurent is getting married in the main clause. At this point, it would no longer be felicitous for him to use the presentational construction, because the information that someone is getting married is already known. Remember that all the information contained in the presentational cleft is supposed to be new to the addressee.

Whereas the presentational cleft is an example of sentence focus, the **c'est**-cleft is what Lambrecht (1994) classifies as an *argument focus* construction. In the **c'est**-cleft construction, there is only one part of the sentence that is in focus; the speaker assumes that the addressee already has knowledge of the other part of the assertion. The focus happens to be whatever argument follows **c'est** (as mentioned above, this category includes noun phrases, prepositional phrases, adverbial phrases, or verb phrases beginning with **en**). Whatever information follows **qui** or **que** is considered to be presupposed. The combination of the presupposed section of the cleft and the focus (the element following **c'est**) is what makes the assertion informative. In contrast to the presentational construction, where the entire sentence is in focus, here it is only the argument following **c'est.**

Despite the prevalence of the **c'est**-cleft in French, this construction is rarely explained with great detail in textbooks, most likely because of its complexity. Smits (1989) laments: "The cleft construction is one of the constructions that has given linguists many a headache over the years" (203). Textbook writers seem not to know what to say about it. For example, two widely-used advanced grammar review textbooks, *L'Essentiel de la grammaire française* (Hoffmann and Schultz) and *La Grammaire à l'œuvre* (Barson), summarize the **c'est**-cleft in only one sentence. In *La Grammaire à l'œuvre*, the **c'est**-cleft is included within a larger description of demonstrative pronouns as a device "pour présenter (identifier) un nom" (122). In *L'Essentiel de la grammaire française*, **"Ce + être + qui/que"** is described as being used "pour mettre une expression en valeur" (146). It is doubtful that these explanations are sufficient for students to understand the function of the **c'est**-cleft in discourse.

Students should understand that the purpose of the **c'est-**cleft is to isolate one element of a sentence and give it special emphasis. In English, accentuating any particular word or phrase within a sentence is not a problem, as a pitch accent may be inserted wherever one wishes. Consider the following example from Nick Hornby's novel *High Fidelity*. The narrator is describing a new woman he has met who seems to be attracted to him: "And she liked me. She liked ME. SHE liked me. She LIKED me. Or at least, I think she did. I THINK she did" (20). Note that in each case the word in capital letters (in italics in Hornby's original) represents what is in focus; it denotes what the speaker believes to be the information that the addressee is lacking in order to have knowledge of a particular assertion. The presuppositions for each utterance are as follows:

• She liked ME.
  *Presupposition:* She liked somebody (x); (x) = me.
• SHE liked me.
  *Presupposition:* Somebody (x) liked me; (x) = she.
• She LIKED me.
  *Presupposition:* She felt something (x) toward me; (x) = feelings of liking.
• I THINK she did.
  *Presupposition:* I had opinion (x) about her liking me; (x) = think it is true.

In French, one does not have the luxury of using a pitch accent to emphasize a particular element within a sentence, as French prosody simply does not work like this. Specifically, as many linguists have pointed out (see Carduner and Hagiwara 1982; Tranel 1987), French does not allow words that are not at the end of rhythmic groups to be accented. Therefore, if one wants to emphasize a word that is not at the end of a rhythmic group, there needs to be a device to put the said word into such a position. The **c'est-**cleft exists precisely for this purpose.

There are two cases in which the use of the **c'est-**cleft is obligatory: to put *subjects* into focus, as in (18):

(18) C'est MARIE qui déteste Jean.

or to put an *unbound pronoun* into focus, whether it be a subject or an object. Unbound pronouns are pronouns that can exist on their own, without being attached to anything. Examples are tonic pronouns (**moi, toi,** etc.) and **cela, ceci,** and **ça.** Bound pronouns (such as subject and direct- and indirect-object pronouns), also referred to as *clitics,* are unable to stand alone; they must always be attached to a a verb. Example (19) contains an unbound pronoun in focus position:

(19) C'est LUI qu'elle déteste.

In contrast, as mentioned above, there are no such restrictions in English on where one may insert a pitch accent. (20) contains a pitch accent on a subject and (21) on an unbound object pronoun:

(20) MARY hates John.
(21) She hates HIM!

It is interesting that English allows both the it-cleft (the equivalent of the **c'est**-cleft) or the canonical sentence in similar contexts, as demonstrated in (22):

(22) I heard that Mary hates John.
No, she hates ME. / No, it's ME/I that she hates.[9]

French sometimes allows both structures as well, but, as mentioned above, not when the focused element is a bound pronoun or when it is the subject of the verb. In fact, it is even preferable to use the canonical version of the utterance when the focused element naturally falls at the end of a rhythmic group. For example, most French speakers would prefer (b) over (a) as an answer to (23), even though both responses are possible:

(23) Tiens, t'as vu ma sœur au resto hier?
(a) Non, c'est ton FRÈRE que j'ai vu.
(b) Non, j'ai vu ton FRÈRE.

Note that there is nothing that requires or motivates the use of the **c'est**-cleft in this situation; the word **frère** is able to receive a pitch accent due to its occurrence at the end of a rhythmic group.

There are two main types of **c'est**-clefts: the variable-fulfillment (VF), and the corrective (CC) **c'est**-clefts, as discussed in great detail in Katz (1997, 2000a, and 2000b). The variable-fulfillment cleft, a term coined by Declerck (1988), is the most frequently found **c'est**-cleft in French (see Katz 1997). In these cases, whatever follows **c'est** is the variable that fulfills the assertion; it is the element that, in conjunction with what is already known (whatever is contained in the relative clause), makes the proposition informative. The example given in the introduction to this chapter, and repeated in (24), contains a VF:

(24) Quel joli chapeau! Où tu l'as acheté?

      C'est ma mère qui me l'a offert.

In this **c'est**-cleft, it is presupposed that the hat has come from somewhere (the speaker obtained it somewhere). What is unknown is its provenance. Therefore the missing variable (x), where x = **ma mère,** is put into focus position to combine with the presupposition (x **me l'a offert**) to form the assertion.

    The corrective cleft (CC) is not as prevalent as the VF; however, it plays a significant role in discourse. Its purpose is to correct a faulty assertion contained in the preceding discourse. Whatever is found following **c'est** is in focus as the corrected element. Consider the following example from the film Les Compères. In this exchange between a Mafia thug and a journalist, the thug uses the CC to correct what he considers to be the journalist's mistaken assertion:

(25) THUG:     Le patron veut te parler.

     JOURNALIST: Je n'ai rien à lui dire.

     THUG:     C'est LUI qui parlera.

The journalist has mistakenly taken for granted that he would be the one speaking; the purpose of the CC is to correct this assumption. Notice that the pitch accent on the argument in focus within the corrective cleft is usually stronger than what one finds in a typical variable-fulfillment cleft.

    Finally, there is the causal **c'est**-cleft, which corresponds to the "that's why" construction in English. (26) is an attested example of this type of cleft:

(26) C'est pour ça que je bois de l'eau. (Minnesota Corpus, Kerr 1983)

The causal **c'est**-cleft is found primarily in the spoken language. Its equivalent in written French would be (27) or (28):

(27) C'est pour cela que je bois de l'eau.

(28) C'est à cause de cela que je bois de l'eau.

Another interesting observation about this construction is that there are times when that which follows **qui** or **que** may not actually be presupposed, as in the exchange contained in (29):

(29) Je ne suis pas très contente de vivre ici. C'est pour ça que je cherche un nouveau poste pour l'année prochaine.

The addressee may not already know that the speaker is planning to look for another job, but the speaker uses the **c'est**-cleft construction nonetheless. This is an example of what Lambrecht (1994) calls pragmatic accommodation. According to Lambrecht, presuppositions are sometimes exploited for communicative purposes (65). In these cases, speakers assume that their addressees will accommodate them and accept what is found in the relative clause as already known information, even if it is not actually presupposed.

## GOING BEYOND: FOR THE ADVANCED LEARNER

### More on the C'est-Cleft

One must be careful not to confuse the **c'est**-cleft with other constructions that appear to have the same structure. For example, certain sentences may be ambiguous when extracted from a written passage without context, as in (30):

(30) C'est un pull que ma mère m'a donné.

This sentence could be a cleft construction when found in a context such as the one in (31):

(31) A: Tu as reçu un chapeau pour ton anniversaire?
     B: Non, c'est un PULL que ma mère m'a donné.

Otherwise, it could be a noun phrase that contains a restrictive relative clause, as in (32):

(32) A: Qu'est-ce que c'est?
     B: C'est un pull que ma mère m'a donné.

Whether (30) is a cleft construction is obvious in the spoken language due to its intonation; the cleft construction has a strong accent on **pull.** In the restrictive relative clause, however, one finds only the normal stress that occurs on the last syllable of a rhythmic group.

Another type of cleft look-alike is what Katz (2000b) calls the **pas parce que** construction. This construction, which is often found in advertisements, looks like but is not a **c'est**-cleft. Take, for example, two billboards found in Montreal, given in (33) and (34):

(33) C'est pas parce qu'on pédale sans permis que tout est permis.

(34) C'est pas parce qu'on est prudent que c'est plat.

At first glance both (33) and (34) appear to be **c'est**-clefts. One indication that they are not clefts is that it is impossible to "uncleft" them into canonical sentences that contain the same meaning, which is a requirement of the cleft.

If these examples were **c'est**-cleft constructions, the presupposition in (33) would be: "everything is permitted for some reason (x)"; the focus (x) would be "not because people ride without permits." The assertion would therefore be: "Everything is permitted, but not because people ride without permits." Clearly this is not the intended meaning of the advertisement. Similarly, in (34), the presupposition would be: "It's uncool for some reason (x);" and the focus (x) would be: "not because people are careful." Therefore, the assertion would be: "It is uncool, but not because people are careful." Again, this meaning is not the intention of the advertisement. The message of (33) is that just because people ride without permits does not mean that everything is permitted, and (34) seeks to affirm that just because you are careful, that does not make you uncool.

Knud Lambrecht has pointed out to us (personal correspondence) that utterances containing **pas parce que** may be ambiguous when they are taken out of context, because, conceivably, they could be interpreted as **c'est**-clefts. Take for example, an utterance such as (35):

(35) C'est pas parce qu'il est riche qu'elle l'aime.

The **pas parce que** interpretation would be that just because he is rich does not mean that she loves him. The **c'est**-cleft interpretation, however, would have an entirely different meaning: that she does indeed love him, but not because he is rich (but for some other reason). The only way to know whether a sentence is a **pas parce que** construction or a cleft is to look at its context (if it is written) or to listen to its intonation (if it is spoken) to hear if it contains the prominent pitch accent found in the **c'est**-cleft.

Another type of cleft look-alike is the continuous cleft, as found in (36):

(36) Qui c'était au téléphone?

    C'était ta mère, qui voulait que tu rentres pour le dîner.

If one reads this exchange out loud, it is clear that the intonation is different than that of the **c'est**-cleft. The English translation would not be "It was your MOTHER who wanted you to come home for dinner" (with a pitch accent on *mother*), but instead, "It was your mother, who wanted you to come home for dinner," with a pause after *mother*. When in doubt as to whether a given sentence is a **c'est-**cleft or not, it is helpful to read it out loud to see whether it has the prosody of the cleft, or to "uncleft" it into one clause to see whether it will have the same meaning.[10]

### More on Dislocations

One of the problems that learners experience when acquiring spoken word-order constructions is that they do not always receive feedback when they make errors. Thus, at times they may overgeneralize rules and produce utterances that native speakers find odd. Yaguello (1998, 35–36) describes an example of this phenomenon related to left dislocations. She explains:

> «Brechat, je l'aime,» dit en soupirant notre jeune invitée américaine avant de reprendre le bateau pour le Continent. La formulation fait sourire, évidemment. Mais en quoi est-elle fautive? En français parlé, et notre Alexandra l'a bien compris, il est règle de «disloquer» l'énoncée en détachant le thème et en «doublant» celui-ci par un pronom qu'on place dans la position syntaxique adéquate (ici complément d'objet). Ainsi,
> **J'aime Natacha**
> donne naturellement
> **Natacha, je l'aime**
> tandis que
> **J'aime la France**
> donne
> **La France, je l'aime.**
> Par contre
> **J'aime le chocolat**
> donne
> **Le chocolat, j'aime ça**
> plutôt que
> **Le chocolat, je l'aime.**

Yaguello brings up two interesting issues here. First, as she highlights in the **chocolat** example, it is incorrect to use the corresponding direct-object pronoun to double the left-dislocated noun when the noun in question refers to a generic category. **Le chocolat, j'aime ça** refers to chocolate in general. **Le chocolat, je l'aime** would be acceptable were it to denote a particular, identifiable piece of chocolate. As Yaguello also points out, if the generic noun in question is a count noun, the dislocated element must be in the plural, as in **Les chats, j'aime ça,** or **les enfants, j'aime ça.** If one were to say **Le chat, j'aime ça,** the referent would not be "cat" in general, but a mass noun, as in a rather unappetizing dinner choice.

Yaguello also posits that the situation gets complicated when the dislocated element is a city. It is fine to say **La France, je l'aime,** but one should not say *****Paris, je l'aime.** Likewise, it is odd to say *****Paris, j'aime ça.** As Yaguello notes, the correct way to express this assertion using dislocation is to say simply **Paris, j'aime,** with no direct-object pronoun contained in the main clause. This is an example of null instantiation, a phenomenon that is found with great frequency in spoken French (see Lambrecht and Lemoine 1995). In fact, Knud Lambrecht (personal correspondence) believes that it is more natural to say **La France, j'aime** than **La France, je l'aime.** Apparently, with places that are not cities, one has the option of saying either.

Anglophone speakers of French often struggle when they try to say the equivalent of *Paris is beautiful.* There is no such problem with countries (or states or continents); for example, *France is beautiful,* may be translated into **La France est belle** without any difficulty. One does not have the option of this construction, however, with cities. Both *****Paris est beau** and *****Paris est belle** are ill-formed. Thus, one can choose among **Paris est une belle ville, Paris, c'est une belle ville,** or **Paris, c'est beau.** Even though cities are either masculine or feminine (for example, Paris is masculine, while Rome is feminine), because they are never found with a determiner (with the exception of certain cities where the determiner is a part of the name, as in **Le Havre, La Rochelle,** and **La Nouvelle-Orléans**), French speakers have difficulty modifying them with adjectives that agree in gender. Most native speakers of French would be more apt to accept **Paris est magnifique** than **Paris est beau,** since the gender of the adjective **magnifique** is not discernible. Still, **Paris, c'est magnifique** seems more natural than **Paris est magnifique,** and this use of a left dislocation is found with great frequency in spoken French.

## CLASSROOM APPLICATIONS

The issue of whether learners should receive explicit instruction in order to integrate dislocations and cleft constructions into their spoken repertoire has been hotly debated. Obviously, students do not need to learn every pragmatic property of these constructions, especially at the earlier levels of instruction. At the same time, they should become aware that such constructions exist, and they should begin to get a feel for them through receiving a good deal of input. Some scholars believe that receiving input is the best way for students to master sentence-level constructions (see Barnes 1990; Ferdinand 2002; and Sleeman 2004). Other studies (see Harley and Swain 1984 on French immersion programs in Canada), however, have shown that input may not be sufficient for leading students to master discourse-level phenomena.

In fact, one of the strongest arguments for explicit instruction is based on the occurrence of mistaken hypotheses caused by transfer and overgeneralization. For example, Bley-Vroman (1986) discusses the famous example of a foreigner who assumes that the English word "hello" may be used in both greeting and parting, because this practice occurs in his native language. Even if this speaker does not ever receive input—hearing someone say "hello" when leaving—he may not correct his faulty hypothesis unless it is pointed out to him that he is making an error.

Similarly, the **c'est-**cleft is an example of a syntactic construction that exists in what is called "free variation" with another construction in English, but not in French. Free variation means that speakers have the choice between two different grammatical constructions to express the same assertion in a particular discourse setting. Native speakers of English may assume that because they can express an utterance in either the clefted or canonical form in English, they have that same option in French. As we have shown above, however, this is simply not the case. There are several reasons why learners may not realize that the canonical form can be inappropriate. First, native speakers tend to understand the intended message, even if the learners incorrectly use the canonical form. Second, learners often see the canonical structure in the written language and do not realize that it would not be used in spoken French. If nobody ever tells learners that their speech sounds stilted, how will they know that it is? At the very least, students need to be made aware that there is not a one-to-one correspondence between word-order constructions in English and in French.

How can textbooks and teachers provide students with input as well as explicit instruction about the occurrences of the various constructions described in this chapter? As mentioned above, explanations do not need to be long or complicated, especially at early levels of instruction. Succinct and accessible descriptions that raise students' consciousness of how constructions function in discourse should be adequate. For example, to teach left dislocations, students should read or hear a passage that contains several; then they should be asked to hypothesize the use of this construction in discourse. Next, by participating in discourse-based activities, students should get a sense of how the particular constructions function in discourse. Students should not be required to produce output immediately.

Blyth (2000) suggests that there should be a variety of input-type activities included right after a given grammar explanation, so that students have a chance to see the construction in context before they are required to produce it. According to Blyth, the production activities that one currently finds in most textbooks may be easily transformed into structured-input activities. Activity 6.1, created following Blyth's guidelines and using the same directions as his activity (1999, 197–198), exposes students to left dislocations:

● ● ● ● ●

**Activity 6.1: Votre avis: êtes-vous d'accord ou pas d'accord?**
(structured input)

Points de vue. Indiquez si vous êtes d'accord ou pas d'accord avec les commentaires suivants.

| | | |
|---|---|---|
| 1. Le français, c'est une très belle langue. | D'accord | Pas d'accord |
| 2. Les gros mots, c'est plus typique chez les hommes. | D'accord | Pas d'accord |
| 3. L'anglais, c'est une langue qui remplace beaucoup d'autres langues. | D'accord | Pas d'accord |
| 4. Les adolescents, ils parlent une langue différente que celle de leurs parents. | D'accord | Pas d'accord |
| 5. Les professeurs, ils font plus d'attention à la grammaire que nécessaire. | D'accord | Pas d'accord |
| 6. Les devoirs, cela ne sert à rien. | D'accord | Pas d'accord |
| 7. Le café, c'est important pour l'énergie. | D'accord | Pas d'accord |
| 8. Le vin, c'est bon pour la santé. | D'accord | Pas d'accord |

Activity 6.2 is another structured-input activity to teach left dislocations that students may do either with a partner or as a survey activity. Students first read the following stereotypes about Americans. Then they

ask their partners whether the statements describe them personally and/or the Americans they know.

• • • • •

**Activity 6.2: Les stéréotypes.** (structured input)

Choose the most appropriate answer from the list provided, or come up with your own response.

Modèle: Les Américains aiment manger au McDo.

      a. Moi, je trouve ça abominable.

      b. Moi, je préfère Burger King.

      c. Moi, j'adore manger au McDo.

Réponse: Alors, pour moi, c'est (c). Moi, j'adore manger au McDo.

1. La plupart des Américains aiment le sport.

    a. Moi, j'aime le sport.

      *Follow-up:* Quels sports (est-ce que) vous préférez?

    b. Moi, je n'aime pas le sport.

    c. (à vous)

2. Il n'y a pas beaucoup d'Américains qui sont bilingues.

    a. Ma mère, elle (ne) parle aucune autre langue.

    b. Ma mère, elle parle d'autres langues.

      *Follow-up:* Lequelles?

    c. (à vous)

3. La famille américaine ne mange plus ensemble.

    a. Chez moi, nous, on ne mange pas ensemble.

    b. Chez moi, nous, on prend le dîner ensemble.

      *Follow-up:* Combien de fois par semaine (est-ce que) vous mangez ensemble?

    c. (à vous)

4. Les Américains sont obsédés par les microbes. Souvent ils prennent plusieurs douches par jour.

    a. Moi, je prends une douche tous les jours.

    b. Moi, je (ne) prends pas toujours de douche.

    c. Moi, je prends plusieurs douches par jour.

      *Follow-up:* Combien? Et pourquoi???

    d. (à vous)

5. Les Américains sont nuls quand il s'agit de l'histoire.

    a. Moi, je connais la date de la Déclaration de l'Indépendance.

      *Follow-up:* C'était quand?

   b. Moi, je suis nul(le) en histoire.

   c. Moi, je m'en fiche de l'histoire.

   d. (à vous)

6. Les Américaines sont moins chics que les Françaises.

   a. Les Françaises, elles s'intéressent plus à la mode.

   b. Les Américaines, elles préfèrent être à l'aise.

   c. Moi, je préfère vivre aux États-Unis.

   d. Moi, je préfère vivre en France.

   e. (à vous)

Note that as a follow-up activity, students may wish to share their findings with the class. They will naturally be drawn into using left dislocations to do so, as the appropriate way to report on others' opinions would be to use utterances of the form: **Robert, il aime le sport, surtout le base-ball.**

A discourse analysis activity, such as Activity 6.3, would be appropriate for more advanced students who are studying the pragmatic roles of left dislocations in discourse. Note that this activity is constructed using authentic materials, and that students are functioning as researchers; their task is to work with data to form hypotheses and find examples.

$$\bullet \quad \bullet \quad \bullet \quad \bullet \quad \bullet$$

**Activity 6.3: Ils donnent leur avis, les Français.** (discourse analysis)

The following interviews (also available on tape) were conducted with young French nationals following the September 11th attacks on the United States (see Katz 2004). In these excerpts, find examples of left dislocations and then decide whether they are used to (a) introduce a referent as a topic, (b) provide a contrast, or (c) indicate turn-taking.

1. JOURNALISTE: À votre avis, pourquoi le réseau Al-Qaïda a-il ciblé les États-Unis et pas un autre pays peut-être?

    N:        Mais enfin, vous savez que le onze septembre on n'était pas très fiers ici en France; on croyait bien qu'on allait vraiment avoir des attentats. Pendant deux semaines là, à Paris je veux dire, il y avait une très mauvaise ambiance. On était tout à fait . . . il y avait cette peur qu'on pouvait sentir pendant au moins quinze jours. Ensuite la vie a repris le dessus. Mais, en tout cas, pour nous, **les attentats islamistes,** on sait ce que c'est. **Moi,** je me suis dit, bon là c'est New York, demain ça peut être Paris. Voilà.

2. JOURNALISTE: Tu as beaucoup consulté les médias dans cette période-là. Je ne sais pas si tu te souviens, mais deux jours après les attaques, *Le Monde* a publié une première page avec un gros titre «Nous sommes tous Américains». Qu'est-ce que ça t'a évoqué? Est-ce que tu es d'accord?

S:    **Moi**… je crois que j'ai fait partie des gens au départ qui ont trouvé ça un peu… démago en fait, parce que… finalement je trouve que la France… a tendance à critiquer quand même pas mal les États-Unis à plein d'égards, et j'ai trouvé que **ce terme «on est tous des Américains»**, c'était un peu tiré par les cheveux et un peu démago. Et en fait à la réflexion, au vu de ce que **moi**… j'ai pu ressentir en apprenant la nouvelle alors que je n'avais pas réellement de vrais contacts aux États-Unis, si c'est vrai que j'ai quand même de la famille mais pas à New York directement… avec le recul, je comprends que ce soit un geste de solidarité que les médias… enfin un message que les médias aient voulu faire passer.

Right dislocations may be taught in a similar manner. Again, in the early stages of instruction, students should become aware of the existence and general pragmatic properties of this construction, and then at more advanced levels, they should begin analyzing its use in discourse. Activity 6.4, a structured-input exercise, could be used as early as the elementary level, and Activity 6.5 should be reserved for more advanced students.

• • • • •

**Activity 6.4: Votre réaction.** (structured input)

What is your reaction to the following comments? Choose from the given answers or create your own response.

1. Les Français dépensent une grande partie de leur salaire sur la nourriture. C'est une des choses les plus importantes de la vie pour eux.
   a. Ils sont fous, les Français. Voyager, c'est plus important que manger.
   b. Ils ont raison, les Français. Manger bien, ça fait très plaisir.
   c. (à vous)
2. Votre mère vous a donné les clés de sa voiture pour le week-end.
   a. Elle est très gentille, ma mère.

    b. Elle est folle, ma mère. Je conduis comme un fou/une folle.

    c. (à vous)

3. Notre professeur de français, il/elle insiste qu'on parle français tout le temps dans sa classe.

    a. Il/Elle a raison, lui/elle. C'est comme ça qu'on apprend à parler.

    b. Il/Elle est trop sévère, lui/elle. Ça va intimider les étudiants.

    c. (à vous)

4. Johnny Depp a décidé de vivre en France.

    a. Il a pris une bonne décision, lui. Sa femme est française, tu sais.

    b. Il a tort de quitter les États-Unis, lui.

    c. (à vous)

5. Michael Jackson a un nouveau CD qui vient de sortir.

    a. Je m'en fiche, moi.

    b. Je vais l'acheter, moi.

    c. Il est fou, lui.

    d. (à vous)

In Activity 6.5, advanced students watch a short film clip (2−3 minutes) that contains several examples of right dislocations. Students are told to note the ones that they hear. Then they analyze the discourse, using the guidelines provided below. The clip should be shown several times so that students become familiar with the context and have time to write down what they hear.

• • • • •

**Activity 6.5: On écoute bien, nous.** (discourse analysis)

Watch the film clip, writing down any right dislocations (of the form: je ne sais pas, moi) that you hear. Afterward, with a partner, decide whether each example you have found is used to (a) introduce or re-affirm a topic for discussion; (b) clarify the identity of a given referent; (c) give additional information about a referent; (d) fill discourse space; or (e) close discourse.

Teaching the presentational and **c'est**-cleft constructions at the elementary level is not appropriate, as clefts are too complex, both structurally and pragmatically. It is essential, however, to present at least the **c'est**-cleft at more advanced levels. One way to begin making students aware of the properties of the **c'est**-cleft is to elucidate the differences between French and English intonational patterns. A "garden-path" technique for teaching grammar, in which students are led to make errors and are subsequently corrected, can be effective here. This type of activity can work well for the **c'est-**cleft. For example, students could be asked to translate sentences from English into French in which the cleft is not used in English but is obligatory in French (for example, when one wants to put the emphasis on a bound pronoun or the subject of a sentence), as demonstrated in Activity 6.6:

• • • • •

### Activity 6.6: Les traductions. (garden pathing)

Translate the following sentences into French.

1. —Your earrings are beautiful.
   —Thanks. I got them at the little boutique downtown.
   [*Answer:* —**Tes boucles d'oreille sont belles.**
   —**Merci, je les ai achetées dans une petite boutique en ville.**
   Note that the cleft, **C'est dans une petite boutique en ville que je les ai achetées,** does not seem to work particularly well here.]
2. —Did you see my brother at the pool?
   —No, I saw your sister.
   [*Answer:* —**Tu as vu mon frère à la piscine?**
   —**Non, j'ai vu ta sœur.** or **Non, c'est ta sœur que j'ai vue.**
   Both the cleft and canonical sentence are acceptable here.]
3. Do you like my shirt? My mother gave it to me.
   [*Answer:* **Tu aimes ma chemise? C'est ma mère qui me l'a offerte.**
   Only the cleft is appropriate here.]
4. —Why are you crying?
   —I love you, not him.
   [*Answer:* —**Pourquoi tu pleures?**
   —**C'est toi que j'aime, pas lui.**
   Again, only the cleft is appropriate here.]

Students usually make the mistake of translating the third and fourth examples without the cleft. Thus, it is important for the students to read their French translations out loud, so that they can hear that they are using an impossible intonation in French. Students should then be asked to hypothesize when one should use the cleft. An overhead, along the lines of the following, would be useful as a post-activity, post-hypothesizing reinforcement:

---

**Overhead 7: Les phrases clivées en *c'est***

C'est _____ que/qui _____

C'est **Robert** qui est français.

   [Students identify **Robert** as a noun.]

C'est **avec LUI** que je suis allé au restaurant.

   [Students identify **avec lui** as a prepositional phrase.]

C'est **là** qu'il m'a dit qu'il n'aimait pas la cuisine amércaine.

   [Students identify **là** as an adverb.]

C'est **en mangeant ses pâtes** qu'il s'est rendu compte qu'en fait la cuisine américaine n'est pas si mauvaise que ça.

   [Students identify **en mangeant ses pâtes** as a verb phrase.]

---

Once students have received explicit instruction about the syntactic and prosodic structure of the **c'est**-cleft, they should be ready to move on to more discourse-based activities, in which they are led to discover the pragmatic properties of this construction. Activity 6.7 is an example of a discourse-based task.[11]

• • • • •

**Activity 6.7: Video clefts.** (discourse analysis)

In this activity, students watch short video clips in which the actors use **c'est**-clefts. The students, who have the opportunity to view the clips several times, are instructed to write down the clefts as they hear them. The **c'est**-clefts are highlighted in the following two examples, the first one being from *Le Dîner de cons*.

Clip 1:

In this clip, Pierre Brochant and Juste LeBlanc have convinced François Pignon to call his colleague, Lucien Cheval, to try to find out the address of the lothario who may have seduced Brochant's wife.

CHEVAL: Pignon . . .

PIGNON: Lucien, je te rappelle parce que j'ai un service à te demander.

CHEVAL: D'accord. Mais à une condition.

PIGNON: Laquelle?

CHEVAL: C'est que tu cries: «Allez l'OM!»

PIGNON: Quoi?!

CHEVAL: Je veux t'entendre crier «Allez l'OM!»

| LEBLANC: | Ben, allez-y! Allez-y, mon vieux! Allez l'OM, Allez l'OM! Allez! |
| BROCHANT AND LEBLANC: | Allez l'OM! Allez L'OM! Allez! Allez l'OM! Allez l'OM! Allez! Allez l'OM! Allez! |
| PIGNON: | **C'est vraiment pour vous que je le fais, Pierre!** Allez l'OM. |
| CHEVAL: | Oh, toi, tu dois avoir quelque chose de sérieux à me demander. |
| PIGNON: | Oui, Lucien, c'est très important. |
| PIGNON: | Je t'écoute. |

Source: Transcription taken from http://www.humnet.ucla.edu/web/elma/ diner_vera-mec/Diner8_print.htm

Clip 2:
In the second clip, from Les Compères and mentioned earlier, the Mafia thugs accost the journalist as he is leaving his hotel in Nice:

| THUG: | Le patron veut te parler. |
| JOURNALIST: | Je n'ai rien à lui dire. |
| THUG: | **C'est LUI qui parlera.** |

After viewing these clips, students are asked to determine what the cleft accomplishes in each case. It is likely that they will give one of the following answers: to correct something, to emphasize something, or to identify something or someone. These are all possible interpretations. Students should understand that not all **c'est-**clefts have the same purpose (note that in clip 1, one finds a VF-cleft, and in 2, a corrective cleft), but what is important for students to realize is that in each case, the **c'est-**cleft singles out one person, thing, place, or idea, isolates it, and gives it a special pitch accent.

Another useful exercise is for students to translate these clefts and their surrounding discourse into English, focusing on what people would actually say in spoken English. In these clips, clefts in English would sound stilted and odd, and it is useful for students to arrive at this conclusion themselves. It is important that students be guided to figure out the use of the cleft themselves. The professor acts as a facilitator but does not provide students with an explicit explanation of the pragmatic properties of the cleft.

• • • • •

**Activity 6.8: Les corrections.** (structured output)

Activity 6.8, also appearing in an earlier version in Katz 2002a and reprinted with the permission of the *French Review*, again involves providing students with a short film clip. It is not necessary that this clip contain any clefts. A three- or four-minute scene is sufficient, preferably one where there is a lot of action. After watching the video, students are put into groups and asked to make a list of *incorrect* assertions about what happened in the video. As they do this, the instructor circulates through the class and chooses and corrects the grammar in certain selected sentences and has students put them on the board (perhaps one assertion from each group). It is vital that the instructor choose utterances that can be easily corrected by **c'est**-clefts. So, for example, an incorrect assertion could be something along the lines of (a):

(a) François veut crier «Allez l'OM!»

This assertion should be corrected using the **c'est**-cleft, as in (b):

(b) Non, c'est Pierre qui veut que François crie «Allez l'OM!»

After all the sentences are written on the board, students correct them using the cleft construction. Although this activity practices the corrective cleft and not the VF, which is the one found more often in discourse, it is a good place to start. The corrective cleft is not difficult to create; its function in discourse is obvious, and its intonation is striking.

How, or even whether, to teach the **il y a** cleft is debatable. Since this construction is found only in the spoken language (or in written form when reflecting the spoken language), and with much less frequency than left or right dislocations or the **c'est**-cleft, it is not a structure that needs to be studied until the most advanced levels of instruction. It is probably in the students' best interest simply to have their attention drawn to it and the differences between it and the **c'est**-cleft. Students could hypothesize these differences through analyzing carefully structured data, as in Activity 6.9:

• • • • •

**Activity 6.9: Les phrases clivées.** (consciousness-raising)

The presentational cleft and the **c'est**-cleft are used in different discourse settings. Compare the (a) responses, which contain the presentational cleft, with the (b) responses, which contain the **c'est-**cleft. Specifically, what is presupposed in each of the (a) responses, and what is presupposed in each of the (b) responses? What generalizations can you make about the use of these two constructions in discourse?

1. a. —Qu'est-ce qui ne va pas? Tu as l'air triste.

   —J'ai mon chien qui est mort.

   b. —J'ai entendu dire que tu as perdu un de tes animaux domestiques.

   —Oui, c'est mon chien qui est mort.

2. a. —Fais tes devoirs.

   —Écoute, il y a le téléphone qui sonne!

   b. —Écoute, il y a quelqu'un à la porte!

   —Non, c'est le téléphone qui sonne.

Finally, as a culminating activity, Activity 6.10 summarizes the properties of the various word-order constructions presented in this chapter. This type of activity reflects the guidelines given in McCarthy and Carter 1995.

● ● ● ● ●

**Activity 6.10: La bonne réponse.** (consciousness-raising)

For each of the following utterances, choose the appropriate response(s) and the corresponding reason(s) for each response.

1. Tu as l'air triste. Qu'est-ce qui ne va pas?
2. Désolé; je viens d'apprendre ce qui est arrivé à ton chat.
3. Parle-moi de tes animaux.

Responses:

    a. J'ai mon chien qui est mort.

    b. Il y a mon chien qui est mort.

    c. C'est mon chien qui est mort.

    d. Mon chien, il est mort.

    e. Il est mort, mon chien.

Reasons:

    i. Everything is new information.

    ii. Something is being introduced as a topic for conversation.

    iii. Only one part of the assertion is missing.

    iv. Something is being corrected.

## CONSOLIDATION EXERCISES

1. The following is an example of a pragmatically odd passage in English (along the lines of what is presented in McCarthy and Carter 1994). Using your native speaker intuitions (if you are anglophone), describe what is odd about the letter. Then correct it, using the appropriate word-order constructions.

Dear Nicole,
It is to you that I am writing this letter in response to your email message. What's outside my window is a big yard that Emma just loves and is playing in now. When it is full of pecans is in the fall. It is you who must come and visit. What we have is plenty of room. You, I would love to see.
Love,
Louis

Next, analyze the following French excerpt, which is similarly odd, changing what is necessary to make it more pragmatically appropriate:

LOUIS:   Comment ça va?
NICOLE: C'est moi qui vais bien, et toi?
LOUIS:   Comment je vais est bien.
NICOLE: Ce week-end, qu'est-ce que tu fais?
LOUIS:   Il ya ce week-end que ma mère vient.
NICOLE: C'est au restaurant qu'on devrait aller.
LOUIS:   Oui, mais la viande, ma mère ne l'aime pas.
NICOLE: Un restaurant végétarien, je le connais.
LOUIS:   Super. Alors, c'est nous qui dînons ensemble ce week-end.
Nicole: Une bouteille de vin, je l'apporterai au restaurant.

2. For each of the following conversations, decide which of the word-order constructions provided is the most appropriate pragmatically. Sometimes more than one answer is possible. Explain your choices, and then compare them with those of native speakers of French. If they think that more than one answer is correct, ask them which one sounds the most natural to them.

   a. *Context*: Two friends looking at a photograph of Constance.
   Tu connais Constance, non? C'est la meilleure amie de Florence.
   1. Oui, c'est elle qui est devenue actrice.
   2. Oui, il y a Constance qui est devenue actrice.
   3. Oui, Constance, elle est devenue actrice.
   4. Oui, elle est devenue actrice, Constance.

b. *Context:* In a restaurant, two friends are looking at a menu.

Qu'est-ce qu'on prend, alors?

1. Tiens, c'est le steak tartare qui est excellent.

2. Tiens, il y a le steak tartare qui est excellent.

3. Tiens, le steak tartare, il est très bon.

4. Tiens, il est très bon, le steak tartare.

c. *Context:* Two students discussing their homework for the next day.

Je suis obligée de lire ce poème de Baudelaire pour mon cours demain.

1. Ah bon? C'est mon professeur qui a écrit un article sur ce poème.

2. Ah bon? J'ai mon professuer qui a écrit un article sur ce poème.

3. Ah bon? Mon professeur, il a écrit un article sur ce poème.

4. Ah bon? Il a écrit un article sur ce poème, mon professeur.

d. *Context:* A French person commenting on American hygiene.

Les Américains, ils sont fous, toujours en train de se laver les mains. Ils ont peur des microbes, quoi.

1. À mon avis, c'est les Français qui sont fous.

2. À mon avis, il y a les Français qui sont fous.

3. À mon avis, les Français, ils sont fous.

4. À mon avis, ils sont fous, les Français.

3. Translate the following attested **pas parce que** expressions into English.

a. C'est pas parce que c'est du bio que c'est nécessairement bon! (Lapin Gourmand)

b. C'est pas parce que c'est gros que c'est meilleur! (Lapin Gourmand)

c. C'est pas parce que c'est drôle qu'on rit. (oserchanger.com)

d. C'est pas parce qu'on est petit qu'on ne peut pas être grand. (adage)

e. C'est pas parce que je suis pauvre que je vais me priver. (titre d'un livre)

f. C'est pas parce que le chacal a mauvaise haleine qu'il faut l'empêcher de bailler. (African proverb)

4. Come up with discourse environments where the following utterances would be appropriate in English. Then translate your English interactions into French.

a. My MOTHER speaks French.

b. My FATHER taught me to drive.

c. That's why I like him.

d. That's why I like HIM.

e. The more you EAT, the hungrier you get. (Note: this is a famous French proverb.)

5. Decide if the following utterances including **c'est** are (a) **c'est**-clefts; (b) **c'est** + noun + a restrictive relative clause; (c) **c'est** + noun + a continuous relative clause; (d) one is unable to tell without hearing the intonation.

a. *Context:* A wife asks her husband the following question as he returns to the house:

> WIFE:       Qui était dans le garage?
>
> HUSBAND: C'était le voisin qui est venu voir si son chat était sous notre voiture.

b. *Context:* Two friends are discussing what they did over the weekend.

> AUDREY:    Vous êtes allés au cinéma ce week-end, toi et Fred?
>
> ARIANE:    Oui, c'est un film d'Almadovar qu'on a vu.

c. *Context:* A friend is trying to make her friend understand that the latter's dog is vicious.

> MÉLISSA:   J'aime Rosco.
>
> EMMA:     Oui, mais c'est un chien qui mord tout le temps.

d. *Context:* A friend notices a ring on her friend's finger.

> FRIEND A:  C'est quoi, ça?
>
> FRIEND B:  C'est un cadeau que Philippe m'a offert.

e. *Context:* A husband and wife are standing on their back porch.

> WIFE:       Regarde ce qu'on voit dans le jardin.
>
> HUSBAND: Oui, c'est les chats qu'on préfère.

f. *Context:* One friend is about to play a song for another.

> FRIEND A:  Écoute cette chanson.
>
> FRIEND B:  Oui, c'est Marie qui chante en français.

## TYPICAL STUDENT ERRORS

Imagine that your students have made the mistakes provided below, each of which is pragmatically ill-formed. Correct each utterance, and then come up with an explanation for your students as to why each one is "wrong."

1. *Context:* A student is asked with whom he went to the movies.
   Je ne suis pas allé au cinéma. Mon frère y est allé.

2. *Context:* A student's friend is ready to leave a party, but she isn't.
   Juste parce que tu veux partir ne veut pas dire que je suis prête à partir.

3. *Context:* A student is asked what he thinks of New York City.
   New York, je la déteste.

4. *Context:* A student is asked what it is she does not like about New York.
New York est laid.

5. *Context:* A student is asked what he thinks about the concept of exams.
Les examens? Je les déteste.

### Corrections of Student Errors (answers may vary)

1. Ce (n)'est pas moi qui suis allé au cinéma; c'est mon frère.
2. Ce (n)'est pas parce que tu veux partir que je suis prête à partir.
3. New York, je déteste.
4. New York, c'est laid. or: New York c'est une ville laide.
5. Les examens? Je déteste ça.

### DISCUSSION TOPICS / PROJECTS

1. There has been some disagreement among linguists as to the level at which one should begin teaching word-order constructions. Kerr (2002) and Blyth (1999) differ, with Blyth calling for some exposure to word-order constructions as early as the first semester of instruction and Kerr believing that it is better to wait until the intermediate level. Of the topics introduced in this chapter, which do you feel should be taught during the first year, and which do you think should not be covered until much later? Why?

2. Some would argue that it is not vital to focus on word-order constructions at all, since using the wrong construction does not necessarily mean that the message is lost. How important is pragmatic accuracy? Could the same be said about other types of accuracy, for example pronunciation? What about grammar (for example, is it truly necessary to use the subjunctive if one can be understood without it)?

3. Have you recognized mistakes or pragmatically odd habits in your own French after reading this chapter? Record a conversation between you and a French person, and then listen to it to see if you find any inconsistencies in register or the use of grammatical structures. Then have a French person listen to the conversation, asking him or her to point out anything that sounds "non-native." Did you come up with the same things?

4. The increase in the use of e-mail and chat forums for discussion has had an effect on awareness of differences between the spoken and written languages. Ask native French speakers to send you e-mail messages

that they have received from casual friends, or go to a French chat room, and analyze the use of spoken forms throughout.

5. Linguists have struggled with some of the differences between the French **c'est**-cleft and the English it-cleft. At times, the two seem to function in the same way, because both French (obligatorily) and English (optionally) use the cleft, as in (a):

> a. —Is your mother making dinner?
>
> —No, it's my dad who's cooking tonight.
>
> (or: No, my DAD is cooking tonight.)
>
> —C'est ta mère qui prépare le dîner?
>
> —Non, c'est mon père qui fait la cuisine ce soir.

However, at other times, the it-cleft is impossible in English, whereas the **c'est-**cleft is required in French, as in (b):

> b. —What a great sweater. Where did you get it?
>
> —My MOTHER gave it to me.
>
> (! It's my mother who gave it to me.)
>
> —Quel joli pull. Tu l'as acheté où?
>
> —C'est ma mère qui me l'a offert.

Based on our earlier discussion of cleft types, do you have any ideas as to why the first example works both with or without the cleft in English, and why the cleft is impossible in English for the second?

## FURTHER READING

### On Spoken French

Ball, Rodney. *Colloquial French Grammar: A Practical Guide*. Oxford: Basil Blackwell, 2000.

Batchelor, R. E., and Offord, M. H. *Using French: A Guide to Contemporary Usage*. Cambridge: Cambridge University Press, 2000.

### On Teaching Spoken Grammar and the Problems with Textbooks

Herschensohn, Julia. "Linguistic Accuracy of Textbook Grammar." *Modern Language Journal* 72 (1988): 409–414.

Joseph, John E. "New French: A Pedagogical Crisis in the Making." *Modern Language Journal* 72 (1988): 31–36.

McCarthy, Michael, and Ronald Carter. "Spoken Grammar: What Is It and How Can We Teach It?" *ELT Journal* 49 (1995): 207–218.

Walz, Joel. (1986). "Is Oral Proficiency Possible with Today's French Textbooks?" *Modern Language Journal* 70 (1986): 13–20.

## On Teaching Word-Order Constructions

Blyth, Carl. "Toward a Pedagogical Discourse Grammar: Techniques for Teaching Word Order Constructions." In *Form and Meaning: Multiple Perspectives*. AAUSC Issues in Language Program Direction, edited by James Lee and Albert Valdman, 183–229. Boston: Heinle, 1999.

Kerr, Betsy. "Variant Word-Order Constructions: To Teach or Not to Teach? Evidence from Learner Narratives." In *Pedagogical Norms for Second and Foreign Language Learning and Teaching*, edited by Susan Gass, Kathleen Bardovi-Harlig, Sally Sieloff Magnan, and Joel Walz, 183–200. Amsterdam: John Benjamins, 2002.

## On Dislocations and Clefts

Ashby, William J. "The Syntax, Pragmatics, and Sociolinguistics of Left- and Right-Dislocations in French." *Lingua* 75 (1988): 203–229.

Barnes, Betsy K. "Apports de l'analyse à l'enseignement de la langue." *French Review* 64 (1990): 95–107.

Katz, Stacey. "A Functional Approach to the Teaching of the French C'est-cleft." *French Review* 74 (2000): 248–262.

———. "Categories of C'est-cleft Constructions." *Revue Canadienne de Linguistique* 45 (2000): 1001–1021.

Lambrecht, Knud. *Information Structure and Sentence Form*. Cambridge: Cambridge University Press, 1994.

# 7 · Interrogative Constructions

### OVERVIEW / KEY CONSIDERATIONS

The following grammatical topics are covered in this chapter:

- Interrogative markers: **est-ce que,** inversion, intonation, and tag questions
- Yes-no questions
- Content WH-questions
- Identifying WH-questions
- Spoken interrogative forms: anteposition and postposition

### DIFFICULTIES FOR THE LEARNER

Linguists, as well as instructors, are often perplexed when attempting to understand and elucidate the intricacies of interrogative structures. There are several reasons for the difficulty. To begin, there are many different ways of saying *what* in French (**qu'est-ce qui, qu'est-ce que, que, quoi,** and **quel**), and to make matters worse, they all begin with **qu.** In addition, sociolinguistic factors play an important role in determining which interrogative forms should be used in particular communicative settings. One cannot, or should not, teach interrogative constructions without considering factors such as whether the discourse is written or spoken, and whether the situation is formal or informal. It is important to keep in mind Batchelor and Offord's (2000) categorization (see Chapter 6) of register as being either R1 "informal," R2 "neutral," or R3 "formal," as each register has a preference (or sometimes a requirement) for certain interrogative forms.

Unfortunately, many textbooks lead students to conclude that interrogative forms are interchangeable and that students may randomly choose to use the form they prefer or find easiest. Because of the inadequacies of textbook explanations, many students learn to produce forms that sound stilted and bookish, instead of natural and appropriate. Thus, learners need to become sensitive to the forms that are appropriate in different discourse environments.

## BASIC FORMS AND MEANINGS

There are three types of questions in French: yes-no questions, Content WH-questions, and Identifying WH-questions. WH-expressions are called "WH" because many of these expressions begin with these letters in English (*who, what, where, when, why*). In this section, we describe the basic properties of each group, beginning with yes-no questions.

Yes-no questions are the simplest of French questions, and students do not usually have too much difficulty grasping their formation. French textbooks tell the learner that there are four basic ways of asking a yes-no question in French. The first three ways are (1) by inserting **est-ce que** before the declarative form of the sentence, (2) by inverting the subject and verb, and (3) by adding a rising intonation to the declarative sentence. These techniques are illustrated below:

(1) Est-ce que tu aimes les chats?     **(est-ce que)**
(2) Aimes-tu les chats?                (inversion)
(3) Tu aimes les chats?                (intonation)

It is important to point out that in order to use inversion in a question that contains a nominal subject (not a pronoun), the noun remains in sentence-initial position and the corresponding subject pronoun must be added and inverted with the verb, as for example in a question such as **Le chat, mord-il?** In addition, if the verb ends in a vowel and, because of inversion, is followed by a pronoun that also begins with a vowel (**il[s], elle[s], on**), **-t-** is inserted between them for the sake of pronunciation, as, for example, in a question such as **Le bébé, parle-t-il?** Note that the inverted form is used primarily in the written language or in a formal spoken setting (R3).

There is a fourth way of asking a yes-no question, which includes adding a "tag expression" to the end of the question. It is surprising that textbooks continue to teach the tag expression **n'est-ce pas?** as a question-forming tool, because French people rarely use this phrase, except, perhaps, in a formal speech setting or in writing. Example (4) contains a question formed using **n'est-ce pas?:**

(4) Tu aimes les chats, n'est-ce pas?

We discuss this issue further in the Meanings in Context section below. For the moment, we will point out that **non?** has replaced **n'est-ce pas?** in most contexts as the appropriate tag question expression in spoken French, as demonstrated in (5):

(5) Tu aimes les chats, non?

The four yes-no question-forming techniques are summarized below:

### Yes-No Question Formation

---

1. **Est-ce que**
   **Est-ce que tu aimes les chats?**
2. Inversion
   **Aimes-tu les chats?**
3. Intonation
   **Tu aimes les chats?**
4. Tag question
   **Tu aimes les chats, non?**

---

Forming questions becomes infinitely more complicated when one wants to know not simply yes or no, but the answer to questions beginning with WH-expressions. We have grouped French WH-expressions into two categories: *Content WH-expressions,* such as **combien, comment, où, pourquoi,** and **quand,** which elicit a place, time, reason, price, or attribute, and *Identifying WH-expressions,* which are used to identify a particular entity: **qui, que, qu'est-ce qui, quoi, quel, lequel,** etc.

There are four ways of forming Content WH-questions. The first two involve using **est-ce que** or inversion, as in (6) and (7):

(6) Pourquoi est-ce qu'il part?          (**est-ce que**)
(7) Pourquoi part-il?          (*inversion*)

WH-questions with **est-ce que** are considered to be neutral (R2), whereas inverted WH-questions may be considered either R2 or, in most cases, R3 (formal).

The other two techniques for forming Content WH-questions are called *anteposition* and *postposition* (which is also known as *in situ*). In these question types, which are found only in informal speech (R1), the word order of the rest of the utterance is the same as what one would find in a declarative sentence. Anteposition, which most speakers consider less "proper" than postposition, means that the WH-expression is found at the beginning of the question, as in (8):

(8) Comment il est?          (*anteposition*)

whereas postposition means that the WH-expression occurs at the end of the question, as in (9):

(9) Il est comment?          (*postposition*)

These question types differ from intonational yes-no questions in two ways. First, they do not have a rising intonation; their prosody is the same as that of a declarative sentence (with a descending intonation at the end). Second, as we discuss in the following section, many speakers consider these forms to be "non-standard."

In the Meanings in Context section, we discuss the differences in the use of various interrogative structures in context. For the moment, it is important to note that **est-ce que** is used in both written and spoken French, that inversion appears primarily in the written language, and that anteposition and postposition occur predominantly in the spoken language. The following table summarizes the formation of Content WH-questions:

## Content WH-Expression Question Formation

Content WH-expressions: **comment, combien, où, pourquoi, quand**

1. **Est-ce que** (used in both spoken and written French)
   **Comment est-ce qu'il s'appelle?**
2. Inversion (used primarily in written French)
   **Comment s'appelle-t-il?**
3. Anteposition (used only in spoken French)
   **Comment il s'appelle?**
4. Postposition (used only in spoken French)
   **Il s'appelle comment?**

---

The Identifying WH-expressions (interrogative expressions that are varieties of the English interrogatives *who[m]*, *what*, *which*, and *which one[s]*) differ from Content WH-expressions, because Identifying WH-expressions function as either the subject, direct object, or object of a preposition within a given question. Their forms also differ, based on their grammatical role in the sentence.

*Who*(m) is arguably the least difficult of Identifying WH-expressions, since it has the same form (**qui**) whether it is a subject, object, or object of a preposition, as demonstrated in (10)–(12):

| | |
|---|---|
| (10) Qui parle français? | (**qui** = *subject*) |
| (11) Qui aimes-tu/est-ce que tu aimes? | (**qui** = *direct object*) |
| (12) Avec qui sors-tu/est-ce que tu sors? | (**qui** = *object of the preposition* **avec**) |

**Qui est-ce qui** as a subject is found only in formal (usually written) speech, as in (13):

| | |
|---|---|
| (13) Qui est-ce qui connaît le président? | (**qui est-ce qui** = *subject*) |

We do not advocate teaching **qui est-ce qui** to beginning or intermediate students. In the Meanings in Context section below, we show that **qui** as a direct object or as the object of a preposition may be found in anteposition or postposition (without being followed by inversion or **est-ce que**) in informal spoken French.

The forms of the French equivalent of the English interrogative *what?* are much more complicated. The subject form is always **qu'est-ce qui,** in all registers and spoken/written forms, as in (14):

(14) Qu'est-ce qui arrive?                  (**qu'est-ce qui** = *subject*)

As a direct object, the standard form is **que,** usually found as **qu'est-ce que,** except in formal writing and speech (where **que** is followed by inversion of the subject and verb). (15) and (16) illustrate the use of **que** and **qu'est-ce que:**

(15) Que veux-tu?                           (**que** = *direct object*)
(16) Qu'est-ce que tu veux?                 (**qu'est-ce que** = *direct object*)

As the object of a preposition, the corresponding form is **quoi,** as in (17):

(17) De quoi parles-tu/est-ce que tu parles?

In the Meanings in Context section below, we discuss how **quoi** has begun either to replace or to exist alongside the direct object interrogative form **que** in the spoken language. We also describe how inversion and **est-ce que** are being used less and less in the spoken language, even when questions contain Identifying or Content WH-expressions.

**Quel,** the last interrogative form that means *what* (and also *which*), cannot exist without an accompanying noun. This noun is found either immediately after it, as in (18):

(18) Quel chien est-ce que tu préfères/préfères-tu?

or following the verb **être,** as in (19):

(19) Quelle est la date aujourd'hui?

Students sometimes are confused as to whether they should use **Quel** or **Qu'est-ce qui** to mean *what* as the subject of the verb **être,** as in the English equivalents *What is the date?* and *What is in your mouth?* The rule is that when **être** is followed by a noun phrase, one uses a form of **quel,** and otherwise (usually when **être** is followed by a prepositional or adjectival phrase), **qu'est-ce qui** is the appropriate interrogative expression. This distinction is illustrated in (20)–(22):

(20) Quelle est la date?                    (*noun phrase*)
(21) Qu'est-ce qui est dans ta bouche?      (*prepositional phrase*)
(22) Qu'est-ce qui est bizarre?             (*adjectival phrase*)

Finally, students often have difficulty distinguishing between the various interrogative forms of **quel** and those of **lequel.** It is important that they realize that **quel,** a determiner, always occurs with a noun, and that **lequel,** a pronoun, replaces a noun. This contrast is demonstrated in (23) and (24):

(23) Quelle femme est dans le bus?
(24) Laquelle est dans le bus?

It is helpful for students to learn that **lequel** and its forms are translated into English as *which one(s)*, and not *which* or *what.*

Finally, there is an interrogative construction designed precisely for asking for a definition: **Qu'est-ce que c'est qu'un(e)** or **qu'est-ce qu'un(e).** These expressions are illustrated in (25)–(26):

(25) Qu'est-ce que c'est (qu)'un lit abattant? [**un lit abattant** = *a* "Murphy bed"]
(26) Qu'est-ce qu'un lit abattant?

As we discuss in the Meanings in Context section, there is an informal way of asking for a definition, which is of the form: **C'est quoi, un(e)...** as in (27):

(27) C'est quoi, un lit abattant?

The interrogative structure of Identifying WH-expressions in standard French (which includes R2 and R3, but not R1) is outlined below:

### Interrogative Structure of Identifying WH-Expressions in Standard French

Who:
1. **Qui** (subject)
   **Qui** aime le fromage?
2. **Qui est-ce qui** (subject)
   **Qui est-ce qui** aime le fromage?
3. **Qui** (object)
   **Qui** est-ce que tu as vu?
   **Qui** as-tu vu?
4. **Qui** (object of a preposition)
   **Avec qui** est-ce que tu sors?
   **Avec qui** sors-tu?

What:

1. **Qu'est-ce qui** (subject)
   **Qu'est-ce qui** (ne) va pas?

2. **Que/Qu'est-ce que** (object)
   **Que** veux-tu?
   **Qu'est-ce que** tu veux?

3. **Quoi** (object of a preposition)
   **À quoi** est-ce que tu penses?
   **À quoi** penses-tu?

4. **Qu'est-ce que c'est que/Qu'est-ce que** (definition)
   **Qu'est-ce que c'est qu'**un lit abattant?
   **Qu'est-ce qu'**un lit abattant?

Which/What:

   **Quel(s)/quelle(s)**
   **Quelle** est la date aujourd'hui?
   **Quelle** date est-ce que tu veux que je réserve?
   **Quelle** date veux-tu que je réserve?

Which one(s):

   **Lequel/laquelle/lesquels/lesquelles**
   **Laquelle** est-ce que tu préfères?
   **Laquelle** préfères-tu?

---

## MEANINGS IN CONTEXT

As mentioned above, interrogative expressions are one of the most difficult constructions to teach, both because of their morphological complexity (particularly for identifying WH-expressions) and the considerable differences between their written and spoken forms. In fact, spoken and written French have diverged so much in terms of what is considered acceptable that it is difficult to construct a *pedagogical norm*, that is, an agreed-upon pedagogical model for students to imitate, on which linguists, instructors, and native speakers agree (see Magnan and Walz 2002). Part of the reason for the dissension is the variety of attitudes toward the different ways of asking questions. Many speakers frown upon and consider certain forms to be substandard, such as the spoken forms mentioned above (for example, **Comment il est?**). Other forms, such as inversion, are held in high esteem and used by speakers who pay close attention to speaking "properly." Valdman (2000) explains that "les Français de la classe moyenne s'entendent généralement pour valoriser l'inversion, pour caractériser **est-ce que** comme neutre, **in situ** [postposition] comme familière et l'**antéposition** comme populaire ou relâchée et pour stigmatiser les variantes d'**est-ce que** [such as **ce que c'est que**] comme franchement vulgaires" (260).

Di Vito (1997) claims that there is not a sharp division between the interrogative forms that are found in spoken vs. written French. In her study, she analyzed a large number of both spoken data (categorized into interviews, conversations, news broadcasts, and conferences) and written data of many genres (18th–20th century theater, folklore and fairy tales, detective novels, 18th–20th century prose, magazines, official correspondence, and travel guides) to compare the occurrences of inversion, questions using **est-ce que,** and questions with a simple subject-verb structure. One of Di Vito's most interesting findings is that within the spoken language, the genre in which questions were found played a large role in determining the interrogative form used: "One clear distinction between . . . spoken genres . . . is the amount of preplanned language used. Conversations and interviews are examples of spoken discourse in which two or more interlocutors are involved in a relatively unplanned, interactive linguistic exchange. On the other hand conferences and news broadcasts are typically noninteractive discourse contexts in which the speakers often refer to—and, at times read from—a written script. This possibility of incorporating planned language into one's speech permits, of course, the use of more cognitively complex syntactic patterns, including various VS [inverted] interrogative structures" (96–97).

In addition, Di Vito found the occurrence of **est-ce que** in the spoken language most frequently in interviewer questions (97). She postulates that **est-ce que** is used in spoken French in the following situations (98):

1. When the speaker wishes to indicate to his addressee that he is going to be asking a lengthy question, so the addressee will know to pay attention to the beginning of the question;
2. For the speaker to buy some time while formulating his question;
3. To mark questions as being hypothetical (in more abstract/philosophical questions);
4. As an emphatic device (to put particular stress on a question).

In addition, Di Vito found a striking absence of the expression **est-ce que** in written texts: "Whereas both **est-ce que** and simple SV [subject-verb] syntax are common in the spoken corpora, simple SV structures are consistently preferred over **est-ce que** in all written genres. Of course, in such cases a written question mark clearly signals interrogation, and there is no need to buy time. This might explain the low frequency of **est-ce que** in written texts" (101). This finding is surprising, since, as we discuss below, many linguists identify **est-ce que** as the structure that is found with overriding frequency in both spoken and written French.

Di Vito's conclusions are important because she questions the long-standing notion that spoken and written French have markedly different forms. One can postulate that the French used in casual spoken conversations is distinctly different from that found in "standard" written texts. However, there is a lot of spoken French that is more like written French and written French that is meant to resemble the spoken language. Thus, it is important to consider factors other than the simple spoken vs. written context or formal vs. informal setting when choosing interrogative forms. The particular pedagogical goal of this book, however, is to provide guidelines for teaching students to express themselves appropriately in the situations in which they are most likely to find themselves, in both academic and social settings. It is doubtful that elementary- or intermediate-level students will be conducting interviews or giving conference papers in French. Likewise, they do not need to develop a highly sophisticated writing style right away. These skills may be developed over time, if necessary.

One of the most fascinating phenomena that linguists have discovered is that most people are truly unaware of what they actually say. Every linguist has a story about how a speaker will vehemently deny using a particular structure or expression and then go on to use it in the very next sentence without even realizing it. Well-educated French speakers are particularly guilty; they tend to monitor their spoken French very carefully in formal situations but speak quite differently when they let their guard down. Knud Lambrecht (personal correspondence) recounts the following anecdote involving a student in his Grammar of Spoken French class: "The students had to tape a conversation and transcribe it, and one student taped her French boyfriend in a conversation with another Frenchman. After transcribing the conversation, the student noticed that her boyfriend never used the negative particle 'ne' and told him so. Her boyfriend angrily answered, 'J'te crois pas!'" Sometimes the only way to prove to speakers that they have or have not used a given structure is to play back a recording of them speaking. Even then, though, many speakers insist that the recording is inaccurate; they had simply made an error and do not normally speak in this manner.

Authors of French textbooks tend to focus on what they believe one should say, rather than on how native speakers actually express themselves. The continued pedagogical focus on structures such as inversion and **n'est-ce pas** reflects the prescriptivism so common in French culture. Corpora of spoken French, however, show that these structures are rare in naturally occurring discourse (note that we are describing conversational spoken French only, not formal spoken discourse or the written language). According to Knud Lambrecht (personal correspondence), there are only a half-dozen examples of pronoun-verb inversion in the Minnesota Corpus (Kerr 1983).

On the one hand, teaching non-standard/familiar structures to beginning and intermediate students is not a pedagogically sound suggestion. On the other hand, since many grammar explanations in textbooks simply do not correspond to the real world of French discourse, this is an issue that needs to be addressed. Consider, for example, the following models of spoken French that appear in various textbook conversations:

(28) —Tu vas passer ton bac cette année, n'est-ce pas?
    —Bien sûr! Sans le bac, on ne peut pas entrer à la fac. (Thompson/Phillips, *Mais oui!* 141)

(29) Bernard et Christine font les provisions ensemble: «Qu'en penses-tu?» (Terrell et al., *Deux mondes*, 236)

(30) A: Quel film as-tu vu récemment?
    B: Voyons... moi? J'ai vu *La Belle et la Bête* avec mes petits cousins.
    A: Comment l'as-tu trouvé?
    B: Je l'ai trouvé médiocre. Tu l'as vu? (Magnan et al., *Paroles*, 191)

Although grammatically correct, these utterances are not accurate representations of how most French speakers would converse. These exchanges appear more natural and less stilted as repeated below in (28a)–(30a):

(28a) Tu vas passer ton bac cette année, non?
(29a) Qu'est-ce que tu en penses?
(30a) A: Quel film est-ce que tu as vu récemment?

B: Voyons… moi? J'ai vu *La Belle et la Bête* avec mes petits cousins.

A: Comment tu l'as trouvé?

B: Je l'ai trouvé médiocre. Tu l'as vu?

Note that it is difficult to reconstruct these dialogues without more information about the discourse contexts in which they are found and the backgrounds of the speakers (age, educational background, class, etc.).

Even when textbooks attempt to distinguish between spoken and written forms, they do not always follow up the grammar descriptions with appropriate activities. For example, in *Allons-y*, the authors correctly point out that inversion is primarily a written form: "In French, inversion is commonly seen in writing. It is therefore most important for you to recognize it when you read. In everyday conversation, either intonation or **est-ce que** are the preferred interrogative forms" (292). Surprisingly, the textbook then provides two activities where students are obliged to use inversion to form spoken questions. The instructions for the first activity are as follows:

---

**I. Comment?** Votre grand-père n'entend pas bien! Chaque fois que vous lui demandez quelque chose, il vous demande de le répéter. La deuxième fois, utilisez **est-ce que** pour poser la question.
Modèle:—As-tu un Walkman?
    —Comment?
    —*Est-ce que tu as un Walkman?* (293)

---

Perhaps the grandfather does not understand the initial question because he would not expect his grandchild to be asking him a question using inversion. The second activity is similarly unnatural:

---

**J. Questionnaire.** Utilisez l'inversion pour poser des questions.
Modèle:Demandez à un(e) autre étudiant(e) s'il (si elle) est américain(e).
    *Es-tu américaine?* (293)

---

Source: *Allons-y! Le français par étapes* (with Audio CD), 6th edition, by Bragger/Rice. © 2004. Reprinted with permission of Heinle, a division of Thomson Learning: www.thomson.com. Fax 800–730–2215.

It is disconcerting to see students being instructed to create and practice forms that they would never use while actually conversing. Instead, why not include a written exercise to practice inversion?

In a communicative language program, students should learn to use language appropriately in various settings. Activities such as the two above undermine this goal. In the Classroom Applications section below, we provide suggestions for leading students to discover the communicative purposes that are reflected in the various interrogative forms. In choosing to use inversion, speakers are at the same time conveying to their addressees that the conversation is meant to be formal. If this is their goal, then there is no problem. However, most American students do not find themselves in formal speech settings with great frequency, especially when they are twenty years old and wearing a backpack.

## GOING BEYOND: FOR THE ADVANCED LEARNER

It is important to address the question of whether learners should be encouraged to incorporate non-standard grammatical forms and lexical items into their developing language systems. Valdman (2000) explains that "il est clair que les locuteurs natifs ne s'attendent pas à retrouver leur propre comportement langagier chez des locuteurs alloglotes, en particulier chez ceux qui ont acquis leur maîtrise de la langue principalement en salle de classe. Au contraire, ils s'attendent à ce que ceux-ci parlent 'mieux' qu'eux, c'est-à-dire qu'ils aient acquis une variété de la langue dans laquelle certaines variantes sont gommées, c'est-à-dire, une variété neutre" (649). In other words, many French native speakers, arguably known for their prescriptive bias, want learners to speak the French language "properly." To be fair, French speakers are equally hard on themselves; for example, it is not uncommon to hear a well-educated and cultivated French person admit, "Moi, je (ne) parle pas bien le français." Thus the question is whether to teach students to use structures that French people employ regularly but consider to be non-standard, in particular, the anteposition or postposition of Content and Identifying WH-expressions combined with a declarative word order, as in **Pourquoi il part?** or **Il mange quoi?**

The data show that these constructions are omnipresent in native speaker discourse. Therefore, it can be argued that advanced students should have the opportunity to be exposed to such structures, even if they are not required to incorporate them into their own speech. If students wish to use these forms, they should ask themselves the following questions:

1. Am I speaking to a friend, a peer, a family member, or someone with whom I can converse casually?
2. Is the setting informal? (Formal settings would include the classroom, an interview, a business meeting, etc.)

If the answer to both questions is affirmative, it is probably acceptable for them to use the non-standard question forms.

There are various points that should be made about the choice of the antepositioning vs. the postpositioning of Content WH-expressions. First, as some linguists have pointed out (Ball 2000; Lindsy Myers, personal correspondence), **pourquoi** is almost always found in anteposition, whereas **quand** is primarily found in postposition. **Où, combien,** and **comment** are more flexible. Although these expressions are usually found in postposition, they can also occur in anteposition (however, as Valdman 2000 points out, when the WH-expression is anteposed, these utterances may be considered **populaires** rather than **familières**). Below are some excerpts from the Minnesota Corpus (Kerr 1983) that illustrate these tendencies (note also the absence of the negative particle **ne** and the use of left and right dislocations):

1. **Pourquoi:** Found in sentence-initial position (anteposition).
   (a) *Context:* The speakers are tasting food that somebody's husband has prepared.
   
   M: Pourquoi tu ris?
   
   C: Pour rien, c'est très bon.
   (b) *Context:* The speakers are discussing a French film that is playing in an American city.
   
   M: Et pourquoi ils ont pas mis le titre français? Les autres, ils l'ont mis entre parenthèses.
   
   C: Parce qu'ils avaient honte de la traduction.
   (c) *Context:* M. refills her dish when the hostess goes into the other room.
   
   C: Pourquoi tu en prends quand Betsy n'est plus là?

M: Mais non, j'en ai pris.

C: Depuis tout à l'heure, tu vois pas que tu es la seule à bouffer!

(d) *Context:* One of the speakers has said "yogurt" instead of "yaourt."

M: Alors pourquoi tu dis yogurt, toi?

C: Parce que en anglais c'est yogurt!

(e) *Context:* The speakers are discussing wisdom teeth.

M: Et pourquoi tu en as pas, toi?

E: Ben, parce que je suis pas sage!

2. **Quand:** Found in sentence-final position (postposition).

*Context:* Speakers are comparing air fares.

E: C'était 198 dollars, aller-retour, y avait un prix spécial, et c'est...

C: C'était quand?

E: C'était pour Noël.

3. **Où:** Usually found in sentence-final position (postposition).

(a) *Context:* The speakers are discussing the high rent that one of them used to pay for an apartment.

E: Et comment c'est que tu payais si cher? C'était où?

(b) *Context:* The speakers are discussing the musical talent of E's husband.

C: Mais il est musicien professionnel?

E: Non!

C: Il joue où?

(c) *Context:* The speakers are talking about where one can find a particular type of honey in the United States.

E: Alors vous trouvez ça où?

M: Oui, alors c'est le problème.

4. **Comment:** Usually found in sentence-final position (postposition).

*Context:* Discussing types of **poinçons.** (**un poinçon** is a type of brand mark that is found on silverware or other silver/gold pieces)

C: Alors le poinçon pour l'argent c'est pas le même que pour l'or, hein!

E: Non, c'est différent.

C: Le poinçon d'argent, c'est comment?

E: Euh, je sais plus.

5. **Combien:** Usually found in sentence-final position (postposition).

*Context:* Speakers are discussing apartments that they have rented.

C: Oui mais alors ma chambre, elle était toute petite, pour le prix que je payais.

E: Tu payais combien alors?

C: Je payais 175 dollars.

Using anteposition and postposition with Identifying WH-expressions is considered more stigmatized than with Content WH-expressions, especially with the word **quoi.** As mentioned above, one often finds **quoi** as a direct-object interrogative expression in informal varieties of spoken French. Lindsy Myers (personal correspondence) has pointed out that **quoi** is always found in postposition when it is a direct object. One would never find an utterance such as (31), for example:

(31) *Quoi tu manges?

The following examples from the Minnesota Corpus illustrate the use of **quoi** in discourse:

6. **Quoi:** Used as a direct object (always in postposition).
   (a) Context: Speakers are discussing how impossible it is to find **lardons** in the United States.
      C: Tu sais ce que je fais moi, quand il faut des lardons, pour n'importe...
      M: Oui.
      E: Oui. Tu prends quoi?
      C: Je prends du bacon, puis je roule, je le roule.
   (b) Context: Speakers are discussing the difference in the way they pronounce the word **poireaux.**
      M: Tu dis poireaux?
      C: La soupe aux poireaux, oui.
      M: Ah! Décidément!
      C: Tu dis quoi, toi?
      M: Poreaux!
      C: Poreaux?! Oh c'est poireaux!

It should be pointed out that as the object of a preposition, **quoi** may be found either in postposition, as in example (32) from the Minnesota Corpus:

(32) Context: One speaker is asking another about her graduate studies.
      M: Alors tu vas faire ta thèse sur quoi, toi?

or in anteposition, as in the following fabricated but acceptable context:

(33) Context: A discussion about a book one of the speakers has read.
>A: J'ai lu un très bon livre de Nick Hornby pendant mes vacances.
>B: Ah bon? De quoi il s'agit?

As mentioned earlier, another very productive use of **quoi** in non-standard French is in the context of asking for a definition. The Minnesota Corpus contains many examples of **C'est quoi... ?** where more formal French would require **Qu'est-ce que (c'est que)... ?** Several examples are given below:

7. **C'est quoi... :** Used for definitions.
   (a) Context: One speaker does not know what cranberries are.
   >E: Et c'est quoi le cranberry?
   >C: C'est bon ça cranberry.
   (b) Context: The speakers are discussing a favorite recipe of M's.
   >M: Les tajines tunisiens.
   >C: C'est quoi?
   >M: Les tajines, c'est des genres de râgouts... c'est pas vraiment du râgout.

**Qui** as a direct object or as the object of a preposition in spoken French may be found either in anteposition or in postposition. The following examples from the Minnesota Corpus illustrate anteposed and postposed **qui** as the object of a preposition:

8. **Qui:** as the object of a preposition.
   Context: The speakers are talking about a book that has been made into a movie.
   >M: Madame Rosa, enfin ça a gagné le prix Nobel en...
   >E: Oui?
   >M: ...soixante-seize, je crois.
   >C: J'ai une élève qui m'en a parlé...
   >E: Le prix Nobel?
   >C: ...ce matin.
   >M: De la littérature française. Madame, Madame Rosa. Alors...
   >E: C'est de qui?

To summarize, the following table presents the familiar forms of WH-questions (both Content and Identifying) that are commonly found in spoken French.

## Familiar Spoken Forms of WH-Questions

Content WH-expressions

1. **Pourquoi:** anteposition only
   **Pourquoi** tu fais ça?

2. **Quand:** postposition only
   Tu viens **quand?**

3. **Où:** postposition preferred, but anteposition possible
   Tu vas **où?**
   **Où** tu vas?

4. **Comment:** postposition preferred, but anteposition possible
   Il est **comment?**
   **Comment** il est?

5. **Combien:** postposition preferred, but anteposition possible
   Ça coûte **combien?**
   **Combien** ça coûte?

Identifying WH-expressions

6. **Quoi:** postposition only for direct objects; anteposition or postposition for objects of prepositions
   On fait **quoi?**
   Tu parles **de quoi?**
   **De quoi** tu parles?

7. **C'est quoi** + noun: used for definitions
   **C'est quoi** un lit abbatant?

8. **Qui:** anteposition or postposition for direct objects or objects of prepositions
   **Qui** vous avez vu?
   Vous avez vu **qui?**
   **De qui** tu parles?
   Tu parles **de qui?**

---

Finally, consider a conversation overheard in a Parisian café. Two young men have been sitting on the **terrasse** for quite some time, and one of them is getting antsy. He asks his friend, **Qu'est-ce qu'on fait maintenant?** but does not receive much of a response. A little later on, he asks, a little less patiently, **On fait quoi maintenant?** It is unclear why both the **est-ce que** question and the postposed interrogative question are used in a similar context, since the co-occurrence cannot be based on either register or spoken/written distinctions. Di Vito (1997, 99–100) has pointed out that the expression **qu'est-ce que** is found with great frequency across genres of spoken and written French and that it is often linked to some relatively fixed expressions (as in, for example, **qu'est-ce que ça veut dire?**). Yet this explanation does not account for this speaker's using both **Qu'est-ce qu'on fait** and **On fait quoi** in a similar context. Either the two forms are in free variation, meaning that they are interchangeable, or the difference between them is pragmatic, that is, based on what the speaker believes his addressee already knows or how the speaker expects or wishes his addressee to answer the question.

Currently there is research being done on issues such as these, which involve the pragmatic properties of the different types of interrogative constructions (see Myers). Coveney (1996) has contributed insights to this growing body of scholarship, and Valdman (2000) provides a chart that delineates the pragmatic properties of interrogative constructions based on Coveney's work. As Valdman points out, however, it would be virtually impossible to incorporate all these complicated rules and hypotheses into a pedagogical norm and expect students to learn them (661). What is crucial for students to know is that one would not find **Que faisons-nous?** used in the same discourse environment as **On fait quoi?** and **Qu'est-ce qu'on fait?** As McCool (1994) points out, after he and a colleague gave a conference presentation entitled "Teaching Street French": "At the close of an interesting question and answer period, I was astounded by the number of high school teachers who approached us to say that they were unaware that inversion was becoming less common in the spoken language. Obviously, teachers of French need to be aware of differences of style and register" (59). He calls for textbooks to help bridge this gap, for the sake of both teachers and students.

## CLASSROOM APPLICATIONS

The prospect of teaching interrogative expressions may seem daunting, but the key is not to try to present everything at once. It is important for teachers to distinguish between the three categories of interrogative expressions described above: yes-no, Content WH-expressions, and Identifying WH-expressions; and to teach each group separately. Yes-no questions, the easiest, should be taught first, and teachers should make their students aware that the most common way of asking yes-no questions in spoken French is by using intonation. Despite Di Vito's (1997) findings mentioned above, **est-ce que** should be taught early on as the expression that appears in both spoken and written discourses and serves as a neutral variant with respect to register. As Ball (2000) explains, "Questions with **est-ce que** bridge the division between standard and colloquial French and are appropriate in a variety of contexts and situations" (27). We agree with Valdman (2000) and McCool (1994) that it is better to wait until students are learning to write before teaching them the rules of inversion.

Valdman (2000) provides some useful guidelines for teaching WH-expressions. He feels that instructors should first help students acquire WH-expression vocabulary: "À ce stade de l'apprentissage de la langue où le lexique doit recevoir la priorité serait soulignée l'acquisition des adverbes, pronoms et adjectifs interrogatifs (**comment, où, quand, pourquoi; qui, quoi; quel, lequel**)" (661–662). Although Valdman does not differentiate between Content WH-expressions and Identifying WH-expressions, we feel that it is more effective to teach them separately, since they do not follow exactly the same patterns. Valdman advocates teaching certain questions as lexical items instead of grammatical constructions during the early stages of instruction: "Les expressions lexicalisées courantes contenant l'inversion, telles que **Comment allez-vous?, Quelle heure est-il?** forment des agglomérats acquis au même titre que des mots individuels et non pas comme des constructions syntaxiques. Elles constituent ainsi des éléments du vocabulaire de base" (662). Some would argue that French speakers are more likely to say **Quelle heure il est?** or **Il est quelle heure?** instead of **Quelle heure est-il?,** but all three forms are acceptable. What is important is that students learn these questions as blocks of vocabulary without concentrating on their internal structure. Already knowing these expressions will make the acquisition of the grammatical rules that govern interrogation easier later on, since students will already have acquired some intuitions.

### Activities

As we have mentioned in earlier chapters, textbooks rarely provide students with the opportunity to receive enough input before asking them to produce output. We have constructed Activities 7.1 and 7.2 (below) to give students structured input containing the constructions **qu'est-ce que** and **qu'est-ce qui,** which they tend to confuse. Before doing these activities, students should participate in consciousness-raising activities that focus on the properties of the two constructions. They should be guided to hypothesize that **qu'est-ce que** is used when *what* is not the subject of the sentence, and **qu'est-ce qui** is used when *what* is the subject. Note that we do not advocate teaching beginning students **que** as an interrogative expression, because it is found only in formal speech and writing. Overhead 8 provides a model for presenting this grammar point to students:

---

### Overhead 8: Qu'est-ce que vs. Qu'est-ce qui

CLAUDE:     Qu'est-ce que tu veux manger?
STÉPHANE: Je ne sais pas. Qu'est-ce qui est dans ton frigo?

Questions:
1. How would you translate **qu'est-ce que** and **qu'est-ce qui** into English?
2. Why do you think that Claude uses **qu'est-ce que** and Stéphane **qu'est-ce qui** to form their questions?
3. How would you formulate a grammatical rule that distinguishes **qu'est-ce qui** from **qu'est-ce que?**

---

• • • • •

**Activity 7.1: Interrogatoire 1 (Qu'est-ce que).** (structured input)

Choose the response that best describes you, or create your own response.

1. Qu'est-ce que vous aimez faire pendant le week-end?
   a. regarder du sport à la télé.
   b. aller au centre commercial.
   c. étudier à la bibliothèque.
   d. manger dans un bon restaurant.
   e. (à vous)
2. Qu'est-ce que vous mangez le matin?
   a. des œufs.
   b. des céréales.
   c. de la pizza froide.
   d. un steak.
   e. (à vous)
3. Qu'est-ce que vous regardez à la télé?
   a. des feuilletons.

   b. les infos.

   c. des matchs de base-ball/basket/football américain.

   d. des émissions de télé-réalité.

   e. (à vous)

4. Qu'est-ce que vous aimez faire pendant les vacances d'été?

   a. voyager.

   b. travailler.

   c. suivre des cours.

   d. dormir.

   e. (à vous)

5. Qu'est-ce que vous portez pendant le week-end?

   a. un t-shirt et un jean.

   b. un complet.

   c. un pyjama.

   d. un maillot de bain.

   e. (à vous)

6. Qu'est-ce que vous préférez comme animal?

   a. les serpents.

   b. les chats.

   c. les singes.

   d. les chiens.

   e. (à vous)

• • • • •

**Activity 7.2: Interrogatoire 2 (Qu'est-ce qui).** (structured input)

Choose the response that best describes you, or add your own response.

1. Qu'est-ce qui est important pour vous dans la vie?

   a. la liberté.

   b. la justice.

   c. le chocolat.

   d. le base-ball.

   e. l'amour.

   f. (à vous)

2. Qu'est-ce qui se passe chez vous pendant le week-end?

   a. une grande fête.

   b. rien.

   c. un dîner avec des amis.

    d. du bricolage.

    e. (à vous)

3. Qu'est-ce qui est dans votre chambre?

    a. un lit.

    b. un bureau.

    c. une affiche.

    d. un gros serpent.

    e. (à vous)

4. Qu'est-ce qui est dans votre sac à dos?

    a. un portable.

    b. des cahiers.

    c. un sandwich de la semaine dernière.

    d. un balladeur.

    e. (à vous)

5. Qu'est-ce qui se passe à deux heures du matin dans votre ville?

    a. Tout le monde sort des bars.

    b. Il y a beaucoup de monde dans les rues.

    c. Il n'y a personne dans les rues.

    d. Tout le monde dort.

    e. (à vous)

We suggest using similar techniques to introduce other interrogative structures. For example, Activity 7.3 provides students with structured input to distinguish between the use of prepositions followed by either **quoi** (for things) or **qui** (for people):

•  •  •  •  •

**Activity 7.3: La bonne réponse?** (structured input)

Choose the appropriate response to each question. Then, decide whether you agree with the answer.

1. À quoi est-ce qu'on pense souvent?

    a. à son ami.

    b. à son argent.

    _____ C'est vrai.    _____ Ce n'est pas vrai.

2. De qui est-ce qu'on parle de temps en temps?

    a. de sa mère.

    b. de son cours.

_____ C'est vrai.          _____ Ce n'est pas vrai.

3. Avec quoi est-ce qu'un criminel sort souvent?

a. avec sa copine.

b. avec son revolver.

_____ C'est vrai.          _____ Ce n'est pas vrai.

4. Pour qui est-ce qu'on achète un cadeau?

a. pour son anniversaire.

b. pour son prof.

_____ C'est vrai.          _____ Ce n'est pas vrai.

5. Sur quoi est-ce qu'un auteur écrit des romans?

a. sur son enfance.

b. sur ses enfants.

_____ C'est vrai.          _____ Ce n'est pas vrai.

One may use Activity 7.4 as a more advanced input activity after students have had exposure to all the interrogative forms.

• • • • •

**Activity 7.4: L'Américain typique.** (structured input)

The following questions are taken from an interview with Jim, a typical American student. Choose the response that corresponds best to the question.

1. Qu'est-ce que tu aimes?

a. J'aime les vacances.

b. J'aime ma copine.

2. Qui est-ce que tu as vu au cinéma?

a. J'ai vu mon ex-copine.

b. J'ai vu le nouveau film de Spielberg.

3. Qu'est-ce que tu détestes?

a. J'ai horreur de mon cousin, Robert.

b. Je n'aime pas trop les olives.

4. À quoi pensez-vous?

a. Je pense à mes amis.

b. Je pense à mes cours d'été.

5. Qu'est-ce qui est dans ta voiture?

a. Quelques vidéos, c'est tout.

b. J'ai laissé ma copine dans ma voiture.

Activity 7.5 also provides the opportunity for students to focus on differentiating between interrogative expressions that they might confuse.

● ● ● ● ●

**Activity 7.5: Quelle est la question?** (structured input)

Choose the appropriate interrogative expression to complete these questions asked during an interview with a college student.

1. (Qu'est-ce qui/Qu'est-ce que) se trouve dans la chambre?
   Il y a des affiches.
2. (Qu'est-ce qui/Quelle) est la date de ton anniversaire?
   C'est le 15 août.
3. (De quoi est-ce que/Qu'est-ce que) tu parles avec tes amis?
   On parle du film qu'on vient de voir.
4. (Quelle/Laquelle) fille est-ce que tu veux inviter au cinéma?
   La blonde de mon cours de chimie.
5. (Qu'est-ce que c'est que/Quel est) l'amour?
   Je n'ai aucune idée.

At this point, students should be ready for some output activities for teaching interrogative expressions. Unfortunately, most textbooks provide mechanical drills rather than true structured-output activities. There are two types of activities that typically follow textbook explanations about interrogatives. The first kind of activity (for yes-no questions) is one where students are asked to convert utterances or already existing questions into questions using **est-ce que** or inversion, as in the following examples:

---

Supply the corresponding question, using **est-ce que** or inversion:
Modèle: Elle parle français.   →
   *Parle-t-elle français?* or *Est-ce qu'elle parle français?*

Convert the following questions (which use inversion) into questions using **est-ce que:**
Modèle: Parle-t-elle français?   →
   *Est-ce qu'elle parle français?*

---

Mechanical exercises of this type may (or may not—see Wong and Van-Patten 2003) be effective for allowing students to practice forming questions using **est-ce que** or inversion. They are, however, rather dull and inappropriate within a communicative framework. It really does not make much sense pedagogically for students to learn a skill that they will never need to use.

Structured-output activities, like structured input, should begin with easier exercises and then culminate with more complex tasks. Activity 7.6, for example, allows students to produce natural-sounding discourse after focusing on a few models of questions created using **est-ce que.** Note that this activity could be done even at an early level, as long as the verb list is appropriate.

• • • • •

**Activity 7.6: Trouvez un colocataire.** (structured output)

Est-ce que vous cherchez un(e) camarade de chambre?
Est-ce que vous savez les qualités importantes chez un(e) camarade de chambre?
Est-ce que vous êtes difficile à vivre?

*Step 1:* Make a list of 8–10 questions to help you screen potential roommates, using **est-ce que** to begin each question. Some verbs are given to help guide you.

Verbs: **aimer, détester, manger, fumer, boire, prendre, regarder, écouter, payer, gagner, être, avoir, sortir, partir**

Modèle: Est-ce que tu aimes écouter de la musique à trois heures du matin? Est-ce que tu as des animaux domestiques?

*Step 2:* Pose your questions to various classmates, taking note of their responses.

*Step 3:* Is there anyone in the class with whom you could or could not live? Why or why not? What have you learned about your classmates? Do you think that you are **difficile à vivre** or **facile à vivre?**

Another typical activity that one finds in elementary French books, often immediately after the grammar presentation, involves having students fill in missing interrogative expressions to complete questions. The activity contained below exemplifies this type of exercise:

---

Complete the following conversation by inserting the missing interrogative expressions:

- _____ tu veux faire ce soir?

- Je ne sais pas. _____ va sortir avec nous?

- Randall et Christine ont envie d'aller au cinéma. _____ film veux-tu voir?

- Ça m'est égal. _____ joue au Clairmont?

---

An activity like this does not lead students to master interrogative forms; rather, it tests whether they have already learned these forms. Note also that students are required to select their answers from a plethora of choices, which may be overwhelming.

It is better not to ask students to produce too many forms at once. Activities 7.7 and 7.8 are provided as samples to teach interrogative expressions. Note that Activity 7.7 focuses on Content WH-expressions and Activity 7.8 on Identifying WH-expressions.

• • • • •

### Activity 7.7: **Maman veut savoir.** (structured output)

Imagine that you are a mother who is trying to find out more about your college-aged son/daughter's life.

*Step* 1: Make a list of 7–10 questions that you would like to ask your child, using some of the interrogative expressions and verbs listed below, as well as the expression **est-ce que,** to form your questions.

Interrogative expressions: **comment, combien, où, pourquoi, quand**
Verbs: **manger, boire, étudier, sortir, téléphoner, s'habiller, acheter,** etc.

*Step* 2: Interview a partner, using the questions you have prepared.

*Step* 3: With your partner, choose the four questions (from both lists combined) that you think would be the most difficult for a college student to answer.

*Step* 4: Ask these questions to the class, allowing your classmates to answer them. Did they provide acceptable answers? Why or why not?

• • • • •

**Activity 7.8: Le jaloux/La jalouse.** (structured output)

*Step* 1: Using the following interrogative expressions and verbs, make a list of questions that a jealous boyfriend or girlfriend might ask his/her partner after they have spent an evening apart.

Interrogative expressions: **qui, qu'est-ce que, qu'est-ce qui, quel, avec qui, de quoi,** etc.
Verbs: **sortir, regarder, dîner, danser, parler,** etc.

Modèle: Qu'est-ce que tu as fait après le dîner?

*Step* 2: With a partner, come up with suitable answers to these questions.

Activities 7.9 and 7.10 are designed for advanced learners in order to give them exposure to various types of authentic discourse (spoken vs. written and formal vs. informal). Note that students are not asked to produce these constructions but to analyze their use in discourse; the goal is for students to work as researchers who, by analyzing discourse, develop hypotheses.

• • • • •

**Activity 7.9: Les entretiens.** (discourse analysis)

Interviews are interesting, because they are conducted orally but are often presented to the public in written form. Compare the following two interviews, one with Jean-Claude Van Damme and the other with Jacques Chirac. There are some significant differences between them, both in content and form. Comment on the following issues: register (whether the discourse is informal, neutral, or formal, or whether it varies), the features of spoken French that are present, and whether there are any surprising components (for example, formal elements mixed in with informal discourse, etc.). Hypothesize why some forms (such as inversion) may appear unexpectedly in certain contexts. We have included only a sampling of some of the questions that are asked in these interviews. To view each interview, go to the Web page provided.

1. *Interview with Jean-Claude Van Damme*

Questions:

Ça ne vous ennuie pas que dans «Tiens, voilà du boudin», on dise qu'il n'y en a pas pour les Belges?

Votre pire douleur physique?

Van Damme, c'est votre vrai nom?

Et vos deuxièmes prénoms?

À part Van Damme, vous avez un pseudo de rêve?

Votre dernier rêve devenu réalité?

Avez-vous une religion officielle?

etc.

Source: http://www.zepngreg.ch/vandamme.htm (Première n° 267 de juin 1999)

2. *Interview with Jacques Chirac*

Interview accordée par M. Jacques Chirac, Président de la République, à M. Adar Primor du quotidien israélien «Haaretz».

Palais de l'Élysée, mardi 19 juillet 2005

Questions [some of which have been shortened]:

Monsieur le Président, par rapport au terrorisme, il existe une question qui intéresse les Israéliens en particulier, est-ce que les Européens, et notamment les Français, vont désormais après les attentats de Londres mieux comprendre les Israéliens qui doivent faire face au terrorisme palestinien? Par exemple, avez-vous plus de compréhension pour l'élimination ciblée des terroristes dans les territoires palestiniens?

Ces attentats rapprochent-ils l'analyse française du terrorisme de celle d'Israël, des États-Unis, du Royaume-Uni?

Comment qualifieriez-vous les relations bilatérales entre Israël et la France? Y-a-t-il une perspective d'amélioration?

Où en est le processus de paix?

À propos justement du Premier ministre, je suis sûr vous suivez les grandes difficultés auxquelles il doit faire face. Est-ce que vous avez changé votre avis sur le Premier ministre? Est-ce que vous regrettez les critiques du passé?

Qu'est-ce qui va se passer si jamais, après cet engagement, le Premier ministre décide d'en terminer là et s'il n'y a pas d'enchaînement?

Pourquoi la France connaît-elle un regain d'actes antisémites?

etc.

Source: http://www.elysee.fr/elysee/francais/interventions/interviews_articles_de_presse_et_interventions_televisees./2005/juillet/interview_accordee_par_m_jacques_chirac_president_de_la_republique_au_quotidien_israelien_haaretz.30785.html (publiée le 22 juillet 2005)

• • • • •

**Activity 7.10: L'interrogatoire.** (discourse analysis)

In the first scene of *Les Compères*, the parents of a runaway youth go to the police station to report their son as missing. A detective meets with them and asks them a series of questions about their son. Students should be instructed to take notes on these questions. The film clip should be played several times to ensure that students receive enough input. Then, students should work in groups to analyze the structure of the questions that they have heard, categorizing them as (a) est-ce que, (b) inversion, or (c) declarative sentence word order. They should make some generalizations about the structures that are used in this particular setting. Might they be more formal than what one usually finds in spoken French? Why?

## CONSOLIDATION EXERCISES

1. Categorize each of the following utterances, which have been extracted from their discourse settings, as (R1 "informal," R2 "neutral," and R3 "formal"):

   a. Veux-tu aller au cinéma avec nous?

   b. S'il te plaît, dis-moi—qui t'a donné ce livre?

   c. Qu'est-ce qu'on mange, alors?

   d. Qui est-ce qui veut du pain?

   e. C'est quoi, un roman à clef?

   f. Qui est-ce que tu aimes?

   g. À quoi Marcel pense-t-il?

2. Classify the following questions as (a) a yes-no question; (b) a Content WH-question; or (c) an Identifying WH-question.

    a. Tu veux lire quel livre?

    b. Il est français?

    c. Combien il a payé?

    d. Elle est comment?

    e. Tu as vu qui à la plage?

    f. De quoi tu parles?

    g. Veux-tu sortir avec nous?

    h. Quand veux-tu qu'on se marie?

    i. C'est quoi, un tatou?

    j. Tu l'as fait où?

    k. Tu aimes les brunes?

3. Give informal (R1) and formal (R3) equivalents of each the following neutral (R2) questions:

    a. Qu'est-ce que tu as fait ce week-end?

    b. Où est-ce que tu as voyagé?

    c. Est-ce que tu n'es pas allé voir l'exposition de Rodin?

    d. Chez qui est-ce que tu es resté?

    e. Quand est-ce que le train est parti?

    f. Pourquoi est-ce que tu as manqué le train?

4. Rewrite the following conversation, transforming the questions into what one would expect to hear in an informal (R1) setting (a conversation between friends).

    GWÉN: Nous voyons-nous ce soir?

    FLO:    Oui. Qu'as-tu envie que nous fassions?

    GWÉN: Je ne sais pas. J'aimerais bien manger dans un bon restaurant.

    FLO:    Quelle sorte de cuisine préfères-tu?

    GWÉN: J'aime tout ce qui est asiatique. Connais-tu un bon endroit?

    FLO:    Dans quel quartier veux-tu sortir?

5. There are times when interrogative expressions occur following **c'est** within the **c'est**-cleft, as in the following two examples taken from the Minnesota Corpus of Spoken French (Kerr 1983). Read through each example, and try to devise a theory that explains why the **c'est**-cleft (boldfaced) is used instead of a typical interrogative construction. Note that the transcript, unlike the excerpts that appear throughout this chapter, has not been simplified and remains in its original form, which includes pauses, sounds other than words, overlapping conversations, etc.

Example 1:

M: Un peu de sérieux les filles, ça divague, ça divague /chuckle/. Ça s'embourbe, même!

C: Ach! Arrête, j'ai mal aux dents!

M: [Mais toi tu as, tu es], tu tu nous couves quelque chose, hein! Entre les dents et le cœur! Elle nous prépare quelque chose, elle. [**C'est quand que tu as rendez-vous chez le dentiste?**]

C: Lundi.

M: Ha ha!

E: Qu'est-ce que tu as? Tu as une

C: Non, j'ai l'impression que c'est soit les dents de sagesse qui poussent

E: Alors là, ah ça c'est, c'est réjouissant, hein!

Example 2:

C: C'est quand Garde à Vue?

E: Garde à Vue, c'est pas cette semaine, c'est l'autre. C'est vendredi, du vendredi, c'est du 16 au au /throat clearing/ au /very elongated vowel/ 22, quelque chose comme ça. Oui je crois que c'est peut-être le 22, donc c'est pendant le week-end, hein. oui . . . et puis jusqu'à mardi, je crois.

M: **Et c'est où que ça joue?**

C: Euh, Bell Museum.

6. In French, is it possible to say both: **Quelle est ta saison préférée?** and **Laquelle est ta saison préférée?** If so, provide discourse contexts for each question.

## TYPICAL STUDENT ERRORS

Imagine that your students have made the mistakes provided below. Each sentence is either grammatically or sociolinguistically ill-formed. A grammatically ill-formed sentence is simply wrong (it would never be acceptable, in any context), whereas a sociolinguistically ill-formed sentence is odd because it violates rules of register. Decide which is the case for each. Finally, come up with an explanation for your students as to why each utterance is "wrong."

1. *Context:* An elementary school student is saying good morning to her teacher.

Salut, monsieur. Es-tu allé au cinéma hier soir?

2. Context: A student is holding up two books to see which one his partner prefers:

Lequel livre veux-tu lire?

3. Context: A student is asking another student about her possessions.

Quel est dans ton sac?

4. Context: A student wishes to know the date.

Qu'est-ce qui est la date aujourd'hui?

5. Context: A student wishes to know whom his classmate saw at a recent party.

Qui est-ce qui tu as vu?

6. Context: A student wishes to know the date.

Qu'est-ce que c'est que la date aujourd'hui?

7. Context: A student has learned a proverb but does not recognize one of the words in it.

Quel est un chacal?

8. Context: A student asks a French friend what she would like to eat.

Quoi veux-tu manger?

9. Context: A student is writing a letter to his prospective host family in which he wishes to know who in the family speaks English.

Qui parlent anglais?

10. Context: A student wants to know who her classmate is thinking about.

Qui penses-tu de?

## Corrections of Student Errors (answers may vary)

1. Bonjour, monsieur. Êtes-vous allé au cinéma hier soir? (*sociolinguistically ill-formed*)

2. Quel livre veux-tu lire? (*grammatically ill-formed*)

3. Qu'est-ce qui est dans ton sac? (*grammatically ill-formed*)

4. Quelle est la date aujourd'hui? (*grammatically ill-formed*)

5. Qui est-ce que tu as vu? (*grammatically ill-formed*)

6. Quelle est la date aujourd'hui? (*grammatically ill-formed*)

7. Qu'est-ce que c'est qu'un chacal? Qu'est-ce qu'un chacal? (*grammatically ill-formed*)

8. Qu'est-ce que tu veux manger? (*grammatically ill-formed*)

9. Qui parle anglais? (*grammatically ill-formed*)

10. À qui est-ce que tu penses? (*grammatically ill-formed*)

## DISCUSSION TOPICS / PROJECTS

1. Some linguists have conducted research that shows that native speakers prefer that non-natives speak "better" than they (the native speakers) do. Above we quoted Valdman (2000), who reports that native speakers prefer that learners speak a more refined and more neutral variant of the target langauge. Do you feel the same way about non-native speakers of English? Would you prefer that they speak a more neutral, "bookish" form of English? Are you put off when they use slang expressions such as "like," or "wanna" or "dude"? If so, why? Is there a time when it is acceptable for learners to use colloquial expressions?

2. Find a conversation from a textbook that you think sounds stilted. Rewrite the conversation to make it more authentic, highlighting elements from the spoken language and at the same time showing where written elements would occur (such as missing **ne**'s, etc.).

3. Watch a scene (approximately five minutes long) from a recent French film, writing down all the questions you hear. What do you notice about the use of inversion, **est-ce que,** and intonation? Do certain characters use one form of interrogation more than others? What does this suggest about the character(s)?

4. Do you agree that inversion is the least important interrogative form for students to learn to *produce*? Should inversion, like the **passé simple,** be a form that is taught for recognition only until more advanced levels of study? In what situations should students use inversion?

5. As we have seen, the French language seems to be undergoing a change with regard to the use of **quoi** as a direct object. Do you think that it will eventually be considered acceptable to write a question such as **Tu as fait quoi?** Why or why not? Do you see any parallels with other grammatical changes that have occurred in French over the last few decades?

6. As mentioned above, **pourquoi** is almost always found in anteposition, while other Content WH-expressions (**comment, combien, où,** and **quand**) tend to be found in postposition. Can you develop a hypothesis as to why **pourquoi** might differ from the other expressions? What might the speaker be expecting from his addressee's answer to a question containing **pourquoi** that could be somewhat different from what one might expect in response to the other interrogative expressions?

7. Some linguists have argued that "free variation" is possible, that is, two different grammatical structures may be appropriate and mean the same thing in the same discourse environment. Others are opposed to this theory, believing that every different construction somehow conveys a different meaning or perspective. Earlier in the chapter, we noted that **Qu'est-ce qu'on fait?** and **On fait quoi?** were both used in the same setting (two friends who were sitting in a café and trying to figure out what to do next). Create a discourse in which each of these utterances might be used, and then survey native speakers to see which structure they prefer. Make sure that you give a sufficient amount of context. Then, decide whether these two constructions indeed appear in different discourse contexts or whether they are in free variation.

## FURTHER READING

### On French Interrogative Constructions

Coveney, Aidan. "The Use of the QU-final Interrogative Structure in Spoken French." Journal of French Language Studies 5 (1995): 143–171.

McCool, George J. "Teaching the Formation of Questions: Lessons from New French." Modern Language Journal 78 (1994): 56–60.

Myers, Lindsy. "WH-Questions in Spoken French." PhD diss., University of Texas at Austin, expected 2007.

Valdman, Albert. "Comment gérer la variation dans l'enseignement du français langue étrangère aux États-Unis." French Review 73 (2000): 648–666.

### On the " Pedagogical Norm"

Magnan, Sally Sieloff, and Joel Walz. "Pedagogical Norms: Development of the Concept and Illustrations from French." In Pedagogical Norms for Second and Foreign Language Learning and Teaching, edited by Susan Gass, Kathleen Bardovi-Harlig, Sally Sieloff Magnan, and Joel Walz, 15–40. Amsterdam: John Benjamins, 2002.

Valdman, Albert. "La notion de norme pédagogique dans l'enseignement du français langue étrangère." In Analyse linguistique et approches de l'oral: Recueil d'études offert en hommage à Claire Blanche-Benveniste, edited by Mireille Bilger, Karel Van den Eynde, and Françoise Gadet, 177–188. Paris: Peeters, 1998.

# 8 · Conclusion

## OVERVIEW / KEY CONSIDERATIONS

This chapter's goal is to summarize our previous discussion of the role of grammar in the communicative classroom and to offer practical suggestions for integrating grammar-focused activities into the communicative framework. The chapter is divided into four sections. The first counters the misconception that the teaching of grammar is incompatible with the communicative method. The second presents different types of syllabi, pointing out their pedagogical goals and the role of grammar within their frameworks. The third section, the most substantial segment of this chapter, suggests ways of adapting and supplementing current textbook materials to reflect recommended methods for teaching grammar. We conclude with a section that contains a brief description of the most important issues for instructors to keep in mind when designing grammar presentations and activities.

## THE COMMUNICATIVE METHOD AND GRAMMAR TEACHING

Communicative language teaching (CLT), with its focus on *communicative competence*, has had a profound influence on the development of language teaching methods and materials over the past three decades. Unfortunately, there are many misconceptions about the tenets of communicative language teaching and how they should be implemented. One of the biggest misunderstandings is the presumption that CLT is incompatible with the teaching of grammar and that this method considers grammatical accuracy unimportant. Savignon (2002), one of the original advocates of CLT (see Savignon 1971, 1972, 1983), tries to clear up some of these erroneous impressions: "While involvement in communicative events is seen as central to language development, this involvement necessarily requires attention to form. Communication cannot take place in the absence of structure, or grammar, a set of shared assumptions about how language works, along with a willingness of participants to cooperate in the negotiation of meaning. In their carefully researched and widely cited paper proposing components of communicative competence, Canale and Swain (1980) did not suggest that grammar was unimportant. They sought rather to situate grammatical competence within a more broadly defined communicative competence. Similarly, the findings of the Savignon (1971) study did not suggest that teachers should forsake grammar instruction" (7). Many scholars and teachers alike, however, have misinterpreted the nature of communicative language teaching, assuming that by performing communicative activities, students will somehow acquire grammatical accuracy.

Part of the confusion may be linked to the ambiguity of the tenets of CLT. According to Omaggio Hadley (2001), "Communicative language teaching, like any instruction oriented towards proficiency goals, is not bound to a particular methodology or curricular design, but represents a flexible approach to teaching that is responsive to learner needs and preferences. In many ways, CLT represents a repertoire of teaching ideas rather than a fixed set of methodological procedures, and as such is not easily defined or evaluated" (118). Consequently, instructors and textbook writers tend to interpret CLT in different ways, which, unfortunately, may result in their abandoning the study of grammar altogether.

As discussed in Chapter 2 however, with the focus on form movement growing in influence, grammar instruction has returned to the forefront of language teaching. More important, researchers and teachers have realized that grammar may be taught in a communicative manner to help students achieve functional objectives. Studying grammatical form need not be incompatible with communicative goals; on the contrary, the concept of grammar as an integral communicative tool is at the core of this framework. Doughty and Williams (1998) assert that "the proposed advantage of focus on form over traditional forms-in-isolation type of grammar teaching is the cognitive processing support provided by the 'overriding focus . . . on meaning or communication.' To state this advantage rather simply, the learner's attention is drawn precisely to a linguistic feature as necessitated by a communicative need" (3). Grammar thus becomes a tool for communicating clearly; it is not an unconnected topic to be studied out of context. In the following section, we discuss how the study of grammar may be better integrated into lesson plans that concentrate on achieving communicative goals.

## TYPES OF LESSON PLANS AND SYLLABI AND THEIR PEDAGOGICAL GOALS

Omaggio Hadley (2001, 462–463) provides some useful guidelines for creating lesson plans, the first four of which are listed below (her final three guidelines are not included here, because they are more geared toward classroom management and self- and course-evaluation than toward the actual creation of lesson plans):

### Omaggio Hadley's Guidelines for Creating Lesson Plans (a partial list)

1. Develop a plan that is contextualized and encourages students to use the language actively to explore a particular theme.
2. Plan activities that will help students reach functional objectives.
3. Plan a variety of activities to accommodate learner differences.
4. Plan activities that are appropriate to the proficiency level of your students.

Source: *Teaching Language in Context*, 3rd edition, by Omaggio Hadley. © 2001. Reprinted with permission of Heinle, a division of Thomson Learning: www.thomson.com. Fax 800-730-2215.

Omaggio Hadley's first guideline, the exploration of a particular theme, is not difficult to implement using most of the textbooks that are on the market today. When one compares today's textbooks to older texts, one immediately sees that they are organized differently. Textbooks from the 1970s and earlier were designed to accommodate a grammatical (often called "structural" or "formal") syllabus; that is, each chapter was developed to support the teaching of a particular grammar point (verb tenses, pronouns, interrogative structures, etc.). Everything revolved around grammar. Today's textbooks, on the other hand, are organized thematically in order to provide students with a meaningful context for language practice and acquisition. In addition, many current textbooks cite introducing students to culture as an important pedagogical goal.

Typical themes for today's elementary level textbooks include introductions/presentations, descriptions of people or places, family/home life, hobbies, eating/drinking, shopping, clothing/fashion, health/body matters, education and school-related activities, traveling, and the arts. Many textbooks also include more abstract themes in later chapters (when students have acquired sufficient language skills to express more complex ideas), such as **Les enjeux du présent et de l'avenir** (*Deux mondes*, Terrell et al.), **Les soucis et les rêves** (*Mais oui!*, Thompson/Phillips), **La qualité de la vie** (*Parallèles*, Fouletier-Smith) / **Qualité de vie** (*Paroles*, Magnan, et al.), **Les immigrés** (*Rapports*, Walz/Piriou), **Le budget, les dépenses et les priorités** (*Thèmes*, Harper et al.), and **Le bonheur, qu'est-ce que c'est?** (*Voilà*, Heilenman et al.). Even the earliest and most basic chapters of many textbooks are designed with the goal of meeting the National Standards' focus on the "5 Cs" (communication, comparisons, communities, connections, and culture), where students are led to develop critical thinking skills through analyzing their own culture in relationship to others.

Culture is central in many books. For example, Walz and Piriou (2003) explain that their text, *Rapports*, "focuses on content rather than language as a basis for instruction. In most cases, this content is the culture of the people who speak the language being learned" (IAE-11). Likewise, Valdman, Pons, and Scullen (2006) explain that *Chez Nous* offers "a richly nuanced focus on the Francophone world through a highly integrative and process-oriented approach to the development of language skills" (xi). Thus, the cultural knowledge that students are expected to acquire is complementary to the development of their language skills, and it is equally important.

The theme- or content-based organization of most elementary French textbooks may be contrasted with the "task-based" syllabi that have become popular in some English as a Second Language (ESL) textbooks and programs. Nunan (2001) outlines the following guidelines for designing a task-based program: "Having specified target and pedagogical tasks, the syllabus designer analyzes these in order to identify the knowledge and skills that the learner will need to have in order to carry out the tasks. The next step is to sequence and integrate the tasks with enabling exercises designed to develop the requisite knowledge and skills." In other words, the syllabus is designed to prepare students for situations they will encounter and tasks they will need to perform in the real world.

There has been some disagreement among researchers, however, as to what exactly constitutes a "task." As Lee (2000) explains, "the consensus is that task-based instruction views language use as a means to an end. Beyond that, variation characterizes the definitions . . . A task is (1) a classroom activity or exercise that has (a) an objective attainable only by the interaction among participants, (b) a mechanism for structuring and sequencing interaction, and (c) a focus on meaning exchange; (2) a language learning endeavor that requires learners to comprehend, manipulate, and/or produce the target language as they perform some set of workplans" (32). Note that ESL programs, especially those designed for second language learners immersed in anglophone countries, recognize that students have practical needs. In fact, many task-based specialists in ESL advocate conducting an in-depth needs analysis of all students enrolled in a given class as a necessary preliminary phase for designing a course. They contend that tasks must be based on student needs in order to be effective. Therefore, the objective is not only to develop the learners' language skills, but also to acclimate the students into the new society and culture. Typical tasks would include, for example, explaining to a barber how one would like one's hair cut, describing to a mechanic what is wrong with one's car, and filling out insurance forms.

In contrast, the goal of acquiring survival skills, although important, is not as urgent in a theme-based foreign language program. Here, students should have the luxury of exploring more intellectually stimulating topics, rather than simply practical matters. It is not that easy, however, to develop theme-based materials at the elementary and intermediate levels. Lee (2000) notes that one challenge of lower-level foreign language programs is to avoid making students, who are limited by their language skills, discuss inane topics. There should be an exchange of meaningful, and interesting, information. Unfortunately, as he points out: "Whereas discussions in history, literature, and linguistics classes purport to clarify the issues, discussions in language classes generally fail to incorporate cognitive, academic goals. Discussions in language classes . . . generally settle for a linguistic goal" (35). How many of us have shuddered, realizing that we have just asked our adult students to describe their ideal picnic or what they might wear if it is cold outside?

Whether a textbook is theme-based or task-based, the various topics and situations that accompany themes or tasks require certain types of grammatical competence. For example, as most textbook writers know, in order to reserve a hotel room or buy a train ticket, a speaker must be able to form questions. A knowledge of past tense forms is necessary for conversations about one's childhood or upbringing. Possessive determiners are needed in order to converse about one's family. Adjective forms are required to describe people or settings. Reflexive verbs are vital for explaining one's daily routine. Dining in a restaurant necessitates the selection of appropriate determiners to precede food items. And, in order to offer an opinion, one needs to know the forms of the subjunctive.

As mentioned in Chapter 2, many textbooks skillfully present vocabulary and provide students with well-conceived activities to help them assimilate the French lexicon. In addition, many textbooks are adept at teaching reading and writing; they often provide relevant, interesting, and pedagogically sound pre- and post-reading/writing activities. Textbooks often fall short, however, when it comes to integrating grammar instruction. Grammar is sometimes conceived of as a necessary evil that, despite its relevance, is isolated and disconnected from the chapter's theme. Some textbooks go as far as to place the grammar descriptions in separate sections at the ends of chapters.

Grammar is sometimes considered a topic to which instructors should not devote precious class time. Terrell, Rogers, Kerr, and Spielmann (2001), for example, explain that in *Deux mondes* "the **Grammaire** section can be used for at-home study, or if instructors so desire, it can be used in class" (p. xiv). The authors' rationale is that the students will pick up grammar through input, a philosophy that is consistent with the *Natural Approach*, based on Krashen's (1982) model, which provides the methodological framework for their book. The authors of *Paroles* (Magnan et al. 2002) explain that "grammar is presented inductively before rules and deductively in rules before examples. The inductive grammar presenta-

tion appears in the **Les mots pour le dire** section in each Dossier. The deductive grammar presentation is found in the **Grammaire** sections" (xii).
Likewise, Heilenman, Kaplan, and Tournier (2006) advise instructors
working with *Voilà* to have students study grammar at home: "Try not to
use class time to explain grammar. The explanations in *Voilà* have been
class-tested and students can learn them on their own" (Instructor's Guide,
15). As we point out (above), however, rather than separating grammar
and content, the two should be integrated.

Returning to Omaggio Hadley's criteria for developing a lesson plan,
most textbooks meet guideline 1: "[developing] a plan that is contextualized and encourages students to use the language actively to explore a
particular theme." Incorporating guidelines 2 and 3, "[planning] activities to help students reach functional objectives" and "[planning] a variety of activities to accommodate learner differences," is more difficult for
instructors, since most textbooks require some enhancement in this area.
Moreover, developing strong and meaningful transitions between activities is an undertaking that even the most experienced instructors find
challenging. If teachers can make a smooth transition between activities
that concentrate on vocabulary or culture to grammar-focused exercises,
then they have succeeded in integrating grammar into their lesson plan.
Interspersing grammar activities that are contextualized and giving attention to their discourse properties when such a treatment is appropriate
make grammar part of the communicative process. The following section
offers suggestions and strategies for adapting a textbook to accomplish
such transitions in order to integrate the teaching of grammar into the
communicative classroom.

## ADAPTING TEXTBOOKS

This section contains suggestions to help instructors modify, supplement, or replace the grammar sections in the textbooks they may currently be using. We aim specifically to accomplish the following goals:

- Make the grammar explanations more inductive.
- Enhance the transitions between communicative activities that do not
  focus on grammar and those that do.
- Improve the sequencing of activities.
- Integrate the consciousness-raising and discourse-based activities intro-
  duced in earlier chapters.

To provide instructors with a model for revamping an already existing grammar section, we have chosen to use a chapter from a popular first-year, university-level textbook. We show how the grammar explanation can be made more inductive and discourse-based; how the mechanical drill-type activities may be replaced by more input-oriented and consciousness-raising kinds of exercises; and how one may create stronger transitions between activities. Furthermore, we select some activities from other first-year textbooks and show how instructors may adapt them as well to make them more task-based.

As already mentioned, our aim is not to criticize individual textbooks for what we perceive to be their inadequacies in teaching grammar. The books from which we have chosen to modify activities or grammar explanations are not necessarily weaker in presenting/teaching grammar than others; in fact, we have selected some precisely because they contain material that can easily be retooled into a more discourse- and task-based framework. Often the other elements of the textbook (for example, the presentation of culture or the readings that are included) are excellent, thus making it worth one's while to rework the grammar sections.

We have chosen to use Exploration 2 from Chapter 5 of Jarvis, Bonin, Birckbichler, and Lair's (2005) *Invitation au monde francophone* (*Invitation*, from this point on) as a model for adapting a textbook's grammar section. Our revisions aim to achieve the following objectives:

• The section will conform more to a discourse-based approach, where grammatical form is linked with meaning.
• Students will be led to induce grammatical rules and functions.
• Activities will be of both the input and output varieties.
• Activities will not be mechanical drills.

As we have stressed above, instructors who prefer a deductive approach and contextualized, highly structured activities might be quite satisfied with a book that is written in a framework such as this one.

The topic of this grammar section is the partitive. The following are the elements that we find problematic:

• The grammar explanation that treats the partitive is unnecessarily complicated, because it is combined with explanations about several other topics (negation, expressions of quantity, and differences between the partitive, the indefinite article, and the definite article).

- The grammar explanation is entirely deductive.
- The exercises that follow the grammar explanation are contextualized, but they are mechanical at the same time.
- Students do not have the opportunity to work with input first. Instead they are expected to produce the target structures immediately after reading about them.
- Students are required to concentrate on too many things at once when doing the initial exercises that follow the grammar description.

We suggest guidelines for making the grammar presentation clearer, less complicated, and more inductive, and we propose activities that will provide a more pedagogically sound learning experience.

The chapter that we have chosen from *Invitation* is well organized. On the first page of the chapter (125) are lists of the chapter's target language functions (such as talking about what one likes to eat, buying food, and ordering in a restaurant), the accompanying vocabulary items (food and food stores), and the chapter's grammatical topics (demonstrative adjectives, the partitive, and the verbs **prendre** and **boire**). The second and third pages of the chapter (126–127) contain images of various French food stores, with food items labeled. Students then are asked to discuss the foods that they like, love, hate, etc. Next, they participate in a role-play (128) where their goal is to find out where various items are located in the supermarket (they ask questions such as **Où sont les petits pois, s'il vous plaît?**). Students are then asked to categorize various types of foods (fruits, vegetables, etc.) through playing a game (129). Next is a cultural note, in English, about meals in France, which highlights the cultural differences between American and French attitudes toward meals and food (130–131). By this point, students have received a good deal of useful cultural information and a solid base of vocabulary. The first grammar section, Exploration 1, which deals with demonstrative determiners, appears next and is followed by Exploration 2, which we will now consider.

Exploration 2, entitled "**Acheter et consommer: Le partitif,**" begins with a brief description of the partitive: "Some things such as coffee, salt, and patience, cannot be counted. In English we often use the words *some, no,* and *any;* or we use the noun alone. We say, for example, *I would like some coffee; we don't have any time; he has no patience; we have money.* In French, the partitive article conveys these meanings" (135). This description is followed by the chart provided below. Four additional points are listed next; each is followed by several examples (which we have omitted here):

### Le partitif

|                              | Affirmatif        | Négatif            |
| ---------------------------- | ----------------- | ------------------ |
| Devant un nom masculin       | du café           | pas de café        |
| Devant un nom féminin        | de la salade      | pas de salade      |
| Devant une voyelle           | de l'eau minérale | pas d'eau minérale |
| ou un **h** muet             |                   |                    |

2.1 Note that after a negative verb, the partitive article becomes **de.**
(. . .)

2.2 **De** is also used in other expression of quantity, weights, measures and serving or packaging sizes.
(. . .)

2.3 Note that when food items are counted as separate items (a loaf of bread, an orange) or used in the plural (some green beans, some fruits), the indefinite article is used.
(. . .)

2.4 Note also the contrast between partitive and definite articles. The partitive is used to indicate an unspecified amount of a noncountable item. If a verb expresses consumption (**acheter, consommer, manger, avoir**), that is a clue to using the partitive. On the other hand, the definite article is used to refer to general categories, such as when talking about likes and dislikes (using verbs such as **aimer, préférer,** and **détester**). (135–136)
(. . .)

Source: *Invitation au monde francophone* (with Audio CD), 2nd edition, by Jarvis/Bonin/Birckbichler/Lair. © 2005. Reprinted with permission of Heinle, a division of Thomson Learning: www.thomson.com. Fax 800-730-2215.

Thus, in this short and extremely dense section, there are several points that the authors want students to understand:

1. When to use the partitive
2. When to use **de**
3. When to use the partitive vs. the indefinite article
4. When to use the partitive vs. the definite article

This is a great deal of information to present to students all at once. We offer the following suggestions for making this material more accessible to students:

• Divide the grammar explanation into several sections.
• Use an inductive approach to impart the information.
• Include exercises that specifically accompany each of the various grammar points (the mass vs. count distinction, **de** after negation, etc.).

To begin, we suggest implementing Overhead 4, from our Chapter 4, which is repeated below. As we mentioned in Chapter 4, this overhead is designed to help students recognize that the partitive is used with mass nouns, as opposed to the indefinite article, which occurs with count nouns.

---

### Overhead 4: L'article indéfini et l'article partitif

### un, une, des vs. du, de la, de l'

*Step* 1: Comparez les deux listes suivantes:

| Liste A | Liste B |
|---|---|
| une carotte/des carottes | du riz |
| une baguette/des baguettes | du pain |
| une bouteille/des bouteilles | de l'eau |
| un steak/des steaks | de la viande |

[Note to instructors: Ask students to generalize: what are the differences between the nouns in List A and the nouns in List B? Goal: Students come up with count vs. mass noun distinction.]

*Step* 2: Décidez lesquels des noms suivants sont nombrables:
Modèle: sandwich → *des sandwichs*

| petit pois | vin | tomate |
|---|---|---|
| croissant | beurre | sel |
| poulet | | |

[Note to instructors: **Poulet** can be both a count noun and a mass noun: for example, it could be **un poulet** if one were to buy an entire uncooked chicken at the supermarket.]

---

Thus, instead of *telling* students about the mass/count distinction, students are *shown* data and asked to figure out the rule themselves.

The mass/count distinction, which distinguishes the partitive from the indefinite article, is the first major grammar point in Exploration 2. Before continuing on to the next point, students should do a few activities to make sure that they have internalized this concept. *Invitation* contains six activities that follow its grammar explanation section. We are not convinced that these activities are sufficient for students to understand and be able to use the grammatical concepts. Activity A (136) is reproduced in part below:

---

**A. Au restaurant universitaire.** You are asking French friends how often the following foods are served in the **restaurant universitaire.** What do they say?
Exemple:  soupe (quelquefois)
　　　　　　　　—*Est-ce qu'il y a souvent de la soupe au menu?*
　　　　　　　　—*Oui, on mange quelquefois de la soupe.*
1. viande (souvent)
2. poisson (rarement)
3. glace (quelquefois)
etc.

---

There are several problems with this activity. First, as the initial exercise of this section, it requires students to produce output immediately without giving them the opportunity to work with input. Second, and perhaps even more important, students may not understand why they are using the partitive here; they may just mechanically insert the masculine/feminine/vowel-preceding forms into the sentences to complete the drill. If the goal is to expose students to the forms of the partitive before teaching its use in discourse, it would make more sense to adapt Activity A into an input exercise, as we suggest in Activity 8.1:

● ● ● ● ●

**Activity 8.1: Au restaurant universitaire.**

How often would your French friends say that the following foods are served in the Resto U?

| 1. de la viande | toujours | souvent | rarement | jamais |
| 2. du poisson | toujours | souvent | rarement | jamais |
| 3. de la glace | toujours | souvent | rarement | jamais |

etc.

*Invitation's* Activity B seems to be out of sequence. Before students have mastered the differences between the partitive and the indefinite article, they must negate sentences that contain the partitive. In addition, Activity B (137) again requires students to produce output immediately, following the pattern shown in the model:

---

**B. Et toi?** Your French friends have asked what American students generally eat. Base your answer on what is usually served in your dining hall or on what you and your friends generally eat. Use the items listed in the preceding activity and add others that fit your situation.

Exemple: *Nous mangeons souvent de la viande, mais il n'y a jamais de poisson au menu.*

---

Not only are students asked to supply the appropriate partitive article before they have had a chance to internalize it, but they also are required to know how to use the zero article **de** after negation simultaneously. This type of activity violates Lee and VanPatten's axiom of having students attend to one grammatical feature at a time. We would suggest omitting this mechanical drill entirely.

Activity C (137), the third exercise provided in this grammar section, is summarized below:

---

**C. C'est moi le chef!** You are planning to make one or more of the following dishes (or one of your favorite recipes) to serve to some French friends. Tell some of the ingredients you'll need to buy.

Exemple: *Je vais préparer une salade. Pour cela, j'ai besoin d'acheter de la salade, des tomates, des carottes . . .*

1. une pizza          2. une salade          3. un sandwich

etc.

---

As a structured-output activity, Activity C is fine, although it should be done only after students have received enough input containing the partitive. Activity C is difficult because students need to choose between the partitive and the indefinite articles without having had the opportunity to learn thoroughly the differences between these forms. We would suggest integrating Activity 4.4 (from Chapter 4 and repeated below) first, and then have students do Activity C (using different food items in each activity). Before students perform Activity C, however, the instructor should ask them to analyze the use of articles in Activity 4.4, looking at why sometimes the partitive is used, and at other times the indefinite article, to accompany various food items:

• • • • •

### Activity 4.4: C'est vous le chef.

Select the ingredient that one does not usually find in each of the following dishes.

Une omelette: des oignons, du fromage, des champignons, du chocolat
Une tarte: de la farine, du sel, du beurre, du poivre
Un sandwich: de la mayonnaise, du maïs, du pain, de la salade
Une salade: des tomates, des pâtes, du pâté, des pommes de terre
Une salade de fruits: des cerises, du raisin, des oranges, des haricots

Follow-up question for students: Some of these food items are preceded by **des** (**des oignons, des champignons,** etc.). How do these nouns differ from the other nouns found in this activity?

There are other activities provided in Chapter 4 that would fit in well here (especially a consciousness-raising activity and/or a structured-output activity). It is important that activities follow a logical sequence and that students not be asked to study or learn more than one concept at a time. For example, after students understand the differences between the partitive and the indefinite article, they then should compare their use in discourse with the definite article. In a similar fashion, students should hypothesize when to use the zero article (**de**) in context, perhaps being asked to analyze an overhead such as the following:

---

### Overhead 9: L'article zéro

Note the articles, which are underlined throughout this passage.
Une description de ma copine, Flo:

Elle boit du vin tous les jours, mais elle ne boit pas de lait.

En fait elle boit beaucoup de vin, souvent une bouteille de vin par jour.

Elle mange beaucoup de pistaches, mais elle ne prend pas de chips pendant l'apéro.

Elle aime bien le café, mais elle n'aime pas le thé.

There are four hypotheses regarding **l'article zéro,** which students should make after studying this description:

1. The partitive article becomes **de** after negation.
2. The partitive article becomes **de** after an expression of quantity.
3. The indefinite article functions in the same way as the partitive (**de** after negation or an expression of quantity).
4. The definite article does not change to **de** after negation.

As straightforward as these rules may seem to instructors, students need to receive a good deal of input to help them internalize these rules. See Chapter 4 for some activities that could be inserted here.

Our main point is that beginning students should learn each piece of the puzzle one by one; they should not be forced to digest too much at once. They should study one part of the paradigm, receive input, and then be asked to produce output. Only after they have grasped the first concept should they move on to the next point. Thus, before asking students to do Activity D from *Invitation* (137, below) or a similar type of exercise (see Activity 8.2 below), the instructor needs to be sure that students have had enough exposure to differences between the partitive/indefinite article and the definite article in discourse (again, see Chapter 4 for activities that could be inserted here):

**D. Préférences et habitudes.** Find out if other students in your class like the following foods and how often they eat them. Tell them about your own preferences.

Exemple: la glace

—*Je mange souvent de la glace. J'adore la glace au chocolat. Et toi?*

—*Moi, je préfère la glace à la fraise.*

1. le poisson          2. le pain français          3. le fromage français
etc.

Activity D could be made less mechanical by adapting it to conform to the structured-output framework. We propose Activity 8.2 as a replacement:

• • • • •

### Activity 8.2: Préférences et habitudes.

*Step* 1: With a partner, make two lists of the things that you both eat often. Make sure that you use the partitive article for nouns you cannot count, and the indefinite article for nouns that are countable. Include 8–10 food items in your list. [Note to instructors: drinks are not included here, since students have not yet studied the verb **boire**.]

| Modèle: | Moi | Mon partenaire |
|---|---|---|
| | du porc | de la glace |
| | du rosbif | des gâteaux |
| | etc. | |

*Step* 2: Compare the two lists. What do your lists say about you and your partner? What kinds of foods do each of you like? For example, you may conclude: **j'aime la viande, mais mon partenaire préfère les desserts.** Remember to use the definite article if you use verbs such as **aimer, adorer,** or **préférer.**

*Step* 3: Make two lists of the foods that you and your partner hate. Use the verb **détester** followed by the definite article. Would you say that your dislikes and likes are typical of Americans? Why or why not?

The authors of *Invitation* provide two final activities, followed by a more open-ended task to complete this section. Activity E (137), which is commendable because it allows students to work with authentic materials, requires students to describe what they would eat for a quick breakfast or for a more leisurely one, using a pamphlet devised by the Comité Français d'Éducation pour la Santé. Activity F (138), which is more structured, contains a shopping list of items that students must buy at an **épicerie,** using expressions of quantity (**une livre de café,** etc.). The culminating activity of this section, entitled **C'est votre tour** (138), consists of a role-play where one student is shopping for various food items and his/her partner must explain that the store has run out of them.

Using a role-play activity to follow up a grammar section is common. Another typical culminating activity found in many textbooks is an open-ended discussion/question section. The goal of both types of activities is to give students the opportunity to pull together the various lexical and grammatical features, along with the cultural content, that they have studied in a particular chapter or section. In addition, both exercise types are considered "tasks," and recent studies (such as Lee 2000) have shown that task-based activities can be particularly effective at the end of a grammar section or chapter. It is important to point out that some researchers distinguish between exercises/activities and tasks. Nunan (2001) explains that "one key distinction between an exercise and a task . . . is that exercises will have purely language related outcomes, while tasks will have non-language related outcomes, as well as language related ones." Thus, for Nunan, exercises/activities may be used to focus on specific vocabulary or a particular linguistic feature, while tasks are usually longer and more concerned with a larger goal, one which tends to require a variety of skills and types of knowledge. Nunan distinguishes between two different types of *pedagogical* tasks (as opposed to *real-world* tasks, which are done outside the classroom):

- Rehearsal task: A piece of classroom work in which learners rehearse, in class, a communicative act they will carry out outside of the class.
- Activation task: A piece of classroom work involving communicative interaction, but NOT one in which learners will be rehearsing for some out-of-class communication. Rather they are designed to activate the acquisition process. (http://www3.telus.net/linguisticsissues/syllabusdesign.html)

Oates and Oukada (2006, 223) regularly provide rehearsal tasks in *Entre amis*, such as the following:

---

### L'addition s'il vous plaît.

Your partner is a waiter/waitress in a French restaurant.

1. After you have looked at the menu . . . , s/he will ask you what you are going to have.
2. Order from the menu.
3. Your partner will then ask you what you want to drink.
4. Order something to drink.
5. When you have finished, ask for the bill.
6. Your partner will verify the items you ordered.
7. Confirm or correct what s/he says.

---

Source: Oates/Oukada, *Entre amis*, Fifth Edition. Copyright © 2006 by Houghton Mifflin Company. Used with permission.

A rehearsal task such as this one is beneficial for students, because it gives them the opportunity to practice an important skill that they will need when they travel to a francophone country. This task would probably be more beneficial than the **C'est votre tour** role-play activity mentioned above, because it allows students to be creative and to take part in a more realistic (and less repetitive) exchange. To make this task even more meaningful, the instructor could precede it by showing a short clip from a French movie so that students are able to see, as well as to hear, how French people actually order in a restaurant.

Activation tasks, on the other hand, are not rehearsals for real-life events; they are often devised as forums for discussing issues of interest. Lee (2000) takes issue with the typical "discussion question" format for eliciting conversation about particular topics, because "communication is not equated with asking and answering questions; rather, communication is defined as the expression, interpretation, and negotiation of meaning" (4). In other words, a successful class discussion should be more than the teacher's asking questions and the students' (often the same ones) volunteering answers. Lee urges that students be given the opportunity to become active participants in communicative tasks. He advises teachers to keep in mind the following when designing task-based activities (34–36):

### Lee's Criteria for Structuring Activities

1. *Identify a desired informational outcome.* What information is supposed to be extracted from the interaction by the learners?
2. *Break down the topic into subtopics.* What are the relevant subcomponents of the topic?
3. *Create and sequence concrete tasks for learners to do, for example, create lists, fill in charts, make tables.* What tasks can the learners carry out to explore the subcomponents?
4. *Build in linguistic support, either lexical or grammatical or both.* What linguistic support do the learners need?

Source: Lee, *Tasks and Communicating in Language Classrooms.* © 2000 McGraw-Hill. Used with permission of The McGraw-Hill Companies.

The following activity, also from *Entre amis* (2006, 222), comes from a well-conceived chapter that compares French and American food preferences and habits. The textbook's **À vous** sections are intended for pairs of students, in order to "personalize the subject matter" for them (IAE-7). In this activity, students work with a partner to respond to a list of questions:

---

### 9. À vous. Répondez.

1. Vos amis prennent-ils le petit déjeuner d'habitude? Si oui, qu'est-ce qu'ils prennent comme boisson?

2. D'habitude, qu'est-ce que vous prenez comme boisson au petit déjeuner? au déjeuner? au dîner?

3. Qu'est-ce que vous avez pris comme boisson ce matin?

4. Qu'est-ce que la plupart des Français prennent comme boisson au dîner?

5. Qu'est-ce que vous allez prendre si vous dînez dans un restaurant français?

6. Si vous commandez un dessert, que prenez-vous d'habitude?

7. Comprenez-vous toujours les menus qui sont en français?

8. Avez-vous appris à faire la cuisine?

---

Source: Oates/Oukada, *Entre amis*, Fifth Edition. Copyright © 2006 by Houghton Mifflin Company. Used with permission.

Although students may find some of these questions stimulating, the activity could be more task-based; specifically, it could allow students to arrive at conclusions that are more complex and thought-provoking.

In order to adapt this activity into a task, modeling the examples suggested by Lee (2000) and Lee and VanPatten (2003), students must negotiate meaning and arrive at their own conclusions. Consider the task below (which is provided in English but which should be done with students in French). Note that it begins with a list of its goals and the procedures that should be followed (this information is for the instructor, not the students). It would be a suitable replacement for Activity 9 above, because it allows students to pull together what they have already read about French and American culinary differences:

• • • • •

### Activity 8.3: Task: A Comparison of American and French Eating Habits.

1. *Desired informational outcome:* Students discuss and analyze whether there are true differences between what Americans and French people eat and how each group conceives of food and eating.

2. *Subtopics*: Students compare an individual American with Americans in general and with French people in general.

3. *Concrete tasks*: Provide students with checklists to focus attention on particular nutritional habits; ask students to create lists, compare data with partners, and then discuss the topics with larger groups.

4. *Lexical and linguistic support*: Vocabulary: food and meals; Grammar: articles (partitive, indefinite, definite, expressions of quantity).

*Step* 1: With a partner, check whether you think that each sentence describes you, your partner, Americans in general, and French people in general.

| | | | | |
|---|---|---|---|---|
| Eat a large breakfast. | Me | My partner | Americans | French people |
| Eat large portions. | Me | My partner | Americans | French people |
| Eat between meals. | Me | My partner | Americans | French people |
| Eat a dessert with both lunch and dinner. | Me | My partner | Americans | French people |
| Drink coffee after lunch and dinner. | Me | My partner | Americans | French people |
| Eat a lot of frozen foods. | Me | My partner | Americans | French people |
| Eat a lot of foods with high fat content. | Me | My partner | Americans | French people |
| Exercise regularly and are concerned with being in shape. | Me | My partner | Americans | French people |
| Walk a lot. | Me | My partner | Americans | French people |

*Step* 2: Make a list of what Americans and French people usually eat for breakfast, lunch, dinner, and snacks.

| | Americans | French people |
|---|---|---|
| Breakfast | | |
| Lunch | | |
| Dinner | | |
| Snacks | | |

*Step 3:* Ask your partner what he or she ate for breakfast, lunch, and dinner yesterday. Did he or she have any snacks?

Breakfast: _____

Lunch: _____

Dinner: _____

Snacks: _____

*Step 4:* Would you say that your partner is a typical American in terms of his or her eating habits? Why or why not? On a scale of 1 (very typically American) to 5 (not very typically American), where would you place your partner? And what about yourself?

*Step 5:* Do you think that American eating habits have changed in your lifetime? How about French eating habits? List the changes.

*Step 6:* If you answered yes in Step 5, what are the social and personal implications of changes in American and French dietary habits? List 3–5 implications.

*Step 7:* Contradictions: Do you find any inconsistencies between American and French attitudes toward food/health/exercise and how Americans and French people actually live their lives? For example, Americans exercise a lot, but they eat more junk food than any other people on the planet. Make a list of 3–5 other contradictions.

*Step 8:* Suggestions: Make a list of 3–5 suggestions to Americans and French people for eating in a healthier manner and developing a healthier lifestyle.

Note that the goal of this task is to facilitate a conversation and to get all students involved in the discussion. Students will work with new vocabulary (food items), become more aware of cultural differences, learn points of grammar (determiners), and practice forming complete sentences. As a follow-up activity, pairs of students could join with other pairs to compare answers. Doing so would facilitate moving from producing sentences to creating connected discourse. Finally, there could be a short class discussion to summarize the findings of the various groups.

Although a task such as this one does not teach grammar per se; it promotes grammatical accuracy for more efficient communication. Students are obligated to attend to many different factors simultaneously; if they have had enough exposure to and practice of the vocabulary and grammar topics before being asked to complete the task, however, they should be ready. It is important to note that performing this kind of task too early would defeat its purpose, which is to tie together all one has learned about a particular topic and to communicate effectively about it. Instructors should plan their lessons to move from short activities that deal with one particular form-meaning connection, to more global, all-encompassing tasks.

## SOME FINAL CONSIDERATIONS

The impetus for this book was to provide instructors with concrete ideas for integrating the study of grammar, especially discourse grammar, into the communicative French language classroom. We must add that there is reason for hope that teaching grammar as communication is catching on. It seems that some textbooks are beginning to rethink how they present grammar, taking into consideration findings in applied linguistics research. For example, in *Rapports* (Walz and Piriou, 2003) and *Voilà* (Heilenman, Kaplan, and Tournier, 2006), one finds sections that point out differences between spoken and written language forms and usage. In *Rapports*, these passages are called **Ce qu'ils disent.** The authors note that "this section appears whenever applicable to explain that spoken French is not exactly like the more formal language taught in textbooks. While students should learn a fairly formal style, these explanations will help them understand what they will hear in a French-speaking country" (IAE-14). The following example from Walz and Piriou (2003, 39) contrasts spoken and written negation:

---

### Ce qu'ils disent

In casual conversations, the French leave out the **ne** of the negation. This is particularly the case with young people. However, they would never write that way, and you must always use **ne** to maintain an appropriate style.

---

| Speaking | Writing |
|----------|---------|
| On mange pas beaucoup. | On ne mange pas beaucoup. |
| Il écoute pas la radio. | Il n'écoute pas la radio. |
| C'est pas un stylo. | Ce n'est pas un stylo. |

Source: Walz/Piriou, *Rapports*, Fifth Edition. Copyright © 2003 by Houghton Mifflin Company. Used with permission.

Unfortunately, even in many texts that attempt to elucidate differences between spoken and written forms, the dialogues provided still are not sociolinguistically appropriate; that is, spoken conversations still contain many elements of written French, despite textbook authors' efforts to represent the spoken language. Textbooks should present what people actually say and then enhance (using highlighting, italics, a different font, etc.) elements of the informal, spoken language that should not be used in writing. Similarly, they could explain in a footnote what one might find in the written language or in a more formal context. In addition, aspects of the written language (such as a missing **ne** or **est-ce que**) could be inserted in parentheses in order to show students where these elements would appear in writing.

Another reason for optimism about the teaching of grammar is that some textbooks, such as Thompson and Phillips's (2004) *Mais oui!*, now make an effort to present inductive grammar explanations along with exercises that include structured input. *Mais oui!*, in fact, introduces every new grammar point with a brief inductive exercise. For example, when teaching students about the differences between **c'est** and **il est,** Thompson and Phillips provide the following introduction (33):

---

### Structure: Identifying people and things (III)

Les expressions **C'est/Il (Elle) est**

Observez et déduisez: Tu connais le monsieur là-bas (*over there*)? C'est un Français. C'est Monsieur Courteplaque, le papa de Marie-Edwige. Il est sérieux et intelligent. Et voilà la femme de Monsieur Courteplaque. Elle est française aussi. Elle est très sympathique. C'est une journaliste.

---

> • Is the expression **c'est** followed by a noun or an adjective? And the expression **il/elle est?**

Source: Thompson/Phillips, *Mais oui!*, Third Edition. Copyright © 2004 by Houghton Mifflin Company. Used with permission.

This technique is effective for focusing students' attention on the differences between **c'est** and **il/elle est,** all within a clearly defined discourse environment. The authors then go on to present the rules deductively. Unfortunately, there is a problem with this particular explanation: it leads students to believe that **c'est** is always followed by a noun. Clearly this is not the case, as one could quite easily add a sentence such as **C'est intéressant, non?** to the end of the paragraph given above. Students should be led to hypothesize that **c'est** may be followed by an adjective when the adjective refers to an entire idea and is not used to describe a particular person, place, or thing.

Although we see why the authors do not want to complicate matters at such an early stage in the curriculum, it is not a good idea to oversimplify explanations and lead students to develop erroneous hypotheses. **C'est** + adjective is a very common construction that students will probably begin hearing almost immediately. Teachers often say things like: **C'est excellent!, C'est parfait!,** or **C'est dommage.** It is confusing and counterproductive for students to construct an inaccurate hypothesis of how grammar functions. On the other hand, this inductive presentation is commendable and a pedagogical step in the right direction.

Unfortunately, many textbooks still present grammar in an entirely deductive manner, accompanied by sentence-level mechanical exercises. Some of these same books are the most creative and sophisticated in terms of their content, which makes the flaws in the grammar instruction particularly disconcerting. As we have stressed throughout this book, instructors who choose or are required to work with textbooks that are deficient in their grammar presentations and exercises will need to develop their own supplementary overheads and activities.

To summarize some of the main points of this book, we urge instructors to follow the guidelines below when they create lesson plans and adapt the grammar sections in their textbooks:

1. Elements of the spoken language may be integrated at every level. As Walz and Piriou (2003) demonstrate in *Rapports*, there is no reason why

students, even those at the beginning level, cannot distinguish between written vs. spoken French and among register distinctions.

2. Students should be encouraged to work as researchers (using authentic materials), even as early as the beginning level.

3. Students should receive a great deal of input, in context, before they are asked to produce grammatical forms. If a textbook does not provide input activities, the instructor should create and implement them.

4. An entire paradigm should not be taught at once. For example, some textbooks have stopped teaching all the direct- and indirect-object pronouns simultaneously. Depending on the students' level, an instructor may consider teaching only a few forms of a verb conjugation at a time.

5. Grammar topics that are rarely used should be eliminated entirely from first-year textbooks. For example, multiple object pronouns of the **Elle lui y en a donné** variety could certainly wait until more advanced levels. In addition, the more obscure uses of the subjunctive should be put off until later.

6. An inductive approach should be used to teach most grammatical items. Students will remember rules better when they have figured them out themselves. Raise students' consciousness about grammatical forms and functions when necessary. Skip the minor points at the elementary level unless they are forms that students will come across frequently.

7. Grammar should be recycled regularly throughout the semester. Certain textbooks (for example, *Chez nous* and *Voilà*) make it a point to keep reintroducing and reusing the same structures. Other books are less attentive to this matter, and instructors must make an effort to integrate earlier material into current lessons.

8. Finally, it is important for instructors never to underestimate the value of an eclectic approach. Variety is essential for maintaining students' interest. In addition, students may have different learning styles (visual, auditory, or kinesthetic), and while some may respond well to a flood of input, others may require a more metalinguistic or hands-on approach.

Nobody ever said that teaching French grammar was going to be easy; however, a combination of knowledge about how the language functions mixed with some strategies for developing meaningful activities can go a long way. We hope that this book has given you the confidence and expertise to teach grammar more communicatively. You should also now be better equipped to answer students' questions about the use of grammar in discourse. Finally, we also hope that the variety of approaches and methods for teaching grammar that we have provided will stimulate your creativity, even when it comes to teaching the least inspiring of grammatical constructions. If you have ever seen your students' eyes start to glaze over during deductively constructed grammar explanations, we think that you will agree that it is worth it to implement some new techniques.

## DISCUSSION TOPICS / PROJECTS

1. It is often said that one cannot properly evaluate a textbook before having the opportunity to teach with it. Have you ever used a promising textbook only to discover that it had serious flaws or drawbacks? What was the problem? Is there any way that this situation could have been avoided?

2. Make a checklist of features that are important to you in a textbook. Then, decide whether the textbook you are currently using meets your criteria. In which areas is your current textbook most lacking? Compare your checklist with those of a few colleagues. Do you have similar requirements? Would you guess that you have a similar teaching style and/or philosophy?

3. Do you see fundamental differences in the way ESL course syllabi (for second language learners who live in the target culture) and foreign language course syllabi should be developed, particularly in regard to task-based instruction? As mentioned above, some proponents of task-based curricula believe that instructors should conduct a needs analysis as the point of departure for any curriculum design. Do you agree that this is necessary for teaching French as a foreign language? What are the needs of students studying French in the United States? How do these needs differ, for example, from that of a businessperson who will be living in France for an extended period of time?

4. Distinguish between the relative merits of rehearsal tasks (for use in the real world) and activation tasks (for language acquisition and class discussion purposes). Do you see a place for both in elementary and intermediate French language programs?

5. If you are not a native speaker of French, for which real world tasks do you feel that your own French classes did not prepare you? Were the deficiencies in grammar, vocabulary, or cultural knowledge? Describe a situation or two where you have found yourself unable to communicate effectively in French. Are there still areas in which you feel inadequate? How could you fill in some of these gaps? Are there areas in

which you are similarly unprepared in your native language? Is the difficulty only because of a lack of appropriate vocabulary, or are there other reasons?

6. It has been said that a good teacher can adapt any textbook to suit his or her needs. Do you agree with this statement, or should it be modified?

7. The issue of oversimplifying grammatical points to make them accessible to students is a problem that many textbook writers face. Do you think that it is better to give students too much or too little information in grammar explanations? Too much information risks complicating matters needlessly for students, and too little information may lead them to develop inaccurate hypotheses. What criteria can textbook authors or teachers employ to decide what constitutes enough information in a grammatical explanation?

8. If you had the choice of using a textbook that contained excellent materials for teaching grammar but weak resources for teaching culture or a textbook that had the opposite problem (excellent cultural materials but poorly constructed grammar presentations and exercises), which book would you choose? Which book would be easier to supplement? Do you find it easier to create sound grammatical resources or to find and design cultural materials and activities? Why?

## FURTHER READING

### Task-based Instruction and Learning

Lee, James F. *Tasks and Communicating in Language Classrooms*. New York: McGraw-Hill, 2000.

Long, Michael. "A Role for Instruction in Second Language Acquisition: Task-based Language Training." In *Modelling and Assessing Second Language Acquisition*, edited by Kenneth Hyltenstam and Manfred Oienemann, 77–99. Clevedon, UK: Mutlilingual Matters, 1985.

Nunan, David. *Designing Tasks for the Communicative Classroom*. Cambridge: Cambridge University Press, 1989.

———. "Communicative Tasks and the Language Classroom." *TESOL Quarterly* 25 (1989): 279–295.

### Syllabus and Curriculum Design

Brown, James Dean. *Elements of Language Curriculum: A Systematic Approach to Program Development*. Boston: Heinle, 1994.

Nunan, David. *Syllabus Design: Language Teaching, a Scheme for Teacher Education*. Oxford: Oxford University Press, 1988.

Richards, Jack C. *Curriculum Development in Language Teaching*. Cambridge: Cambridge University Press, 2001.

# Notes

## CHAPTER 2. WHAT IS GRAMMAR?

1. There is a parallel here with the philosophy that one should not translate vocabulary items for students, the rationale being that it is better for learners to associate the target word with its referent, not with its English translation. Teachers sometimes realize the absurdity of spending thirty seconds trying to act out a particular noun (often unsuccessfully) while students guess what it means, when it would probably have been more efficient and effective simply to provide a two-second, one-word translation of the expression in question.

2. It is worth pointing out here that instructors of English (as a first language!) sometimes have the same complaints about their students' writing skills.

## CHAPTER 3. METHODS FOR TEACHING GRAMMAR

1. Our focus is on first- and second-year college French textbooks, but the same problems exist in high school textbooks as well.

2. An exclamation point is used to denote sentences that may be grammatically correct in another context.

3. There are, however, a large number of ESL methods textbooks.

4. Note that an asterisk is used to denote a sentence that is grammatically incorrect.

5. The term "difficult" is challenging to define (see Hulstijn 1995). We are appealing to teachers' intuitions here, as they have a sense of what students tend to pick up "easily," and what concepts are more challenging.

## CHAPTER 4. ARTICLES

1. It would be possible to translate this sentence as *The snakes are reptiles*, depending on the context. However, it would be very odd to translate it as *The snakes are some reptiles*.

2. It could be argued that in an utterance such as **Je voudrais du vin,** the wine could indeed be identifiable (the speaker could be pointing at a bottle of wine, and everyone would be able to see the wine in question). However, there is a distinction to be made between **le vin,** which would mean all the wine in the bottle (and thus clearly be iden-

tifiable), and **du vin,** which would denote some (an unidentified amount) of the wine in the bottle.

3. Unfortunately, there are some exceptions to this rule, such as **du raisin.** French speakers, however, are beginning to accept **des raisins** as grammatical.

4. The exception to this rule is when the main verb is **être,** as in **Ce n'est pas un chien.**

5. The inspiration for this activity comes from McCarthy and Carter (1995).

6. This is an extended version of an activity presented in Katz 2001.

7. This example comes from Langacker (1987), who created the sentence: "After I ran over the cat with our car, there was cat all over the driveway" (67).

## CHAPTER 5. NARRATIVE PAST TENSES

1. The **passé simple** performs similar functions to the **passé composé** in literary narrative discourse. For more information regarding the use of the **passé simple** in narrative contexts, see Di Vito 1997.

2. Adapted from French 103 class materials—University of Chicago; reprinted with the permission of Nadine O'Connor Di Vito, University of Chicago.

3. Thanks to Nadine O'Connor Di Vito and Claude Grangier of the University of Chicago for sharing their materials with us.

## CHAPTER 6. WORD-ORDER CONSTRUCTIONS IN THE SPOKEN AND WRITTEN LANGUAGES

1. We would like to thank Knud Lambrecht for passing this reference along to us.

2. It should be noted that some linguists have questioned the rationale behind trying to make non-native speakers indistinguishable from native speakers, since this is often an impossible, and not necessarily desirable, goal (see Kramsch 1997).

3. Some linguists refer to these constructions as the "topic" and "antitopic" constructions (Lambrecht 1994) or as left and right "detachments." We will use the term "dislocations" throughout this book, but all these terms are acceptable.

4. Note that the subscript $_i$ is used to indicate that two expressions are co-referential, that is, when they refer to the same entity.

5. Note that a clause almost always contains a subject and a verb, whereas a phrase can consist of a noun and its accompanying determiner (noun phrase), a preposition and a noun (prepositional phrase), etc. A phrase may consist of only one word, as in a proper name or an adverbial expression (*there, here,* etc.).

6. Note that **c'est** almost always replaces **ce sont** in spoken French, even when **le bon usage** would dictate that one should say **ce sont.** Thus in spoken French, one would find, for example, **C'est eux** instead of **Ce sont eux.** Variations on **c'est** are possible, although not all that frequent, within the cleft, as in the following examples:

• **Ça doit être** ma mère qui a fait ça.
• **C'était** lui qui était venu.
• **Ce sera** demain que tu comprendras.

7. Below we present a case where there is no pitch accent following **c'est,** but this phenomenon is rare.

8. As numerous linguists have pointed out (Lambrecht 1994, for example), however, one can find indefinite articles in this position when they refer to a generic category, as in the following example from the film *Les Compères*. After being hit in the head several times with a telephone receiver, a character laments: "Un téléphone, c'est pas fait pour ça." In this case, the speaker is not referring to a specific unidentifiable telephone, but to phones in general.

9. It is important to point out that the English it-cleft is used differently than the **c'est-**cleft in discourse, mainly because it is never required. Sometimes it may sound rather formal; it is often employed as a literary device or found in formal speech. In general, the it-cleft appears to be used more for stylistic reasons than for pragmatic ones, and it is found much less frequently in the spoken language than the **c'est-**cleft.

10. As always, there is an exception to prove the rule. There is one type of **c'est-**cleft that is very rare in French and that is usually found either in written form or at the beginning of a public speech. An example of this type is "C'est en 1900, à la Belle Époque, en plein Art Nouveau que Rodin dévoile sa fameuse 'Porte de l'Enfer'" (Rodin PostcardBook). There is no pitch accent on **1900,** and the information following **que** is not presupposed. Since this utterance may be "unclefted" without any problem, one could argue that it is indeed a cleft. Because it is so rare, we will not worry about it too much here. It is interesting to note that this same structure is also found, albeit infrequently, in English.

11. Activities 6.7 and 6.8 and their accompanying explanations are updated versions of descriptions provided in Katz 2000a, reprinted with the permission of the *French Review*.

# Bibliography

American Council on the Teaching of Foreign Languages. *ACTFL Proficiency Guidelines*. Hastings-on-Hudson, NY: ACTFL, 1986.

Andersen, Roger W. "El desarollo de la morfología en el español como segundo idioma." In *Adquisición del lenguaje—Aquisição da linguagem*, edited by Jürgen M. Meisel, 115–139. Frankfurt am Main: Vervuert Verlag, 1986.

———. "Models, Processes, Principles and Strategies: Second Language Acquisition inside and outside the Classroom." In *Second Language Acquisition—Foreign Language Learning*, edited by Bill VanPatten and James Lee, 45–78. Clevedon, UK: Multilingual Matters, 1990.

———. "Developmental Sequences: The Emergence of Aspect Marking in Second Language Acquisition." In *Second Language Acquisition and Linguistic Theories*, edited by Charles A. Ferguson and Thom Huebner, 305–324. Amsterdam: John Benjamins, 1991.

———. "Four Operating Principles and Input Distribution as Explanations for Underdeveloped and Mature Morphological Systems." In *Progression and Regression in Language*, edited by Kenneth Hyltenstam and Ake Viborg, 309–339. Cambridge: Cambridge University Press, 1993.

Andrews, Barry. "Aspect in Past Tenses in English and French." *International Revue of Applied Linguistics* 30 (1992): 169–189.

Ashby, William J. "The Syntax, Pragmatics, and Sociolinguistics of Left- and Right-Dislocations in French." *Lingua* 75 (1988): 203–229.

Ayoun, Dalila, and M. Rafael Salaberry, eds. *Tense and Aspect in Romance Languages: Theoretical and Applied Perspectives*. Amsterdam: John Benjamins, 2005.

Ball, Rodney. *Colloquial French Grammar: A Practical Guide*. Oxford: Basil Blackwell, 2000.

Bardovi-Harlig, Kathleen. "The Relationship of Form and Meaning: A Cross-sectional Study of Tense and Aspect in the Interlanguage of Learners of English as a Second Language." *Applied Psycholinguistics* 13 (1992): 253–278.

———. "A Narrative Perspective on the Development of the Tense/Aspect System in Second Language Acquisition." *Studies in Second Language Acquisition* 17 (1995): 263–291.

———. "Narrative Structure and Lexical Aspect: Conspiring Factors in Second Language Acquisition of Tense-aspect Morphology." *Studies in Second Language Acquisition* 20 (1998): 471–508.

———. *Tense and Aspect in Second Language Acquisition. Form, Meaning and Use*. Oxford: Basil Blackwell, 2000.

Barnes, Betsy K. "Apports de l'analyse à l'enseignement de la langue." *French Review* 64 (1990): 95–107.

Barson, John. *La Grammaire à l'œuvre*. Fifth Edition. Fort Worth: Harcourt Brace, 1996.

Batchelor, R. E., and Offord, M. H. *Using French: A Guide to Contemporary Usage*. Cambridge: Cambridge University Press, 2000.

Bergström, Anna. "The Expression of Past Temporal Reference by English-speaking Learners of French." PhD diss., Pennsylvania State University, 1995.

Berman, Ruth A., and Dan I. Slobin. *Relating Events in Narrative: A Cross-Linguistic Developmental Study*. Hillsdale, NJ: Lawrence Erlbaum, 1994.

Bley-Vroman, Robert. "Hypothesis Testing in Second-Language Acquisition Theory." *Language Learning* 36 (1986): 353–376.

Blyth, Carl. "Evaluation in Oral Québécois Narratives: The Function of Non-referential Meaning in Discourse." PhD diss., Cornell University, 1990.

———. "A Constructivist Approach to Grammar: Teaching Teachers to Teach Aspect." *Modern Language Journal* 81 (1997): 50–66.

———. "Toward a Pedagogical Discourse Grammar: Techniques for Teaching Word Order Constructions." In *Form and Meaning: Multiple Perspectives*. AAUSC Issues in Language Program Direction, edited by James Lee and Albert Valdman, 183–229. Boston: Heinle, 1999.

———. "Between Orality and Literacy: Developing a Pedagogical Norm for Narrative Discourse." In *Pedagogical Norms for Second and Foreign Language Learning and Teaching*, edited by Susan Gass, Kathleen Bardovi-Harlig, Sally Magnan, and Joel Walz, 241–274. Amsterdam: John Benjamins, 2002.

———. From Empirical Findings to the Teaching of Aspectual Distinctions." In *Tense and Aspect in Romance Languages: Theoretical and Applied Perspectives*, edited by Dalila Ayoun and M. Rafael Salaberry, 211–252. Amsterdam: John Benjamins, 2005.

———, Karen Kelton, and Nancy Guilloteau. *Français interactif*. (2004). http://www.laits.utexas.edu/fi.

Bonin, Thérèse. "The Role of Colloquial French in Communication and Implications for Language Instruction." *Modern Language Journal* 62 (1978): 80–102.

Bragger, Jeannette D., and Donald B. Rice. *Allons-y*. Sixth Edition. Boston: Thomson, 2004.

Brown, James Dean. *The Elements of Language Curriculum: A Systematic Approach to Program Development*. Boston: Heinle, 1994.

Canale, Michael. "From Communicative Competence to Communicative Language Pedagogy." In *Language and Communication*, edited by Jack C. Richards and Richard W. Schmidt, 2–27. London: Longman, 1983.

———, and Merrill Swain. "Theoretical Bases of Communicative Approaches to Second Language Teaching and Testing." *Applied Linguistics* 1 (1980): 1–47.

Carduner, Sylvie, and M. Peter Hagiwara. *D'accord: la prononciation du français international: Acquisition et perfectionnement*. Hoboken, NJ: Wiley, 1982.

Celce-Murcia, Marianne, Zoltán Dörnyei, and Sarah Thurrell. "Direct Approaches in L2 Instruction: A Turning Point in Communicative Language Teaching?" *TESOL Quarterly* 31 (1997): 141–152.

Celce-Murcia, Marianne, and Diane Larsen-Freeman. *The Grammar Book*. Boston: Heinle, 1999.

Celce-Murcia, Marianne, and Elite Olshtain. *Discourse and Context in Language Teaching.* Cambridge: Cambridge University Press, 2000.

Cirko, Leslaw. "Traditional Grammar: A Brake or Stimulus for University Grammar." *Studia Linguistica* 21 (2002): 31–42.

Comrie, Bernard. *Aspect.* Cambridge: Cambridge University Press, 1976.

Connor, Meryl. "A Processing Strategy Using Visual Representation to Convey the *Passé Composé/Imparfait* Distinction in French." *International Revue of Applied Linguistics* 30 (1992): 321–328.

Cook, Guy. *Language Play, Language Learning.* Oxford: Oxford University Press, 2000.

Coveney, Aidan. "The Use of the QU-final Interrogative Structure in Spoken French." *Journal of French Language Studies* 5 (1995): 143–171.

———. "L'Approche variationniste et la description de la grammaire du français: le cas des interrogatives." *Langue Française* 115 (1996): 88–100.

Cox, Thomas J. "How to See What to Say in French." *French Review* 68 (1994): 203–208.

Crookes, Graham. "SLA and Language Pedagogy: A Socio-Educational Perspective." *Studies in Second Language Acquisition* 19 (1997): 93–116.

Dansereau, Diane. "A Discussion of Techniques Used in the Teaching of the *Passé Composé/Imparfait* Distinction in French." *French Review* 61 (1987): 33–38.

———. "Patterns of Second Language Development in French Immersion." *French Language Studies* 2 (1992): 159–183.

Declerck, Renaat. *Studies on Copular Sentences, Clefts and Pseudo-Clefts.* Louvain: Foris, 1998.

DeKeyser, Robert, and Karl Sokalski. "The Differential Role of Comprehension and Production Practice." *Language Learning* 46 (1996): 613–642.

Di Vito, Nadine O'Connor. "Incorporating Native Speaker Norms in Second Language Materials." *Applied Linguistics* 12 (1991): 383–395.

———. "'Present' Concerns about French Language Teaching." *Modern Language Journal* 76 (1992): 50–57.

———. "Using Native Speech to Formulate Past-Tense Rules in French." *Georgetown University Roundtable on Languages and Linguistics* (1995): 188–197.

———. *Patterns across Spoken and Written French.* Boston: Houghton Mifflin, 1997.

Dörnyei, Zoltán, and Sarah Thurrell. "Teaching Conversational Skills Intensively: Course Content and Rationale." *ELT Journal* 48 (1994): 40–49.

Douay, Catherine. "Grammar and Interlocution: English Articles as Markers of Recipient Role." *Revue Québécoise de Linguistique* 29 (2001): 79–94.

Doughty, Catherine. "Instructed SLA: Constraints, Compensation and Enhancement." In *The Handbook of Second Language Acquisition,* edited by Catherine Doughty and Michael Long, 256–310. Malden, MA: Basil Blackwell, 2003.

———, and Jessica Williams. *Focus on Form in Classroom Second Language Acquisition.* Cambridge: Cambridge University Press, 1998.

Dubos, Ulrika. *L'Explication grammaticale du thème anglais.* Paris: Nathan, 1990.

Ellis, Rod. *SLA Research and Language Teaching.* Oxford: Oxford University Press, 1997.

———. "Teaching and Research: Options in Grammar Teaching." *TESOL Quarterly* 32 (1998): 39–60.

———. "The Place of Grammar Instruction in the Second/Foreign Language Curriculum." In *New Perspectives on Grammar Teaching in Second Language Classrooms*, edited by Eli Hinkel and Sandra Fotos, 17–34. Mahwah, NJ: Lawrence Erlbaum, 2002a.

———. "Methodological Options in Grammar Teaching Materials." In *New Perspectives on Grammar Teaching in Second Language Classrooms*, edited by Eli Hinkel and Sandra Fotos, 155–179. Mahwah, NJ: Lawrence Erlbaum, 2002b.

Ferdinand, Astrid. "Acquisition of Syntactic Topic Marking in L2 French." *Linguistics in the Netherlands* (2002): 49–59.

Flashner, Vanessa E. "Transfer of Aspect in the English Oral Narratives of Russian Speakers." In *Transfer in Language Production*, edited by Hans Dechert and Manfred Raupach, 71–97. Norwood, NJ: Ablex, 1989.

Fleischman, Suzanne. *Tense and Narrativity: From Medieval Performance to Modern Fiction*. Austin, TX: University of Texas Press, 1990.

Fotos, Sandra. "Integrating Grammar Instruction and Communicative Language Use through Grammar Consciousness-Raising Tasks." *TESOL Quarterly* 28 (1994): 323–351.

Fouletier-Smith, Nicole. *Parallèles: Communication et culture*. Third Edition. Upper Saddle River, NJ: Prentice Hall, 2004.

Fox, Cynthia. "Communicative Competence and Beliefs about Language among Graduate Teaching Assistants of French." *Modern Language Journal* 77 (1993): 313–324.

Garrett, Nina. "The Problem with Grammar: What Kind Can the Language Learner Use?" *Modern Language Journal* 70 (1986): 133–148.

Gass, Susan, Kathleen Bardovi-Harlig, Sally Sieloff Magnan, and Joel Walz, eds. *Pedagogical Norms for Second and Foreign Language Learning and Teaching*. Amsterdam: John Benjamins, 2002.

Giacomi, Alain. "Étude des structures d'énoncés dans un corpus relevé à Marseille—la subordination." PhD diss., Université d'Aix-en-Provence, 1980.

Giessing, Jürgen. "Learning a Foreign Language in Spite of the Textbook: Further Notes on the Role of Textbooks in Foreign Language Learning." *Praxis des neusprachlichen Unterrichts* 50 (2003): 91–93.

Glisan, Eileen, and Victor Drescher. "Textbook Grammar: Does It Reflect Native Speaker Speech?" *Modern Language Journal* 77 (1993): 23–33.

Grevisse, Maurice. *Le Bon usage*. Louvain-la-Neuve: Duculot, 1993.

———, and André Goosse. *Nouvelle grammaire française*. Louvain-la-Neuve: Duculot, 1995.

Harley, Birgit. *Age in Second Language Acquisition*. Avon, UK: Multilingual Matters, 1986.

———. "Patterns of Second Language Development in French Immersion." *Journal of French Language Studies* 2 (1992): 245–260.

———, and Merrill Swain. "The Interlanguage of Immersion Students and Its Implications for Second Language Teaching." In *Interlanguage*, edited by Alan Davies, C. Criper, and A. P. R. Howett, 291–311. Edinburgh: Edinburgh University Press, 1984.

Harper, Jane, Madeleine Gélineau Lively, and Mary Williams. *Thèmes*. Boston: Heinle, 2000.

Harris, Julian, and André Lévêque. *Basic Conversational French*. New York: Holt, Rinehart and Winston, 1978.

Hatch, Evelyn. *Discourse and Language Education*. Cambridge: Cambridge University Press, 1992.

Heilenman, L. Kathy, Isabelle Kaplan, and Claude Toussaint Tournier. *Voilà.* Fifth Edition. Boston: Thomson, 2006.

Herschensohn, Julia. "The Predictability of the Article in French." In *Contemporary Studies in Romance Linguistics,* edited by Margarita Suñer, 176–193. Washington, DC: Georgetown University Press, 1977.

———. "Linguistic Accuracy of Textbook Grammar." *Modern Language Journal* 72 (1988): 409–414.

Hinkel, Eli, and Sandra Fotos, eds. *New Perspectives on Grammar Teaching in Second Language Classrooms.* Mahwah, NJ: Lawrence Erlbaum, 2002.

Hoffmann, Léon-François, and Jean-Marie Schultz. *L'Essentiel de la grammaire française.* Third Edition. Englewood Cliffs, NJ: Prentice Hall, 1995.

Hornby, Nick. *High Fidelity.* New York: Riverhead, 1995.

Hulstijn, Jan H. "Not All Grammar Rules Are Equal: Giving Grammar Instruction Its Proper Place in Foreign Language Teaching." In *Attention and Awareness in Foreign Language Learning,* edited by Richard W. Schmidt, 359–386. Honolulu: University of Hawaii Press, 1995.

Jarvis, Gilbert A., Thérèse M. Bonin, Diane W. Birckbichler, and Anne Lair. *Invitation au monde francophone.* Second Edition. Boston: Thomson, 2005.

Jespersen, Otto. *Analytic Syntax.* Copenhagen: Levin and Munksgaard, 1937.

Joseph, John E. "New French: A Pedagogical Crisis in the Making." *Modern Language Journal* 72 (1988): 31–36.

Kaplan, Marsha. "Developmental Patterns of Past Tense Acquisition Among Foreign Language Learners of French." In *Foreign Language Learning: A Research Perspective,* edited by Bill VanPatten, Trisha Dvorak, and James Lee, 52–60. Cambridge, MA: Newbury House, 1987.

Katz, Stacey. "The Syntactic and Pragmatic Properties of the C'est-Cleft Construction." PhD diss., University of Texas at Austin, 1997.

———. "A Functional Approach to the Teaching of the French C'est-Cleft." *French Review* 74 (2000a): 248–262.

———. "Categories of C'est-Cleft Constructions." *Revue Canadienne de Linguistique* 45 (2000b): 1001–1021.

———. "Teaching Articles: How Students Can Master the French Determiner System." *French Review* 75 (2001): 290–304.

———. "France After September 11th: From the Perspectives of Young French Adults." *French Review* 77 (2004): 500–512.

Kerr, Betsy. *Minnesota Corpus of Spoken French.* Minneapolis: University of Minnesota, 1983.

———. "Variant Word-Order Constructions: To Teach or Not To Teach? Evidence from Learner Narratives." In *Pedagogical Norms for Second and Foreign Language Learning and Teaching,* edited by Susan Gass, Kathleen Bardovi-Harlig, Sally Sieloff Magnan, and Joel Walz, 183–200. Amsterdam: John Benjamins, 2002.

Kramsch, Claire. "The Privilege of the Non-Native Speaker." *PMLA* 112 (1997): 359–369.

Krashen, Stephen D. *Principles and Practice in Second Language Acquisition.* New York: Pergamon, 1982.

Kumpf, Lorraine. "Temporal Systems and Universality in Interlanguage: A Case Study." In

*Universals of Second Language Acquisition*, edited by Fred Eckman, Diane Nelson, and Lawrence H. Bell, 132–143. Rowley, MA: Newbury House, 1984.

Labov, William. "The Transformation of Experience in Narrative Syntax." In *Language in the Inner City: Studies in Black English Vernacular*, edited by William Labov, 354–396. Philadelphia: University of Pennsylvania Press, 1972.

———, and Joshua Waletsky. "Narrative Analysis: Oral Versions of Personal Experience." In *Essays on the Verbal and Visual Arts*, edited by June Helm, 12–44. Seattle: University of Washington Press, 1967.

Lambrecht, Knud. *Topic, Antitopic and Verb Agreement in Non-Standard French*. Amsterdam: John Benjamins, 1981.

———. "On the Topic of SVO Sentences in French Discourse." In *Coherence and Grounding in Discourse*, edited by Russell Tomlin, 217–261. Amsterdam: John Benjamins, 1987.

———. "Presentational Cleft Constructions in Spoken French." In *Clause-Combining in Grammar and Discourse*, edited by John Haiman and Sandra A. Thompson. Amsterdam: John Benjamins, 1988.

———. *Information Structure and Sentence Form*. Cambridge: Cambridge University Press, 1994.

———. "Topic, Focus, and Secondary Predication. The French Presentational Relative Construction." In *Proceedings of Going Romance 2000*, edited by Claire Beyssade, Reineke Bok-Bennema, Frank Drijkoningen, and Paola Monachesi, 171–212. Amsterdam: John Benjamins, 2002.

———, and Kevin Lemoine. "Vers une grammaire des compléments d'objet zéro en français parlé." In *Absence de marques et représentation de l'absence. Travaux Linguistiques du CerLiCO*, 9, edited by Jean Chuquet and Marc Fryd, 279–309. Rennes: Presses Universitaires de Rennes, 1995.

Langacker, Ronald W. "Nouns and Verbs." *Language* 64 (1987): 53–94.

Lee, James F. *Tasks and Communicating in Language Classrooms*. New York: McGraw-Hill, 2000.

———, and Bill VanPatten. *Making Communicative Language Teaching Happen*. New York: McGraw-Hill, 2003.

Leech, Geoffrey. "Students' Grammar—Teachers' Grammar—Learners' Grammar." In *Grammar and the Language Teacher*, edited by Martin Bygate, Alan Tonkyn, and Eddie Williams, 17–30. New York: Prentice Hall, 1994.

Leow, Ronald. "Attention, Awareness and Foreign Language Behavior." *Language Learning* 47 (1997): 467–505.

———. "Toward Operationalizing the Process of Attention in SLA: Evidence for Tomlin and Villa's (1994) Fine-grained Analysis of Attention." *Applied Psycholinguistics* 19 (1998): 133–159.

Liskin-Gasparro, Judith E. "Narrative Strategies: A Case Study of Developing Storytelling Skills by a Learner of Spanish." *Modern Language Journal* 80 (1996): 271–286.

———. "The Use of Tense-Aspect Morphology in Spanish Oral Narratives: Exploring the Perceptions of Advanced Learners." *Hispania* 83 (2000): 830–844.

Long, Michael. "A Role for Instruction in Second Language Acquisition: Task-based Language Training." In *Modelling and Assessing Second Language Acquisition*, edited by Kenneth Hyltenstam and Manfred Pienemann, 77–99. Clevedon, UK: Multilingual Matters, 1985.

———. "Focus on Form: A Design Feature in Language Teaching Methodology." In *For-*

*eign Language Research in Cross-Cultural Perspective*, edited by Kees de Bot, Ralph B. Ginsberg, and Claire Kramsch, 39–52. Amsterdam: John Benjamins, 1991.

Loschky, Lester, and Robert Bley-Vroman. "Grammar and Task-based Methodology." In *Tasks and Language Learning*, edited by Graham Crookes and Susan Gass, 123–167. Clevedon, UK: Multilingual Matters, 1993.

Lunn, Patricia V. "The Aspectual Lens." *Hispanic Linguistics* 2 (1985): 49–61.

Magnan, Sally Sieloff, and Walz, Joel. "Pedagogical Norms: Development of the Concept and Illustrations from French." In *Pedagogical Norms for Second and Foreign Language Learning and Teaching*, edited by Susan Gass, Kathleen Bardovi-Harlig, Sally Sieloff Magnan, and Joel Walz, 15–40. Amsterdam: John Benjamins, 2002.

Magnan, Sally, Laurie Martin-Berg, William J. Berg, and Yvonne Rochette Ozzello. *Paroles.* Second edition. Fort Worth: Harcourt, 2002.

Master, Peter. "The Effect of Systematic Instruction on Learning the English Article System." In *Perspectives on Pedagogical Grammar*, edited by Terence Odlin, 229–249. Cambridge: Cambridge University Press, 1994.

———. "Consciousness Raising and Article Pedagogy." In *Academic Writing in a Second Language*, edited by Diane Belcher and George Braine, 183–204. Norwood, NJ: Ablex, 1995.

McCarthy, Michael. *Discourse Analysis for Language Teachers*. Cambridge: Cambridge University Press, 1991.

———, and Ronald Carter. *Language As Discourse: Perspectives for Language Teaching*. London: Longman, 1994.

———, and Ronald Carter. "Spoken Grammar: What Is It and How Can We Teach It?" *ELT Journal* 49 (1995): 207–218.

McCool, George J. "Teaching the Formation of Questions: Lessons from New French." *Modern Language Journal* 78 (1994): 56–60.

McKay, Sandra L., and Nancy H. Hornberger. *Sociolinguistics and Language Teaching.* Cambridge: Cambridge University Press, 1995.

Moreau, Marie-Louise. *C'est.* Mons: Éditions Universitaires de Mons, 1976.

Myers, Lindsy. "WH-Questions in Spoken French." PhD diss., University of Texas at Austin, expected 2007.

Nassaji, Hossein, and Sandra Fotos. "Current Developments in Research on the Teaching of Grammar." *Annual Review of Applied Linguistics* 24 (2004): 126–145.

Norris, John M., and Lourdes Ortega. "Effectiveness of L2 Instruction: A Research Synthesis and Quantitative Meta-Analysis." *Language Learning* 50 (2000): 417–428.

Nunan, David. *Syllabus Design: Language Teaching, a Scheme for Teacher Education.* Oxford: Oxford University Press, 1988.

———. *Designing Tasks for the Communicative Classroom.* Cambridge: Cambridge University Press, 1989a.

———. "Communicative Tasks and the Language Classroom." *TESOL Quarterly* 25 (1989b): 279–295.

———. "Aspects of Task-Based Syllabus Design." The English Centre, University of Hong Kong, December 2001. http://www3.telus.net/linguisticsissues/syllabusdesign.html.

Oates, Michael D., and Larbi Oukada. *Entre amis.* Fifth Edition. Boston: Houghton Mifflin, 2006.

Oller, John W., Jr. "Reasons Why Some Methods Work." In *Methods that Work: Ideas for Literacy and Language Teachers*, edited by John W. Oller, Jr., 374–386. Boston: Heinle, 1993.

Omaggio, Alice C. *Teaching Language in Context: Proficiency-Oriented Instruction*. Boston: Heinle, 1986.

Omaggio Hadley, Alice. *Teaching Language in Context*. Third Edition. Boston: Heinle, 2001.

Polanyi, Livia. "Telling the Same Story Twice." *Text* 1 (1981): 315–336.

———. *Telling the American Story: A Structural and Cultural Analysis of Conversational Storytelling*. Cambridge, MA: MIT Press, 1989.

Preston, Dennis R. *Sociolinguistics and Second Language Acquisition*. Oxford: Basil Blackwell, 1989.

Prince, Gerald. *Narratology: The Form and Functioning of Narrative*. Berlin: Mouton, 1982.

———. "Narratology, Narrative, and Meaning." *Poetics Today* 12 (1991): 543–552.

Richards, Jack C. *The Language Teaching Matrix*. Cambridge: Cambridge University Press, 1990.

———. *Reflective Teaching in Second Language Classrooms*. Cambridge: Cambridge University Press, 1994.

———. *Beyond Training*. Cambridge: Cambridge University Press, 1998.

———. *Curriculum Development in Language Teaching*. Cambridge: Cambridge University Press, 2001.

Riggenbach, Heidi. *Discourse Analysis in the Language Classroom*. Ann Arbor: University of Michigan Press, 1999.

Robin, Richard. "Should We Teach Grammar? Part II." (2004) http://www.coas.uncc.edu/linguistics/courses/6163/should_we_teach_grammar.htm.

Robison, Richard. "The Primacy of Aspect: Aspectual Marking in English Interlanguage." *Studies in Second Language Acquisition* 12 (1990): 315–330.

Rosenberg, Samuel N., Mona Tobin Houston, Richard A. Carr, John K. Hyde, and Marvin Dale Moody. *Harper's Grammar of French*. Boston: Heinle, 1991.

Rutherford, William. *Second Language Grammar: Learning and Teaching*. New York: Longman, 1987.

Salaberry, Maximo Rafael. "The Development of Aspectual Distinctions in L2 French Classroom Learning." *Canadian Modern Language Review* 54 (1998): 508–542.

———. "The Development of Past Tense Verbal Morphology in Classroom L2 Spanish." *Applied Linguistics* 20 (1999): 151–178.

———. *The Development of Past Tense Morphology in L2 Spanish*. Amsterdam: John Benjamins, 2000.

———. "Evidence for Transfer of Knowledge of Aspect from L2 Spanish to L3 Portuguese." In *Tense and Aspect in Romance Languages*, edited by Dalila Ayoun and M. Rafael Salaberry, 179–210. Amsterdam: John Benjamins, 2005.

Sanders, Carol. "Sociosituational Variation." In *French Today: Language in Its Social Context*, edited by Carol Sanders, 27–53. Cambridge: Cambridge University Press, 1993.

Savignon, Sandra J. "A Study of the Effect of Training in Communicative Skills as Part of a Beginning College French Course on Student Attitude and Achievement in Linguistic and Communicative Competence." PhD diss., University of Illinois, Urbana-Champaign, 1971.

———. *Communicative Competence: An Experiment in Foreign Language Teaching*. Philadelphia: Center for Curriculum Development, 1972.

————. *Communicative Competence: Theory and Classroom Practice.* Reading, MA: Addison Wesley, 1983.

————. *Interpreting Communicative Language Teaching.* New Haven: Yale University Press, 2002.

Schell, Karyn Anna. "Functional Categories and the Acquisition of Aspect in L2 Spanish: A Longitudinal Study." PhD diss., University of Washington, 2000.

Schiffrin, Deborah. "Tense Variation in Narrative." *Language* 57 (1982): 45–62.

Schmidt, Richard W. "The Role of Consciousness in Second Language Learning." *Applied Linguistics* 11 (1990): 129–158.

————. "Awareness and Second Language Acquisition." *Annual Review of Applied Linguistics* 13 (1993): 206–226.

————. "Attention." In *Cognition and Second Language Instruction,* edited by Peter Robinson, 3–32. Cambridge: Cambridge University Press, 2001.

Sempé, Jean-Jacques and René Goscinny. *Le petit Nicolas.* Paris: Gallimard, 1973.

Sharwood Smith, Michael. "Consciousness-Raising and the Second-Language Learner." *Applied Linguistics* 2 (1981): 159–169.

Silva-Corvalán, Carmen. "Tense and Aspect in Oral Spanish Narrative: Context and Meaning." *Language* 59 (1983): 760–780.

Siskin, H. Jay, Ann Williams-Gascon, and Thomas J. Field. *Débuts.* New York: McGraw-Hill, 2003.

Sleeman, Petra. "Guided Learners of French and the Acquisition of Emphatic Constructions." *International Review of Applied Linguistics in Language Teaching* 42 (2004): 129–151.

Smits, R. J. C. *Eurogrammar: The Relative and Cleft Constructions of the Germanic and Romance Languages.* Dordrecht, Holland: Foris, 1989.

Spada, Nina. "Form-focused Instruction and Second Language Acquisition: A Review of Classroom and Laboratory Research." *Language Teaching* 30 (1997): 73–87.

Swain, Merrill. "Focus on Form Through Conscious Reflection." In *Focus on Form in Classroom Second Language Acquisition,* edited by Catherine Doughty and Jessica Williams, 64–82. Cambridge: Cambridge University Press, 1998.

Terrell, Tracy D., Mary B. Rogers, Betsy J. Kerr, and Guy Spielmann. *Deux mondes.* Fifth Edition. New York: McGraw-Hill, 2005.

Terry, Robert M. "Concepts of Pastness: The *Passé Composé* and the Imperfect." *Foreign Language Annals* 14 (1981): 105–110.

Thogmartin, Clyde. "Tense, Aspect, and Context." *French Review* 57 (1984): 344–349.

Thompson, Chantal P., and Elaine M. Phillips. *Mais oui!* Second Edition. Boston: Houghton Mifflin, 2004.

Tomasello, Michael, and Carl Herron. "Down the Garden Path: Inducing and Correcting Overgeneralization Errors in the Foreign Language Classroom." *Applied Psycholinguistics* 9 (1988): 237–246.

Tomlin, Russell S., and Victor Villa. "Attention in Cognitive Science and SLA." *Studies in Second Language Acquisition* 16 (1994): 183–203.

Toolan, Michael. *Narrative: A Critical Linguistic Introduction.* New York: Routledge, 1988.

Tranel, Bernard. *The Sounds of French.* Cambridge: Cambridge University Press, 1987.

Valdman, Albert. *Introduction to French Phonology and Morphology.* Rowley, MA: Newbury House, 1976.

———. "Classroom Foreign Language Learning and Language Variation: The Notion of the Pedagogical Norm." In *The Dynamic Interlanguage*, edited by Miriam R. Eisenstein, 261–278. New York: Plenum Press, 1989.

———. "Authenticity, Variation, and Communication in the Foreign Language Classroom." In *Text and Context: Cross-disciplinary Perspectives on Language Study*, edited by Claire Kramsch and Sally McConnell-Ginet, 79–97. Lexington, MA: D. C. Heath, 1992.

———. *Bien entendu! Introduction à la prononciation française.* Englewood Cliffs, NJ: Prentice Hall, 1993.

———. "Letter from the President." *American Association of Teachers of French National Bulletin* 23 (1997): 1.

———. "La notion de norme pédagogique dans l'enseignement du français langue étrangère." In *Analyse linguistique et approches de l'oral: Recueil d'études offert en hommage à Claire Blanche-Benveniste*, edited by Mireille Bilger, Karel Van den Eynde, and Françoise Gadet, 177–188. Paris: Peeters, 1998.

———. "Comment gérer la variation dans l'enseignement du français langue étrangère aux États-Unis." *French Review* 73 (2000): 648–666.

———, Cathy Pons, and Mary Ellen Scullen. *Chez nous.* Third Edition. Upper Saddle River, NJ: Pearson, 2006.

VanPatten, Bill. *Input Processing and Grammar Instruction in Second Language Acquisition.* Norwood, NJ: Ablex, 1996.

———. *From Input to Output: A Teacher's Guide to Second Language Acquisition.* New York: McGraw-Hill, 2003.

Vendler, Zeno. "Verbs and Times." *Philosophical Revue* 66 (1957): 143–160.

Vendryès, Joseph. *Le Langage: Introduction linguistique à l'histoire.* Paris: La Renaissance du livre, 1923 and Éditions Albin Michel, 1968.

Walz, Joel. "Is Oral Proficiency Possible with Today's French Textbooks?" *Modern Language Journal* 70 (1986): 13–20.

———, and Jean-Pierre Piriou. *Rapports.* Fifth Edition. Boston: Houghton Mifflin, 2003.

Westfall, Ruth, and Sharon Foerster. "Beyond Aspect: New Strategies for Teaching the Preterite and the Imperfect." *Hispania* 79 (1996): 550–560.

Williams, Jessica. "Focus on Form in the Communicative Classroom: Research Findings and the Classroom Teacher." *TESOL Journal* 4 (1995): 12–16.

Wolfson, Nessa, and Elliot Judd, eds. *Sociolinguistics and Language Acquisition.* Rowley, MA: Newbury House, 1983.

Wong, Wynne. *Input Enhancement: From Theory and Research to the Classroom.* New York: McGraw-Hill, 2005.

———, and Bill VanPatten. "The Evidence is IN. Drills are OUT." *Foreign Language Annals* 36 (2003): 403–423.

Yaguello, Marina. *Petits faits de langue.* Paris: Seuil, 1998.

Yule, George. *Explaining English Grammar.* Oxford: Oxford University Press, 1999.

# Index

articles, 61–66; activities, 38, 85–101, 231–236; definite, 66–68, 70–73, 76; indefinite, 68–73, 76; and other equivalents of "some," 84–85; partitive, 73–76; retention of, 82–84; zero, 77–82

aspect: activities, 125, 130–138; grammatical, 109–115 (*see also* habituality; iterativity; prototype: aspectual marking); lexical, 113–114, 120; and narrative structure, 116–120, 130; order of acquisition, 120–122; visual representation of, 122–125

background. *See* aspect: and narrative structure

**c'est** vs. **il est,** 243–244
cleft constructions. *See* word order constructions
communicative language teaching (CLT), 3, 9–10, 12–13, 15–16, 20–22, 28, 30, 43, 198, 222–223
competence: communicative, 8–9, 20, 22, 222; discourse, 20–21, 22, 148; grammatical, 20, 148, 222, 226; sociolinguistic, 20, 148; strategic, 21; versus performance, 51
**conditionnel** (future in the past), 115–116

consciousness raising (CR), 32, 36–39, 45, 55, 86, 122, 124, 227–228, 245; activities, 89, 92–97, 128–133, 178–179, 205–206, 231, 234–235

deductive approach to grammar instruction, 32, 226–229, 244, 246
determiners, 64
dictogloss, 39, 45–46, 97–98, 136–137
discourse analysis, 39, 42; activities, 98–100, 172–177, 213–215
drills, mechanical, 10, 13–15, 43, 210–211, 228–229, 233, 244

explicit instruction, 3, 10, 14–17, 30, 35–36, 147, 168–169, 176–177; and deductive approach, 32; direct and indirect, 15, 17, 36; of English articles, 63; in grammar consciousness raising, 37; of lexical blocks, 48

focus: argument vs. sentence, 160–161
focus on form, 15–17, 35, 222–223
foreground. *See* aspect: and narrative structure
free variation, 169, 204

garden path technique, 39, 44, 51, 174–175